NATURE GUIDE *to* NEW ENGLAND

Erin McCloskey & Gregory Kennedy

Lone Pine Publishing International

First printed in 2012 10 9 8 7 6 5 4 3 2 1
Printed in China

The Distributor:
Lone Pine Publishing
1808 B Street NW, Suite 140
Auburn, WA 98001

Website: www.lonepinepublishing.com

Publisher's Cataloging-In-Publication Data
(Prepared by The Donohue Group, Inc.)

McCloskey, Erin, 1970–
Nature guide to New England / Erin McCloskey [and] Gregory Kennedy.

p. : col. ill. ; cm.

Includes bibliographical references and index.

ISBN-13: 978-976-650-051-1
ISBN-10: 976-650-051-7

1. Natural history—New England—Guidebooks. 2. Nature study—New England—Guidebooks. 3. New England—Guidebooks. 4. Animals—New England—Identification. 5. Plants—New England—Identification.
I. Kennedy, Gregory, 1956– II. Title.

QH104.5.N4 M33 2012 508.74

Cover Images: Frank Burman, Ted Nordhagen, George Penetrante, Gary Ross, Ian Sheldon
Illustrations: A complete list of illustration credits appears on page 4, which constitutes an extension of this copyright page.

Disclaimer: This guide is not intended to be a "how to" reference guide for food or medicinal uses of plants. We do not recommend experimentation by readers, and we caution that a number of plants in New England, including some used traditionally as medicines, are poisonous and harmful.

PC: 16

Table of Contents

ILLUSTRATION CREDITS

Frank Burman: 125c, 126c, 136a, 137c, 138b, 139a, 139b, 140c, 149a, 152e, 158c, 159a, 159b, 160c, 161b, 162e, 163a, 164b, 165a, 165b, 166b, 166d, 170c, 171, 172e, 173c, 174a, 174c, 175, 176a, 176b, 177a, 177c, 178a, 178c, 179a, 180e, 181c, 182, 183a, 184a, 184b, 185a, 185d, 186, 187a, 187b, 187c, 188d, 189a, 189c, 190, 191a, 191c, 192b, 192c, 193, 194, 195b, 195c, 196b, 196c, 197c, 198a, 198b, 198c, 199, 200, 202c, 204a, 204b

Linda Dunn: 170a, 191b

Tamara Eder: 62c, 187a

Linda Kershaw: 159c, 165c

Ted Nordhagen: 78b, 82c, 83b, 83c, 84a, 84b, 85a, 88b, 92a, 92c, 93b, 94b, 95, 96a, 97a, 98b, 99c, 100, 101a, 101c, 102a, 102b, 103a, 103c, 104a, 106a, 106c, 107b, 107c, 108

George Penetrante: 54b, 55, 123b, 124b, 124c, 126a, 126b, 127a, 127c, 128, 129, 131c, 132, 133a, 134b, 135a, 135b, 137b, 140a, 147b, 159d, 159e, 160a, 160b, 165d, 166c, 170b, 172a, 172b, 172c, 172d, 173a, 174b, 177b, 178b, 179b, 179c, 180a, 180b, 180c, 180d, 181a, 181b, 187d, 188a, 188e, 189b, 192a, 198d, 201, 202a, 202b

Ewa Pluciennik: 93c

Michel Poirier: 110c, 111c, 118b

Gary Ross: 79, 82a, 85c, 88c, 54a, 56, 57, 58, 59, 60, 61, 62, 63, 64, 65, 66, 67, 68, 69, 70, 71, 74, 75, 76, 77, 78a, 78c, 80, 81, 82b, 83a, 84c, 85b, 86, 87, 88a, 89, 90, 91, 92b, 93a, 94a, 94c, 96b, 96c, 97b, 97c, 98a, 98c, 99a, 99b, 101b, 102c, 103b, 104b, 104c, 105, 106b, 107a, 110a, 110b, 111a, 111b, 112, 113, 114, 115, 116, 117, 118a, 118c, 119, 120

Ian Sheldon: 48, 49, 50, 51, 52, 53, 123a, 123c, 124a, 125a, 125b, 127b, 131a, 131b, 133b, 133c, 134a, 134c, 135c, 136b, 136c, 137a, 138a, 138c, 139c, 140b, 144, 145, 146, 147a, 147c, 148, 149b, 149c, 150, 151, 152a, 152b, 152c, 152d, 153, 154, 155, 158a, 158b, 158d, 161a, 161c, 161d, 162a, 162b, 162c, 162d, 163b, 163c, 164a, 164c, 166a, 173b, 176c, 183b, 183c, 184c, 185b, 185c, 188b, 188c, 195a, 196a, 197a, 197b, 202d, 203, 204c

ACKNOWLEDGMENTS

For their time in helping select the species represented in this guide, thanks go to Kurt Schatzl and Joe Martinez of the New England Herpetological Society; Mason Weinrich of the Whale Center of New England; and Elizabeth Fransworth, editor-in-chief of *Rhodora*.

Thank you also to Nicholle Carrière for being such a talented and helpful editor.

calypso

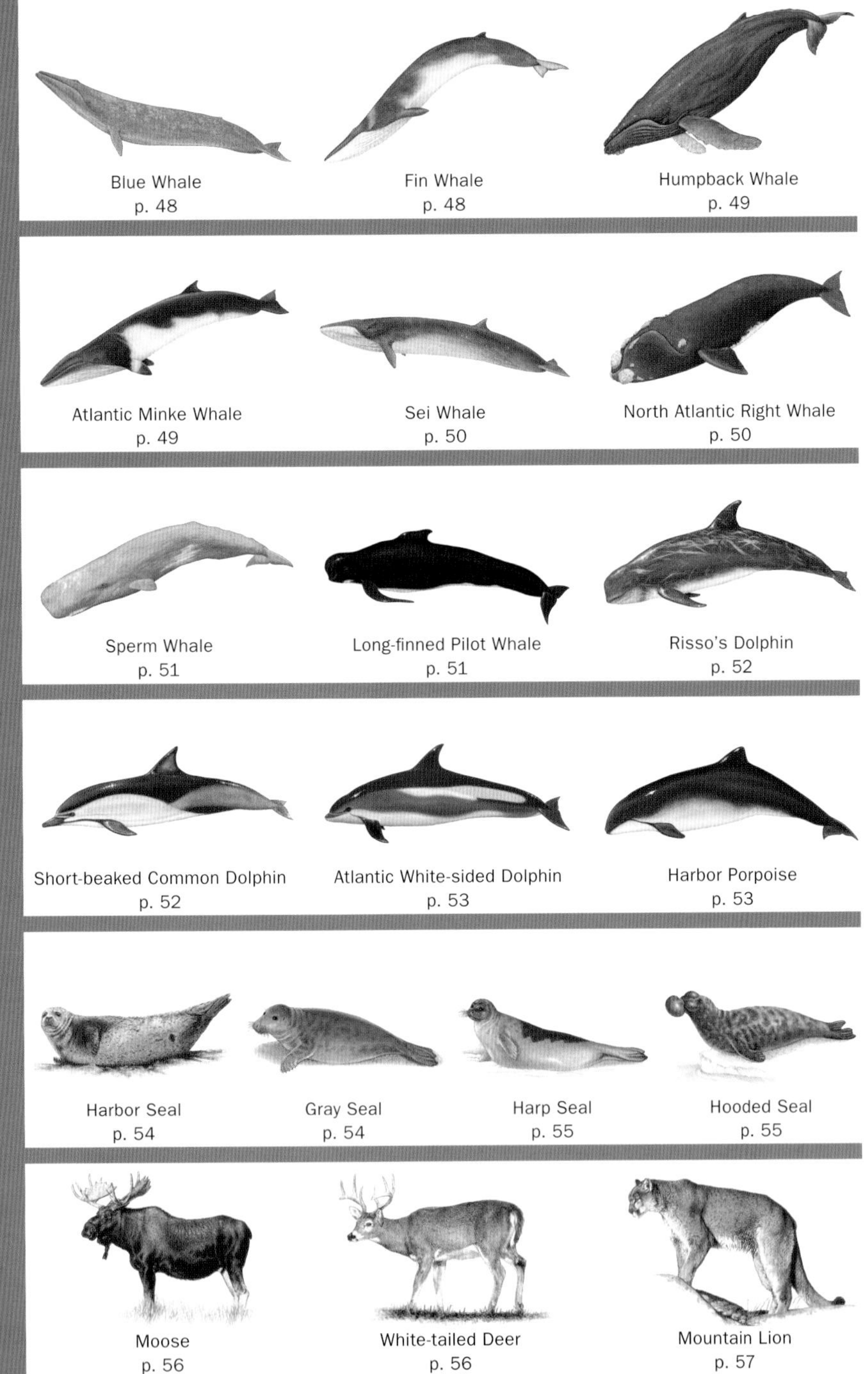

Blue Whale
p. 48

Fin Whale
p. 48

Humpback Whale
p. 49

Atlantic Minke Whale
p. 49

Sei Whale
p. 50

North Atlantic Right Whale
p. 50

Sperm Whale
p. 51

Long-finned Pilot Whale
p. 51

Risso's Dolphin
p. 52

Short-beaked Common Dolphin
p. 52

Atlantic White-sided Dolphin
p. 53

Harbor Porpoise
p. 53

Harbor Seal
p. 54

Gray Seal
p. 54

Harp Seal
p. 55

Hooded Seal
p. 55

Moose
p. 56

White-tailed Deer
p. 56

Mountain Lion
p. 57

Lynx
p. 57

Bobcat
p. 58

Black Bear
p. 58

Coyote
p. 59

Red Fox
p. 59

Gray Fox
p. 59

American Marten
p. 60

Fisher
p. 60

Long-tailed Weasel
p. 60

Short-tailed Weasel
p. 61

Mink
p. 61

Northern River Otter
p. 61

Striped Skunk
p. 62

Raccoon
p. 62

New England Cottontail
p. 62

Snowshoe Hare
p. 63

European Hare
p. 63

Beaver
p. 63

Porcupine
p. 64

Woodchuck
p. 64

Eastern Gray Squirrel
p. 64

Red Squirrel
p. 65

Southern Flying Squirrel
p. 65

Eastern Chipmunk
p. 65

Southern Bog Lemming
p. 66

Meadow Vole
p. 66

Common Muskrat
p. 66

Brown Rat
p. 67

Black Rat
p. 67

House Mouse
p. 67

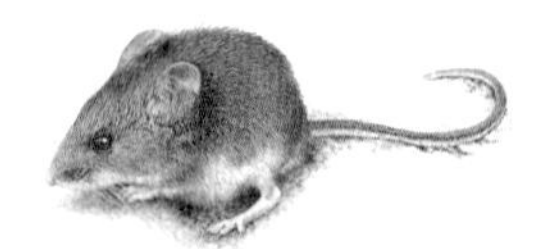
White-footed Mouse
p. 68

Deer Mouse
p. 68

Meadow Jumping Mouse
p. 68

Big Brown Bat
p. 69

Eastern Pipistrelle
p. 69

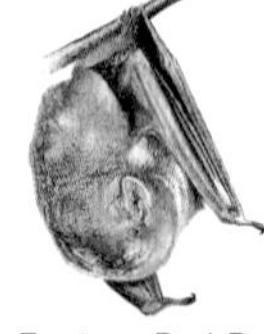
Eastern Red Bat
p. 69

BIRDS

American Bittern
p. 78

Great Blue Heron
p. 78

Great Egret
p. 79

Green Heron
p. 79

Black-crowned Night-heron
p. 79

Turkey Vulture
p. 80

Osprey
p. 80

Bald Eagle
p. 80

Northern Harrier
p. 81

Sharp-shinned Hawk
p. 81

Northern Goshawk
p. 81

Red-shouldered Hawk
p. 82

Red-tailed Hawk
p. 82

American Kestrel
p. 82

Virginia Rail
p. 83

Sora
p. 83

Piping Plover
p. 83

Killdeer
p. 84

American Oystercatcher
p. 84

Spotted Sandpiper
p. 84

Willet
p. 85

Upland Sandpiper
p. 85

Red Knot
p. 85

Sanderling
p. 86

Wilson's Snipe
p. 86

American Woodcock
p. 86

Herring Gull
p. 87

Great Black-backed Gull
p. 87

Common Tern
p. 87

Rock Pigeon
p. 88

Mourning Dove
p. 88

Yellow-billed Cuckoo
p. 88

Barn Owl
p. 89

Great Horned Owl
p. 89

Snowy Owl
p. 89

Barred Owl
p. 90

Long-eared Owl
p. 90

Northern Saw-whet Owl
p. 90

Common Nighthawk
p. 91

Whip-poor-will
p. 91

Chimney Swift
p. 91

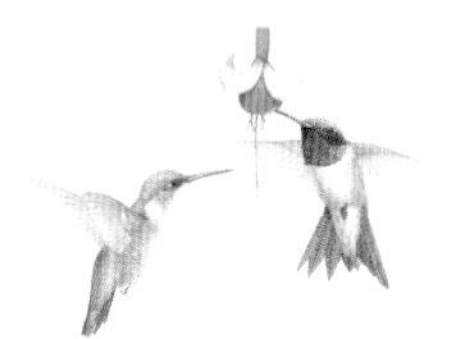
Ruby-throated Hummingbird
p. 92

Belted Kingfisher
p. 92

Red-bellied Woodpecker
p. 92

Downy Woodpecker
p. 93

Black-backed Woodpecker
p. 93

Northern Flicker
p. 93

Pileated Woodpecker
p. 94

Eastern Wood-pewee
p. 94

Alder Flycatcher
p. 94

Eastern Phoebe
p. 95

Eastern Kingbird
p. 95

Northern Shrike
p. 95

Red-eyed Vireo
p. 96

Blue Jay
p. 96

Common Raven
p. 96

Horned Lark
p. 97

Tree Swallow
p. 97

Barn Swallow
p. 97

Black-capped Chickadee
p. 98

White-breasted Nuthatch
p. 98

Winter Wren
p. 98

Golden-crowned Kinglet
p. 99

Eastern Bluebird
p. 99

Veery
p. 99

Hermit Thrush
p. 100

Wood Thrush
p. 100

American Robin
p. 100

Gray Catbird
p. 101

Northern Mockingbird
p. 101

Cedar Waxwing
p. 101

Ovenbird
p. 102

Black-and-white Warbler
p. 102

American Redstart
p. 102

Common Yellowthroat
p. 103

Yellow Warbler
p. 103

Black-throated Blue Warbler
p. 103

Chipping Sparrow
p. 104

Savannah Sparrow
p. 104

Song Sparrow
p. 104

White-throated Sparrow
p. 105

Dark-eyed Junco
p. 105

Scarlet Tanager
p. 105

Northern Cardinal
p. 106

BIRDS

Rose-breasted Grosbeak
p. 106

Indigo Bunting
p. 106

Red-winged Blackbird
p. 107

Eastern Meadowlark
p. 107

Common Grackle
p. 107

Purple Finch
p. 108

American Goldfinch
p. 108

House Sparrow
p. 108

AMPHIBIANS & REPTILES

Red-spotted Newt
p. 110

Blue-spotted Salamander
p. 110

Spotted Salamander
p. 110

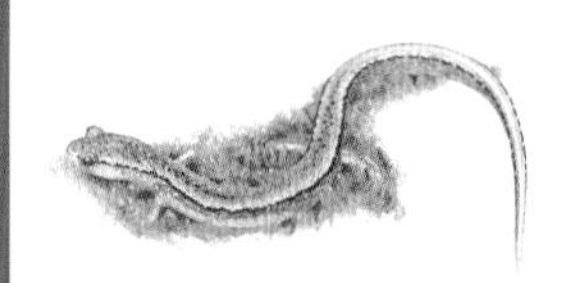
Northern Two-lined Salamander
p. 111

Red-backed Salamander
p. 111

Northern Dusky Salamander
p. 111

American Toad
p. 112

Fowler's Toad
p. 112

American Bullfrog
p. 112

Gray Treefrog
p. 113

Northern Spring Peeper
p. 113

Wood Frog
p. 113

Northern Leopard Frog
p. 114

Pickerel Frog
p. 114

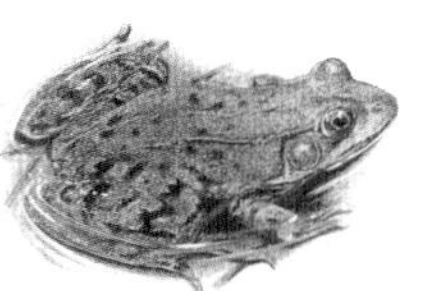
Green Frog
p. 114

Common Snapping Turtle
p. 115

Common Musk Turtle
p. 115

Painted Turtle
p. 115

Blanding's Turtle
p. 116

Spotted Turtle
p. 116

Wood Turtle
p. 116

Eastern Box Turtle
p. 117

Loggerhead Sea Turtle
p. 117

Green Sea Turtle
p. 117

Eastern Garter Snake
p. 118

Ribbon Snake
p. 118

Northern Water Snake
p. 118

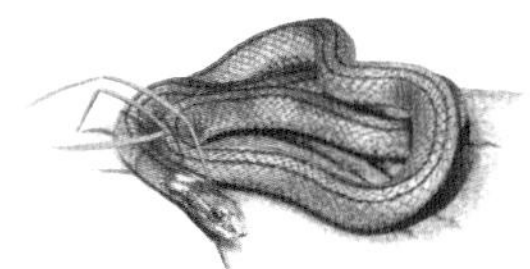
Red-bellied Snake
p. 119

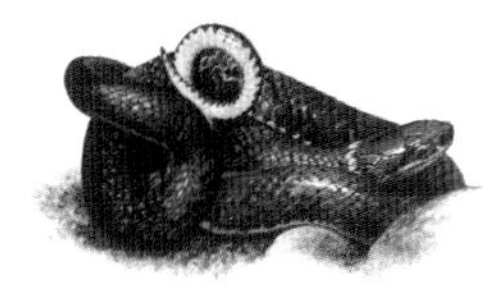
Northern Ring-necked Snake
p. 119

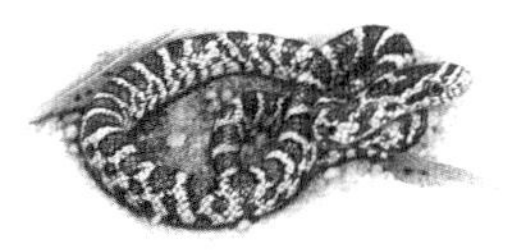
Eastern Milk Snake
p. 119

Black Rat Snake
p. 120

Eastern Racer
p. 120

Timber Rattlesnake
p. 120

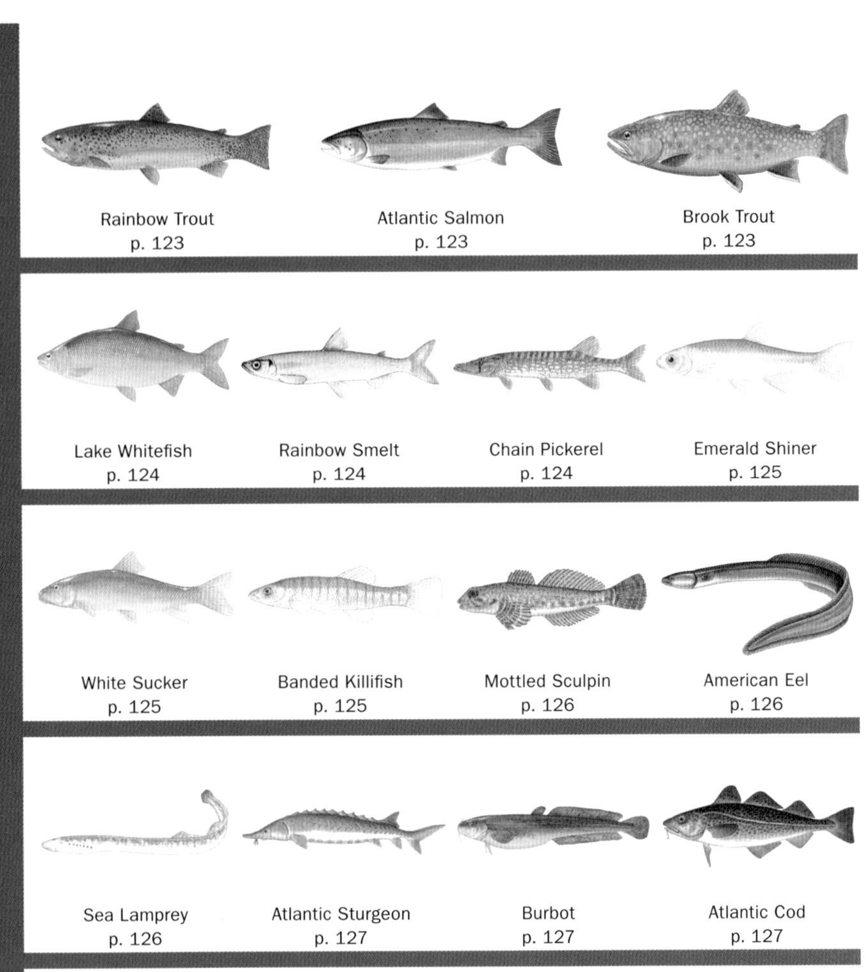

Rainbow Trout p. 123
Atlantic Salmon p. 123
Brook Trout p. 123

Lake Whitefish p. 124
Rainbow Smelt p. 124
Chain Pickerel p. 124
Emerald Shiner p. 125

White Sucker p. 125
Banded Killifish p. 125
Mottled Sculpin p. 126
American Eel p. 126

Sea Lamprey p. 126
Atlantic Sturgeon p. 127
Burbot p. 127
Atlantic Cod p. 127

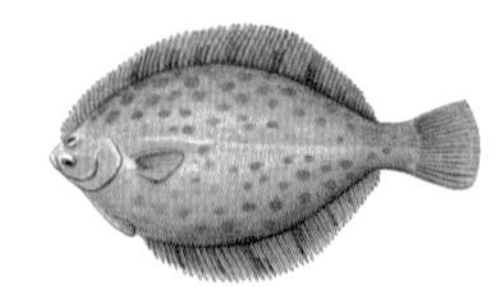

Winter Flounder p. 128

Atlantic Mackerel p. 128

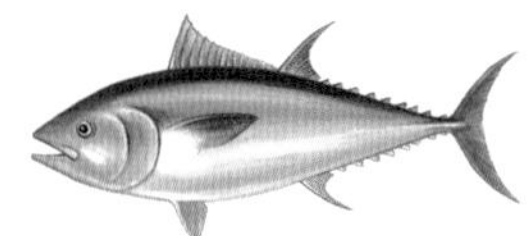

Atlantic Bluefin Tuna p. 128

Alewife p. 129

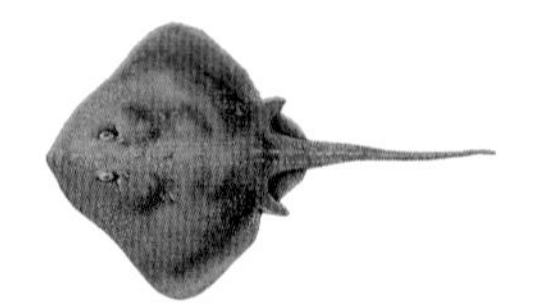

Thorny Skate p. 129

Porbeagle Shark p. 129

Acorn Barnacle
p. 131

Softshell Clam
p. 131

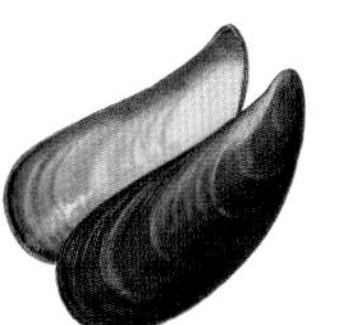
Blue Mussel
p. 131

American Oyster
p. 132

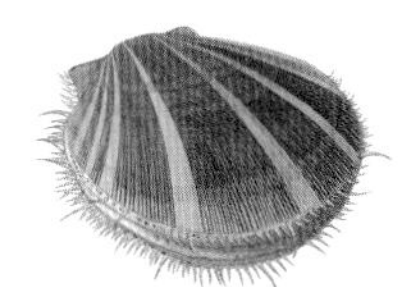
Atlantic Deep-sea Scallop
p. 132

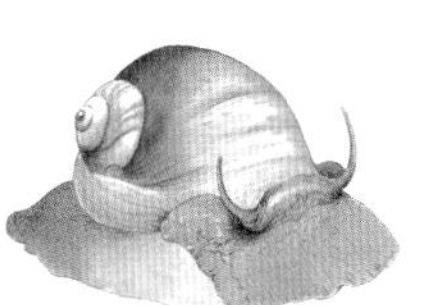
Northern Moon Snail
p. 132

Common Periwinkle
p. 133

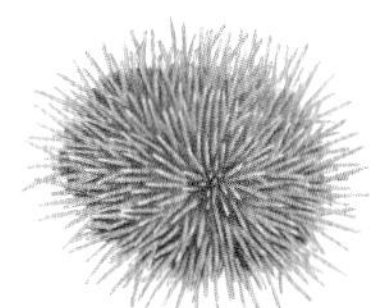
Green Sea Urchin
p. 133

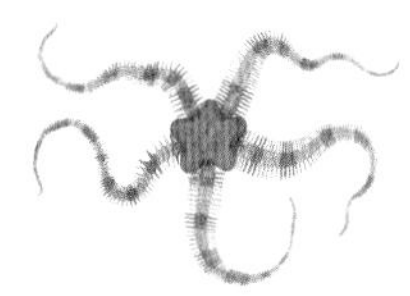
Daisy Brittle Star
p. 133

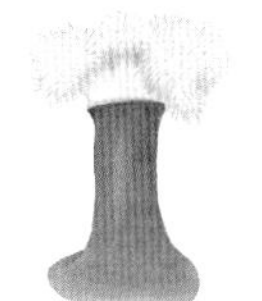
Frilled Anemone
p. 134

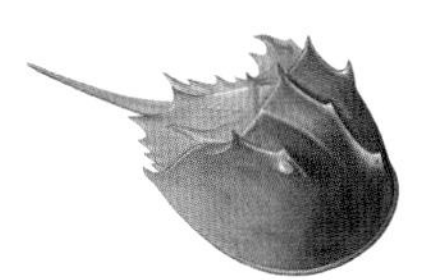
Horseshoe Crab
p. 134

Green Crab
p. 134

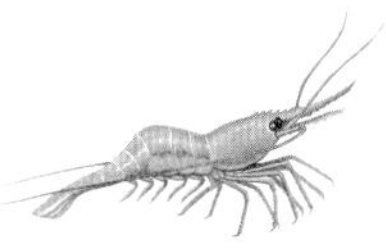
Northern Shrimp
p. 135

North American Lobster
p. 135

Moon Jellyfish
p. 135

Cabbage White
p. 136

Eastern Black Swallowtail
p. 136

Monarch
p. 136

American Copper
p. 137

Karner Blue Butterfly
p. 137

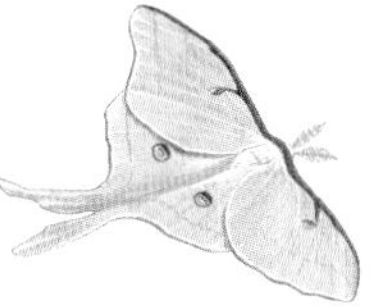
Luna Moth
p. 137

Green Darner
p. 138

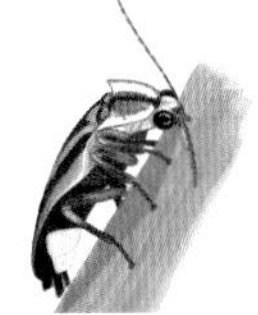
Firefly
p. 138

INVERTEBRATES

Seven-spot Ladybug
p. 138

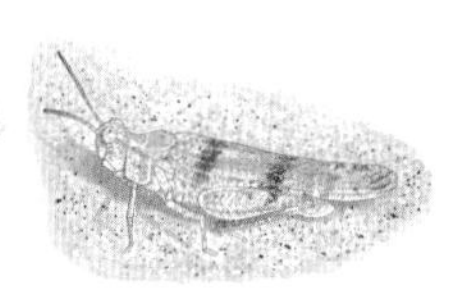
Seaside Grasshopper
p. 139

Saltmarsh Mosquito
p. 139

Eastern Yellow Jacket
p. 139

Honey Bee
p. 140

Horsefly
p. 140

Eastern Daddy Longlegs
p. 140

TREES

Red Spruce
p. 144

Eastern Hemlock
p. 144

Eastern White Pine
p. 145

Red Pine
p. 145

Northern White-cedar
p. 146

Eastern Red-cedar
p. 146

Tulip Tree
p. 147

Sassafras
p. 147

Sycamore
p. 148

American Elm
p. 148

Butternut
p. 149

Shagbark Hickory
p. 149

American Beech
p. 150

White Oak
p. 150

Red Oak
p. 151

Yellow Birch
p. 151

White Birch
p. 152

American Basswood
p. 152

Balsam Poplar
p. 153

Quaking Aspen
p. 153

Black Willow
p. 154

Sugar Maple
p. 154

Red Maple
p. 155

White Ash
p. 149

American Hornbeam
p. 158

Eastern Hop-hornbeam
p. 158

Witch-hazel
p. 158

Spicebush
p. 159

Eastern Baccharis
p. 159

Rosebay Rhododendron
p. 159

Pinxter Flower
p. 160

Mountain Laurel
p. 160

Highbush Blueberry
p. 160

American Mountain-ash
p. 161

Pin Cherry
p. 161

American Plum
p. 161

Chokecherry
p. 162

Downy Serviceberry
p. 162

Black Raspberry
p. 162

Swamp Rose
p. 163

SHRUBS & VINES

Flowering Dogwood
p. 163

Red-osier Dogwood
p. 163

Black Tupelo
p. 164

Winterberry
p. 164

Staghorn Sumac
p. 164

Poison Ivy
p. 165

Buttonbush
p. 165

Southern Arrowwood
p. 165

Nannyberry
p. 166

Bayberry
p. 166

Hog-peanut
p. 166

HERBS, GRASSES, FERNS & SEAWEEDS

Wood Lily
p. 170

Painted Trillium
p. 170

Large-flowered Trillium
p. 170

Yellow Trout-lily
p. 171

False Solomon's-seal
p. 171

Canada Mayflower
p. 171

Bluebead Lily
p. 172

Indian Cucumber Root
p. 172

Sessile Bellwort
p. 172

Grass-pink
p. 173

Calypso
p. 173

Stemless Lady's-slipper
p. 173

Large Purple Fringed Orchid
p. 174

Snowy Orchis
p. 174

Wild Ginger
p. 174

Wild Columbine
p. 175

Marsh-marigold
p. 175

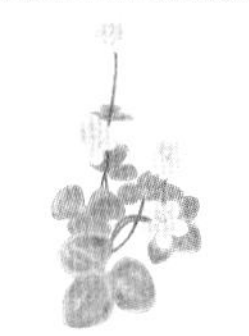
Roundlobe Hepatica
p. 175

Bristly Buttercup
p. 176

Goldthread
p. 176

Red Baneberry
p. 176

Bloodroot
p. 177

Sea Rocket
p. 177

Dutchman's Breeches
p. 177

Pokeweed
p. 178

Prickly-pear
p. 178

Spring-beauty
p. 178

Water Smartweed
p. 179

Shinleaf
p. 179

Spotted Wintergreen
p. 179

Common Wood Sorrel
p. 180

Blue Violet
p. 180

Indian-pipe
p. 180

Pinesap
p. 181

Fringed Polygala
p. 181

Mayflower
p. 181

Fringed Loosestrife
p. 182

Starflower
p. 182

Sea-milkwort
p. 182

Fen Grass-of-Parnassus
p. 183

Common Strawberry
p. 183

Twinflower
p. 183

Beach Pea
p. 184

Lupine
p. 184

Red Clover
p. 184

Purple Loosestrife
p. 185

Fireweed
p. 185

Common Evening-primrose
p. 185

Enchanter's-nightshade
p. 186

Flowering Spurge
p. 186

Spotted Touch-me-not
p. 186

Dwarf Ginseng
p. 187

Wild Sarsaparilla
p. 187

Woolly Sweet-cicely
p. 187

Water Parsnip
p. 188

Cow Parsnip
p. 188

Marsh-pennywort
p. 188

Angelica
p. 189

Indian Hemp
p. 189

Common Milkweed
p. 189

Blue Phlox
p. 190

Sea Lungwort
p. 190

Blue Vervain
p. 190

Wood Sage
p. 191

Wild Bergamot
p. 191

Heal-all
p. 191

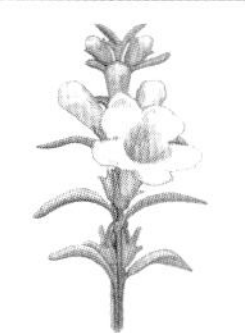
Downy False Foxglove
p. 192

Common Monkeyflower
p. 192

Wood-betony
p. 192

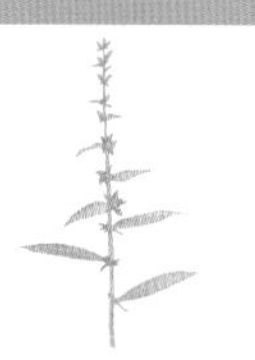
Harebell
p. 193

Cardinal-flower
p. 193

Bluets
p. 193

Partridgeberry
p. 194

Cleavers
p. 194

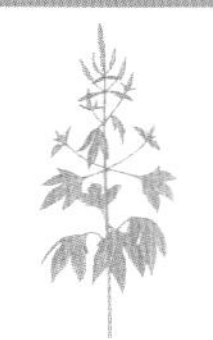
Giant Ragweed
p. 194

Common Yarrow
p. 195

Oxeye Sunflower
p. 195

Golden Ragwort
p. 195

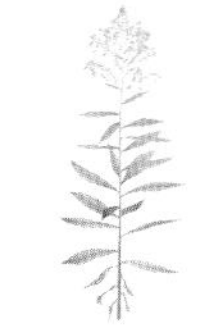
Canada Goldenrod
p. 196

New England Aster
p. 196

Common Boneset
p. 196

Canada Thistle
p. 197

Common Dandelion
p. 197

Black-eyed Susan
p. 197

Broad-leaved Arrowhead
p. 198

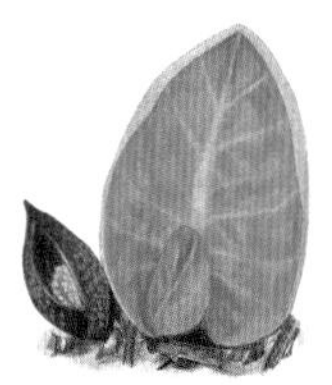
Skunk Cabbage
p. 198

Jack-in-the-pulpit
p. 198

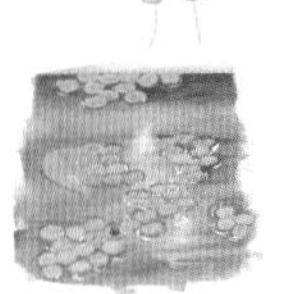
Lesser Duckweed
p. 199

Sea Lavender
p. 199

Ostrich Fern
p. 199

Beach Grass
p. 200

Common Reed
p. 200

Rush
p. 200

Cord Grass
p. 201

Beach Sedge
p. 201

Spike Grass
p. 201

Cottongrass Bulrush
p. 202

Broad-leaved Cattail
p. 202

Eel Grass
p. 202

Rockweed
p. 203

Sugar Kelp
p. 203

Encrusting Corraline Algae
p. 203

Dulse
p. 204

Irish Moss
p. 204

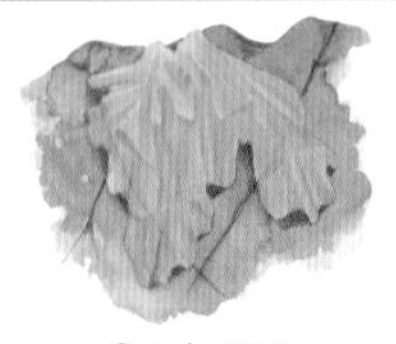
Sea Lettuce
p. 204

INTRODUCTION

Long before the Pilgrims arrived on the *Mayflower* in 1620, the Algonquin peoples were here, descended from nomadic Asiatic groups who left the first human footprints on these lands in 9000 BC, or possibly earlier. They were followed by the Vikings, who quite likely arrived in New England after reaching Newfoundland around AD 1000, and John Cabot is believed to have seen these shores on his second voyage to the New World in 1498. Basque whalers visited the area in the 1500s, and the Spanish, Portuguese and Irish may possibly all have landed upon the coast at various times. A French colony in 1604 failed, but was followed by a successful British colony in 1605. New England went on to become the birthplace of the United States, adding a noteworthy chapter in a much longer natural history.

North Atlantic right whale

In the 300 years since Europeans settled in the region, dramatic ecological changes have taken place in this northeastern corner of the country. Primeval forest was cleared for agriculture by the steadfast colonists, who were not laborshy, and they painstakingly cultivated even the stony hills. The most rapid change occurred from 1750 to 1820, when 75 percent of the arable land was converted to crops and pasture, and the area's virgin forests were reduced from 95 percent of the landscape to a mere 5 percent. Interestingly, a century later, New England returned to being about 75 percent forested after farms were abandoned and people pioneered their way west, lured by the promise of better farmland in the Midwest and the riches of the California gold rush. Abandoned fields became pine stands, and the forestry industry took over where agriculture left off. These second-growth pines reached harvestable size just after the turn of the 20th century. Besides the major stands of eastern white pine,

eastern white pine

coyote

American beech

New England forests feature red oak, red maple, red spruce, paper birch, quaking aspen and eastern hemlock.

By the 1970s, the era of the "tree-hugger," more and more forest was coming under protection. Some forests have recovered so well that there are once again pockets of old-growth yellow birch and sugar maple. The moist forest floor supports luxurious beds of moss, and lichens cover tree trunks and the erupting gnarled roots of giant American beeches. Balsam fir (*Abies balsamea*) and balsam poplar scent the air. The recovering species are mostly birches, white pine, red pine and red oak. The hardwoods—American beech, sugar maple and American basswood—mix with eastern hemlock, white birch and quaking aspen. Northern white-cedar is common on the coast.

sharp-shinned hawk

blue darner

Parts of New England are still busy with human endeavors—industrial, agricultural and urban—yet wild enough for foxes, bears and hawks; other areas are remote enough for rare and elusive species such lynx. Our own backyards host visits from bold and opportunistic animals such as coyotes, deer and many species of birds, insects and rodents. We get to enjoy the great spectacle of migratory birds travelling along the Atlantic Flyway in spring and fall, and see coastal cliffs completely covered in millions of flapping, squawking nesting seabirds. High mountain ranges, such as the northern Appalachian Mountains that reach their highest point at Mount Washington (6288 ft), inspire us to climb them. We can wrap our arms around ancient trees in our great forests and listen to choruses of frogs singing from the wetlands, lakes and rivers. There is much to appreciate and admire in New England.

northern spring peeper

NATURAL REGIONS

The Forests

The **Acadian–New England Forest** is a transitional forest where the boreal spruce-fir forest to the north intermingles with the deciduous forests of the south. The Appalachian Mountains cut through the region, running parallel to the Atlantic Coast, which strongly influences vegetation dynamics in coastal and inland areas. The cardinal directions are distinctly different in New England, with a different ecotype at every corner and elevation. Not only from north to south do we see a transition from cold to warm, but the Appalachians add alpine elevations and have distinctly different forest types on western and eastern slopes.

The mixed forest of hardwoods and conifers of the **Laurentian Plains and Hills** occurs in northeastern Maine and reaches up into Quebec and the Maritime provinces of Canada. New England's mixed forest was once more extensive, and little of the original forest remains. Today, disjunct portions occur in areas such as western Vermont. Much of the old-growth sugar maple, American beech, American elm, ash, yellow birch, white pine and eastern hemlock were cleared for agriculture and by logging, fires, insect infestations and hurricanes, and coniferous forests moved in. Stands of red oak, sugar maple, yellow birch and American elm still exist, and ash and red maple are typical of wet sites.

sugar maple

Along the **Appalachian Mountains**, the mixed coniferous forest of firs, pines, spruces, hemlocks and larch is typical of alpine regions and follows the Appalachians through New England southward. At higher latitudes closer to the Canadian border, these tree species occur at lower elevations. Numerous glacial lakes throughout the region quench the landscape. Tundra-like alpine meadows occur at the highest elevations of the White Mountains in New Hampshire and particularly Mount Washington. Bogs and fens are common. At the extent of the treeline, the harsh climate dwarfs trees into krummholz forests.

Along the western slopes of the Appalachian Mountains and inland are the **Northeastern Highlands**, composed of northern hardwood and spruce-fir forests. This side of the Appalachians is less populated than the eastern slopes and the area extending to the coast. Farming was attempted on these western slopes but was not successful, and the land is mainly forested or urbanized.

The ocean moderates the climate of the region, resulting in more deciduous tree species along the coast, and the climate becomes warmer from southern Maine down the coast. The **Coastal Pine Barrens** of Cape Cod have predominantly oak-pine forests, and groundcover species include bluebead lily, starflower

bluebead lily

and common wood sorrel. Conifers are beginning to fade out of the picture, and the **Oceanic Broadleaf Forest** dominates southern New England. Many plant species find their northern limits here, and tulip trees, basswoods and oaks, tree species more typical of the South, occur in warm microclimates.

With the mixing of forest types, biodiversity increases, and with the conifers come bird species such as nuthatches, golden-crowned kinglets and various wood-warblers intermingling with typically southern birds such as the northern cardinal, scarlet tanager and red-eyed vireo. Wild turkeys and ruffed grouse are game birds in some areas. Characteristic reptiles include the box turtle, snapping turtle, painted turtle, eastern racer, eastern garter snake and timber rattlesnake, and amphibians to discover include the spotted salamander, green frog and American bullfrog. Mammals such as moose, black bears, foxes, showshoe hares, porcupines, fishers, beavers, bobcats, martens, raccoons, squirrels, white-footed mice, northern river otters, skunks and Virginia opossums are found throughout the forests and sometimes in urban settings. The range of the white-tailed deer has expanded northward, displacing the woodland caribou (*Rangifer tarandus* ssp. *caribou*), and coyotes have slipped in where wolves were extirpated, though the wolf has proved to be a survivor, with one paw yet inside the U.S. border.

golden-crowned kinglet

eastern box turtle

The Rocky Shore

The rocky shore is divided into the **spray zone** and the **intertidal zone**. The spray zone lies just beyond the reach of the highest high tides, leaving the vegetation to receive moisture in the form of sea spray or from high, stormy waves or rainfall. White spruce is a dominant tree species in coastal areas owing to its tolerance of sea salt spray. Barnacles and periwinkles cover the rocks.

common periwinkle

The **intertidal zone** lies between the high and low tide lines and has several subzones. The **upper intertidal zone**, also known as the periwinkle zone, is near the high-tide line, and animals and algae here must survive almost half the day without water. Shellfish such as blue mussels must trap sea water or close off fresh water as needed. Periwinkles and dog whelks (*Nucella lapillus*) graze on the thin film of green algae on the rocks and in tidal pools. The **middle intertidal zone**, also called the

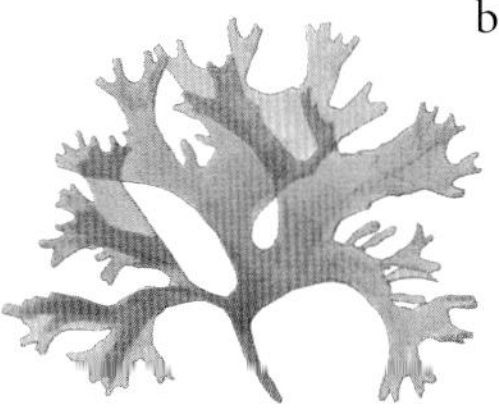

Irish moss

barnacle-rockweed zone, forms the largest part of the intertidal zone. Characteristic flora and fauna are brown algae, predominantly rockweed (*Fucus* spp.) and knotted wrack (*Ascophyllum nodosum*), periwinkles, barnacles, blue mussels, limpets (*Acmaea* spp.) and sea stars. The **lower intertidal zone**, or Irish moss zone, lies just above the low-tide mark. Irish moss, a type of red algae, is only exposed during the very lowest tides. There is higher animal diversity here owing to the stability of the habitat—extreme tidal variations are infrequent, making life in this zone less stressful to organisms. Blue mussels are quite abundant here. The **subtidal zone**, or kelp zone, is always underwater except during the extreme spring tides of winter. This zone extends only as far as sunlight can penetrate, and it is inhabited by leathery kelp and red algae, particularly encrusting coralline algae, as well as sea stars and sea urchins. Flounders and eels enter the intertidal zone at high tide.

Sandy Beaches and Wrack Lines

The **sandy beach** is a zone of constantly shifting unconsolidated material—sand. Created by riparian deposits, coastal erosion or glacial till, the grains of sand are diverse in color. If you look closely, you will notice black, green, red and brown grains from various origins, as well as white or clear grains, which are quartz. The mineral grains dissolve over time, leaving behind mainly quartz granules; thus, older sand is less colorful, and white sandy beaches are old beaches. Also, the coarser the sand, the steeper the face of the beach.

beach pea

raccoon

Dead seaweed and other flotsam collect at the **wrack lines**, attracting little beach fleas or beach hoppers, as well as many other invertebrates, providing food for gulls, terns and shorebirds, as well as raccoons, skunks and various rodents. Pioneer plants on the dunes, a few yards landward and above the reach of the highest storm waves, include beach grass, dusty miller (*Artemisia stelleriana*) and beach pea. The next succession of vegetation grows on the soils stabilized by the pioneer plants and includes coastal species of wild roses (*Rosa* spp.) and goldenrod (*Solidago* spp.), as well as bayberry, poison ivy and coastal grasses.

Salt Marshes

Salt marshes occur in protected bays and estuaries where fresh water flows to the coast and into the ocean—the mixed fresh and salt water is known as brackish water. Tidal flooding and the stream currents deposit significant amounts of minerals and sediment in the shallow waters, forming the base of the marsh. Plants begin to take hold and stabilize the sedimentary floor, then decomposing plant materials start building layers of peat. Salt marshes are one of most highly productive ecosystems owing to the nutrient-rich detritus they produce, and they are often referred to as the "nurseries of the sea" because many young fish and crustaceans can be found in these sheltered, food-rich waters. Many species of shellfish, fish and shorebirds rely on saltmarsh habitat. The highest biodiversity occurs at the marsh edge farthest from the ocean tides, starting with plants such as large reeds, staghorn sumac and bayberry.

cord grass

Salt marshes can typically be divided into three zones. The **upper marsh** is a freshwater zone with freshwater plants, but they are salt tolerant and are submerged during spring and storm tides. These plant species include spike grass, rushes, sea lavender, goldenrod and asters. The **middle marsh**, or salt meadow, is almost dominated by cord grass. In the **lower marsh**, closest to the ocean, cord grass is often submerged. Green algae and small snails are abundant, as is the saltmarsh mosquito.

Tidal Flats

When the lowest tides are out, we can see—and smell—the mud and sand of the low-wave situations in estuaries. These exposed areas are called **tidal flats**. The sediment constantly shifts, so most plants cannot take hold, but free-floating algae—diatoms and dinoflagellates—cover the sand in a greenish yellow sheen, and eel grass is prevalent. Little clams and sea worms dig into the sand—you can see the little breathing holes they create—and crabs, small crustaceans, snails and other mollusks are found throughout the flats.

The Atlantic Ocean

Water temperatures are a main factor determining the range and abundance of marine life, which can also vary with the season. Cold, arctic water from the Labrador Current flows along the eastern Canadian coast and offshore islands, becoming the Maine Current when it enters the Gulf of Maine. This cold current continues south to northern Cape Cod, where it meets the warm Gulf Stream waters. The two currents collide and are redirected east over the Grand Banks, a group of shallow (80 to 330 ft deep) underwater plateaus, before they veer off toward Europe. The mixing of the warm and cold currents over the shallow Grand Banks lifts nutrients off the ocean floor and creates one of the richest fishing grounds in the world.

Cape Cod is a large peninsula extending 60 miles into the open Atlantic Ocean and has only a 3- to 4-foot tide. Its beaches and estuaries are sheltered inside a nook in the Gulf of Maine. Crustaceans are abundant here, including crabs, shrimp and, most famously, the North American lobster. Many species of fish inhabit the offshore waters, and the Atlantic cod is now recuperating from overharvesting, its near disappearance an inconceivable occurrence for anyone who fished for cod when it existed in epic numbers. The coast features many species of seabirds and marine mammals, and birding and whale watching are hugely popular and rewarding activities.

northern shrimp

HUMAN-ALTERED LANDSCAPES & URBAN ENVIRONMENTS

The impact of human activity on natural environments is something we must become increasingly aware of and sensitive to as our populations continue to encroach on wildlife habitat. No description of important habitats would be complete without a mention of towns and cities. Roads, urban and agricultural areas and forestry and mining sites are just a few examples of the impact that humans have on the landscape.

The region has lost much of its original forest to forestry and agriculture; the large, ancient trees were valuable timber and textile for early homesteaders, and the rich soil produced bountiful fruit orchards and hay and vegetable crops. Fire suppression and the restriction of tidal flow into coastal salt marshes bordering the coastal forests has resulted in less biodiverse forests than existed in prehistoric times. Wolves were exterminated and wolverines extirpated; beavers, martens and lynx populations were reduced by trapping and forestry but are making a comeback.

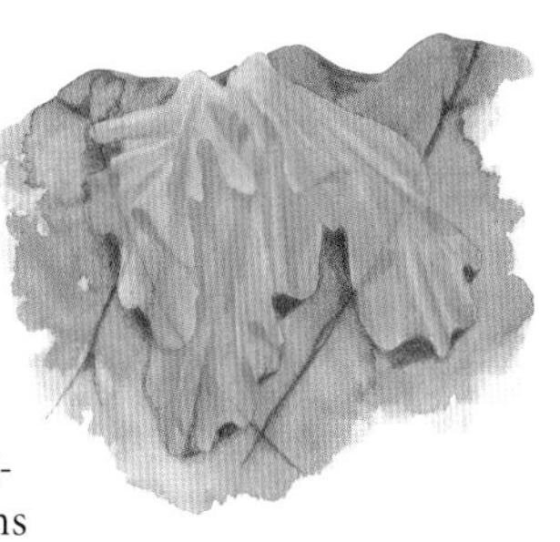
sea lettuce

Biodiversity is at its highest along the suburban fringe, where a botanical anarchy of remnant native plants, exotic introduced plants and hybrids exists. Strategic species, whether native or introduced, take advantage of evolving opportunities for food, shelter and breeding territory. We have established human-made lakes, urban parks, bird feeders, birdhouses and bat houses to deliberately accommodate the species we appreciate, whereas wharves and ports, garbage dumps and even our own homes seem to attract unwanted species we consider to be pests. Many of the most common plants and animals in these altered landscapes were not present before the arrival of settlers and modern transportation. The most established of the introduced species exemplify how co-habitation with humans offers a distinct set of living situations that benefit many plants and animals. The house mouse, brown rat and house sparrow are some of the highly successful exotic animals that have been introduced to North America from Europe and Asia. Exotic and noxious weeds number in the thousands, and insect pests have been either deliberately or accidentally introduced for centuries.

softshell clam

house sparrow

THE SEASONS

moose

The New England forests are famous for their fall color; various glorious shades of red, orange and yellow are even further highlighted in contrast to the evergreen boreal stands that intermingle with the deciduous trees in the transitional forest. Spruce and fir stands are reduced to islands farther south and along the ridges of the Appalachians.

The seasons of New England greatly influence the lives of plants and animals. Although some birds, insects and marine mammals are migratory, most animals are terrestrial and have varying ranges—the range of a large predator can cross multiple state borders, and a whale can travel the length of the North American continent, but a vole's range may encompass only a few square yards. Animals with limited geographic ranges must cope in various ways with the changing seasons.

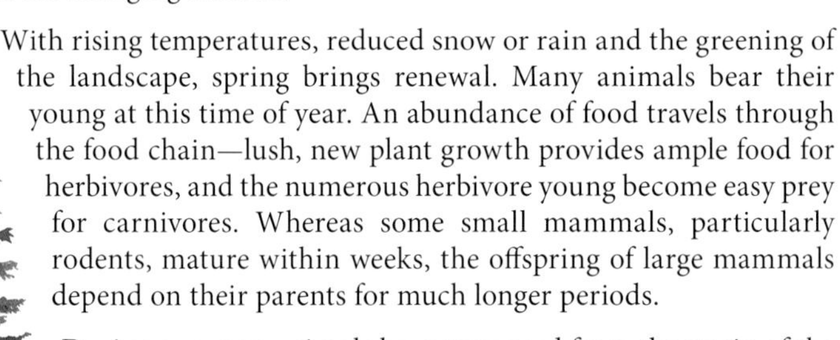
red spruce

With rising temperatures, reduced snow or rain and the greening of the landscape, spring brings renewal. Many animals bear their young at this time of year. An abundance of food travels through the food chain—lush, new plant growth provides ample food for herbivores, and the numerous herbivore young become easy prey for carnivores. Whereas some small mammals, particularly rodents, mature within weeks, the offspring of large mammals depend on their parents for much longer periods.

During summer, animals have recovered from the strain of the previous winter's food scarcity and spring's reproductive efforts, but it is not a time of relaxation. To prepare yet again for the upcoming fall and winter, some animals must eat vast quantities of food to build up fat reserves, whereas others work furiously to stockpile food caches in safe places. Some of the more charismatic species such as white-tailed deer and moose mate in the fall with dramatic ruts, but small mammals such as voles and mice may mate every few months or even year-round.

meadow vole

Summers are warm, but winters are snowy and cold, with extremes of –60°F winter lows to 110°F summer highs. The average winter temperature is below freezing, with heavy snowfall. The long 4- to 5-month growing season was what permitted the first colonies to become established and nurture food crops and orchards.

Higher altitudes and inland areas of New England endure harsher climates than the coast. Winter differs in intensity and duration between these two regions.

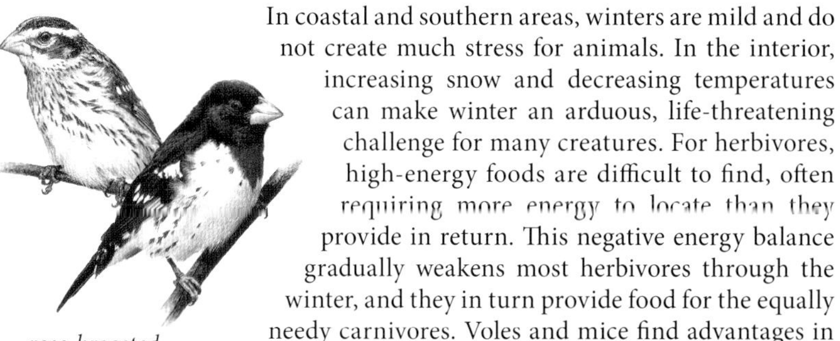
rose-breasted grosbeak

In coastal and southern areas, winters are mild and do not create much stress for animals. In the interior, increasing snow and decreasing temperatures can make winter an arduous, life-threatening challenge for many creatures. For herbivores, high-energy foods are difficult to find, often requiring more energy to locate than they provide in return. This negative energy balance gradually weakens most herbivores through the winter, and they in turn provide food for the equally needy carnivores. Voles and mice find advantages in the season—an insulating layer of snow protects their elaborate trails from the worst of winter's cold. Food, shelter and warmth are all found in the thin layer between the snow and the ground surface, and the months devoted to food storage now pay off.

mayflower

The seasons also affect the array of species found in the region. When you visit natural areas in winter, for example, you will see a different group of species than in summer; many plants die back, migrating animals head south, and other animals become dormant in winter. Conversely, many birds arrive at bird feeders in winter, and certain mammals, such as deer, enter lowland meadows to find edible vegetation, making these species more visible during cold weather.

Spring tides are the highest and the lowest when the moon and the sun (both on the same side of the planet, the moon in front of sun) are aligned with the earth, generating the maximum gravitational pull; neap tides are the most minimal tidal changes, when the sun and the moon are at right angles to each other, cancelling out one another's gravitational pull on the oceans. The moon orbits the earth every 27½ days, changing position daily and rising about 50 minutes later each day. So, at the same point on the earth, tidal changes occur 50 minutes later each day. This explains one tide change every day, but most places have two high and two low tides daily. The second tide is a result of centrifugal force, a whipping effect that occurs as the earth turns.

northern moon snail

No discussion about the weather would be complete without mentioning hurricanes. The Atlantic coast is not immune to the impacts of tropical cyclones and has been hit by several severe hurricanes throughout recorded history. In 1939, a hurricane felled a million sugar maples in Vermont, and trees throughout New England are often pruned by Mother Nature's shears, when high winds rip through the forest.

NATIONAL PARKS, PROTECTED AREAS & OTHER WILDLIFE-WATCHING AREAS

Whether with great foresight or regretful hindsight, many protected areas and parks have been established to conserve areas of wilderness. During the early decades of European settlement, species disappeared because of either habitat loss or deliberate extirpation—for example, the eradication of wolves to prevent livestock losses. Ancient old-growth forests were wiped out when wooded areas were cleared for agriculture and trees cut down for pulp and timber. Today, more natural areas than ever before are being set aside for wilderness conservation, for its intrinsic value as well as for us to appreciate and experience now and into the future.

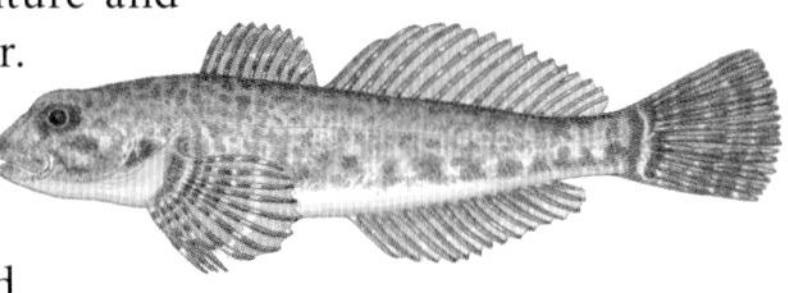

mottled sculpin

New England has many state parks, state forests and state wildlife and wildlife management areas, but many wildlife hotspots and areas of particular natural beauty extend far beyond protected area jurisdictions. For example, the Connecticut River, New England's largest and longest waterway at over 400 mi in length, has been designated an American Heritage River. Starting near the Canadian border, it flows through Vermont, New Hampshire, Massachusetts and Connecticut, and throughout the river valley, anybody who looks skyward in spring or fall can witness the great hawk migrations that follow this flyway. Bird migrations can make wildlife hotspots out of your favorite beach, city park or your own backyard. The many rivers, lakes, mountain trails and miles of coastline throughout New England all invite people to get out and enjoy nature. Below is just a sampling of the parks and natural areas you may wish to explore.

New England aster

Marsh-Billings-Rockefeller National Historical Park, Vermont

Created in August 1992, Marsh-Billings-Rockefeller National Historical Park recounts the conservation history and evolving nature of land stewardship in America. This park has significant heritage value, protecting some of the original homesteads, covered bridges and rambling stone walls in the area, as well as sugar maples and 400-year-old hemlocks. Wildlife also benefits from the protected area, and bobcats have been spotted in the park.

bobcat

Mount Washington and White Mountain National Forest, New Hampshire

red fox

Mount Washington, the highest peak in New England at 6288 ft, lies in the heart of the spectacular White Mountains. Famed not only for its stature, but also for its erratic, often extreme weather, it holds the world record for wind speed (231 mph). The scenic White Mountains strongly define the topography of New Hampshire, covering about a quarter of its area and a small portion of western Maine. White Mountain National Forest's trails and campgrounds encourage the public to enjoy the nature of this spectacular region. A total of 237 bird species, with 145 breeding species confirmed and 11 species unconfirmed, have been recorded in the nearly 800,000 acres of White Mountain National Forest and surrounding areas. Animal species include moose, deer and foxes, and the Kancamagus Highway and the northernmost areas of the national forest are well known for numerous moose sightings.

Acadia National Park and Mount Desert Island, Maine

starflower

Established in 1919, Acadia National Park was the first national park established east of the Mississippi River and remains the only national park in New England. It protects 50,000 acres on a cluster of islands on the Maine coast, with lengths of shoreline, the only genuine fjord in the Lower 48 and innumerable lakes and ponds that host nearly a dozen different species of amphibians and fish. Half of Mount Desert Island lies within the park. The forest was modified by a major fire in 1947 that burned over 10,000 acres (plus 8000 acres outside the park area) and provided an opportunity for yellow and white birches, aspens and red maples to take hold. Red and white spruce, eastern hemlock, white pine and balsam fir dominate in the rest of the park. Among the mountains stands Cadillac Mountain, which, at 1530 ft, is the highest point on the U.S. Atlantic coast. Walk some of the 115 mi of trails to witness the transition between the eastern deciduous and northern coniferous forests, where a high diversity of species of plants and animals are at the edges of their geographic ranges. You can see common woodland flowers such as goldthread, bluebead lily and starflower. In spring, bluebead lily has pale yellow flowers that turn to striking blue, bead-like berries by later summer or early fall, at which time members of the aster family such as black-eyed Susan and New England aster are in full bloom. Twenty-three species of wood-warblers breed in the park, and these offshore islands provide critical nesting habitat for common eiders (*Somateria mollissima*) and other seabirds, raptors and colonial shorebirds, as well as winter habitat for numerous migratory birds. Scores of bald eagles stop here during migration. Mollusks, crustaceans and other marine invertebrates and various seaweeds are to be discovered in the tidal pools of the intertidal zones.

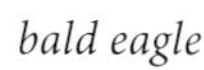

bald eagle

Top Wildlife-watching Sites in New England

Vermont (VT)

1. Missisquoi NWR
2. Groton SF
3. Marsh-Billings-Rockefeller National Historic Park
4. Green Mountain NF

New Hampshire (NH)

5. Mt Washington & White Mountain NF
6. Pawtuckaway SP
7. Clough SP
8. Miller SP & Pack Monadnock Mtn
9. Odiorne Point SP

Maine (ME)

10. Rachel Carson NWR
11. Reid SP & Popham Beach SP
12. Acadia NP & Mount Desert Island
13. Hirundo Wildlife Refuge & Orono
14. Moosehorn NWR

Massachusetts (MA)

15. Moran WMA & Notchview Reservation
16. Arcadia WS
17. Rutland SP
18. Great Meadows NWR
19. Walden Pond
20. Parker River NWR
21. Boston Harbor
22. Daniel Webster WS
23. Wellfleet Bay WS
24. Cape Cod National Seashore
25. Monomoy NWR
26. Martha's Vineyard & Felix Neck WS
27. Nantucket Island

Connecticut (CT)

28. Peoples SF
29. Nepaug SF
30. Simsbury SWA
31. Naugatuck SF
32. Quaker Ridge
33. Hammonasset Beach SP
34. Natchaug SF
35. Barn Island WMA
36. Bluff Point SP

Rhode Island (RI)

37. Buck Hill SMA
38. Ninigret NWR
39. Sachuest Point NWR

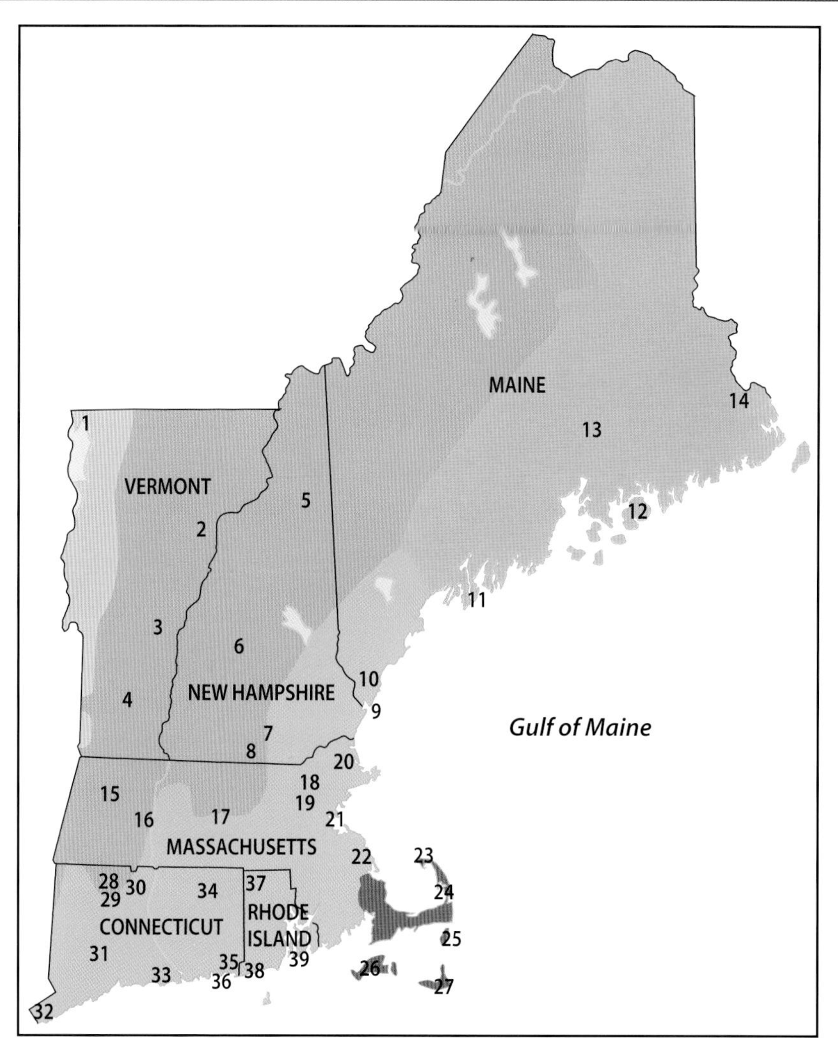

Acadian–New England Forest Ecoregions

- Great Lakes Lowlands
- Northeastern Highlands
- Laurentian Plains & Hills
- Oceanic Broadleaf Forest
- Coastal Pine Barrens

Abbreviations

NF . . . . . National Forest
NP. . . . . National Park
NWR . . . National Wildlife Refuge
SF . . . . . State Forest
SP . . . . . State Park
SWA. . . . State Wildlife Area
WMA . . . Wildlife Management Area
WS . . . . Wildlife Sanctuary

Map is based on *Level III Ecoregions of the Continental United States* (2000) issued by the U.S. Environmental Protection Agency.

Cape Cod National Seashore, Massachusetts

Cape Cod National Seashore comprises over 43,000 acres extending from the shoreline to uplands and provides diverse upland, wetland and coastal habitats, as well as woodlands, pine and scrub oak forests, heathlands, grasslands, sphagnum bogs, swamps, salt marshes and vernal ponds. Within the park are 20 permanently flooded freshwater kettle ponds ranging in size from 2½ to 100 acres and from 6 to 65 ft in depth. There are marine mammals offshore, and hundreds of species of amphibians, reptiles, fish, birds and invertebrates live on the cape among the iconic Cape Cod lighthouses, cottages and beaches. Migratory and nesting shorebirds are of particular importance, with 25 federally protected species occurring in the park, most prominently the threatened piping plover (roughly 5 percent of the entire Atlantic coast population nests here).

red-backed salamander

Boston Harbor Islands National Recreational Area, Massachusetts

The 30-plus islands and numerous peninsulas in Boston Harbor, located in Massachusetts Bay, protect habitat for most of coastal New England's animal species. Birds such as barn owls, common terns and northern harriers, reptiles such as eastern garter snakes and mammals such as eastern cottontails, raccoons, skunks, squirrels and many rodent species inhabit the islands. The islands are believed to have originally been covered with mature forests of typical eastern hardwoods, and though some mixed oak stands remain, the woodlands were cleared for agriculture and today feral fruit trees, herbs, horseradish and asparagus can be found. Patches of undisturbed native flora are rare—most of the islands are covered with grasses and sumac. From the shoreline to the deeps, the waters teem with lobsters, crabs, clams, mussels, jellyfish, sea turtles and fish, and marine mammals such as harbor seals, white-sided dolphins, harbor porpoises and humpback, fin, minke, pilot and right whales. **Stellwagen Bank National Marine Sanctuary**, located at the mouth of Massachusetts Bay, between Cape Cod and Cape Ann, was established in 1992 to federally protect the 842 mi² (638 nautical mi²) of this important marine ecosystem. Supported by the bank, Stellwagen is one of only 14 such marine sanctuaries in the United States.

barn owl

Atlantic minke whale

staghorn sumac

Walden Pond State Reservation, Massachusetts

Henry David Thoreau (1817–62) lived at Walden Pond from July 1845 to September 1847; it is here that he wrote his seminal work, *Walden; or, Life in the Woods* (1854), in which he called for a return to simplicity and respect for nature. Considered by many to be the birthplace of the conservation movement, the pond is surrounded by 333 acres of woodland. Thoreau lived in relative isolation here, but, ironically, his followers now come to the area in droves. Visitors are limited to 1000 at one time. Despite the area's popularity, you can still find the wildlife of Thoreau's time; mammals such as rabbits, gray squirrels and chipmunks are common, and though skunks, raccoons and red foxes are primarily nocturnal, they can sometimes be observed just after sunrise or before sunset. In spring and fall, migratory ducks and geese fly overhead and land in nearby marshes for food and rest. Other birds such as belted kingfishers, black-capped chickadees and red-tailed hawks can often be seen. Pickerel, once the pond's main fish, disappeared around the turn of the 20th century but are now stocked annually.

eastern gray squirrel

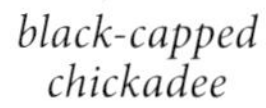

black-capped chickadee

Barn Island Wildlife Management Area, Connecticut

Located in the extreme southeastern corner of the state, in a protected enclave sheltered by headlands, the 1013-acre Barn Island WMA is Connecticut's single largest coastal area managed for wildlife conservation and includes a number of diverse of ecosystems and habitats, with mixed hardwood forests, hilly uplands, open fields, coastal scrub woodlands and thickets and salt, brackish and freshwater tidal wetlands. The conservation area features 36 federally and state-listed animal and plant species that are considered endangered, threatened or species of special concern. Recognized as a globally significant Important Bird Area (IBA), Barn Island hosts the willet, king rail (*Rallus elegans*), seaside sparrow (*Ammodramus maritimus*) and saltmarsh sparrow (*A. caudacutus*), provides feeding habitat for herons, egrets, terns and a number of shorebird species, and supports wintering populations of short-eared owls (*Asio flammeus*) and savannah sparrows. The nutrient-rich tidal saltmarshes also serve as nurseries, spawning grounds and feeding areas for a wide variety of finfish, shellfish and crustaceans. Barn Island gives visitors easy access to some of the state's most extensive saltmarsh communities.

great egret

green crab

The Appalachian Mountains

The Appalachian Mountains, which extend through parts of Maine, New Hampshire, Vermont, Massachusetts and Connecticut, include several mountain ranges and are the most rugged in New England. The Green Mountains of Vermont run north-south from Massachusetts to Quebec, between the Champlain and Connecticut River valleys. The Long Trail, constructed from 1910 to 1930, is the oldest long-distance trail in the U.S. and follows the main ridge of the Green Mountains from the Massachusetts-Vermont border north to Canada. It coincides with the 2175-mile-long Appalachian Trail, which runs from Mount Katahdin in Maine to Springer Mountain in Georgia. The Appalachian Trail crosses 14 states and two national parks, and extends through five of the six New England states, missing only Rhode Island. Gray foxes, deer, black bears, moose, raccoons, skunks and porcupines share the trail. You can take in stunning mountain vistas and see the flora and fauna associated with the trail's hardwood forests and wetlands of rivers and alpine bogs. The trail reaches its highest point of 6288 ft on Mount Washington in New Hampshire's White Mountains.

porcupine

National Wildlife Refuges (NWR)

pinxter flower

The first national wildlife refuge was established by President Theodore Roosevelt on Pelican Island in Florida as a bird refuge. Nationwide, approximately 93 million acres of wilderness have come under NWR protection. There are 32 national wildlife refuges in New England, including Moosehorn NWR in Vermont, Great Meadows NWR and Monomoy NWR in Massachusetts and Sachuest Point NWR in Rhode Island. You can learn more about the wildlife refuges in each state through the U.S. Fish and Wildlife Service website at www.fws.gov/refuges/. A few of the national wildlife refuges in New England are described in detail below.

Missisquoi National Wildlife Refuge, Vermont

One of the best areas for waterfowl and marsh birds in Vermont, and in New England, is the 5650-acre Missisquoi NWR, located in the delta of the Missisquoi River close to Lake Champlain. The name comes from an Abenaki word meaning "land of much grass and many waterfowl"—a description that still rings true. Because dike trails are partly inundated during spring floods, a canoe is the best way to get around. Most trails are accessible by foot in summer, and the refuge is a good place to look for waterfowl, as well as resident northern saw-whet owls and visiting snowy owls.

snowy owl

Rachel Carson National Wildlife Refuge, Maine

Established in 1966 to protect important wetlands for migratory birds, this refuge is named in honor of Rachel Carson (1907–64), a marine biologist who became one of the country's most eminent conservationists and the author of many books. Her influential *Silent Spring* bravely documented the decline of songbirds and drew a connection between the decrease in bird populations and pesticide use. The refuge holds or is adjacent to nesting sites for one-half to three-quarters of Maine's piping plover nests and is restoring native flora.

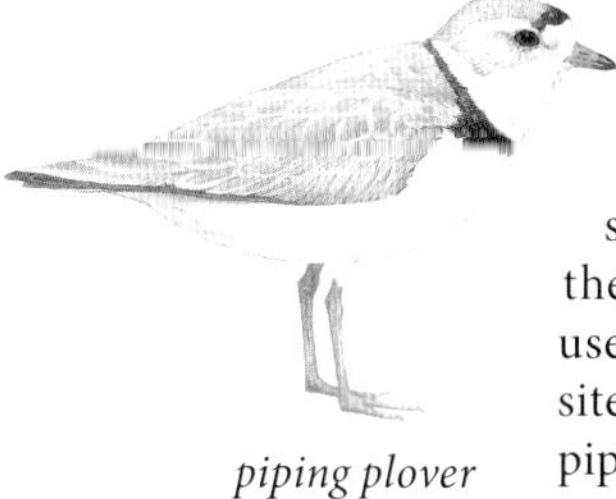
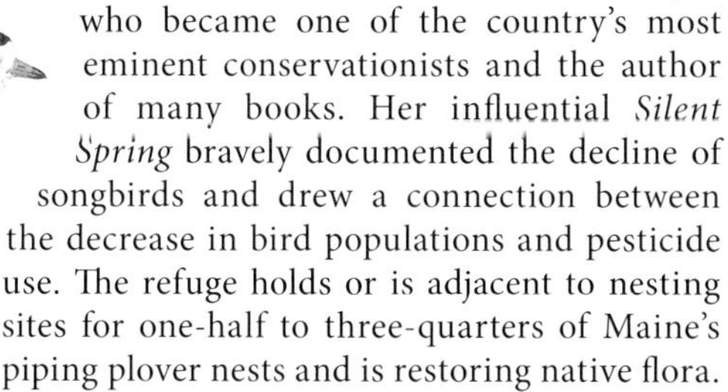

piping plover

Ninigret National Wildlife Refuge, Rhode Island

Ninigret NWR borders the 1700 acres of Ninigret Pond—the largest saltwater pond in the state. The diverse wildlife reflects the varied habitats, which include salt marshes, kettle ponds, freshwater wetlands, maritime shrublands and forests dominated by oak and maple. More than 250 bird species have been recorded, with 70 species nesting in the area. The fall shorebird migration can be spectacular, and endangered piping plovers nest on some of the beaches. Twenty-two mammal species have been observed in the park, including white-tailed deer, coyotes, red squirrels, red foxes, raccoons, striped skunks and river otters. A number of reptile and amphibian species also occur, as do a wide variety of butterfly species.

American copper

chain pickerel

Wildlife Sanctuaries

Wildlife Sanctuaries are found throughout the country and are usually established and managed by trusts, private individuals or large organizations and add to the network of protected areas for nature. Audubon is an example of an organization that has established several sanctuaries in New England to protect bird and other wildlife habitat. Among them are Felix Neck Wildlife Sanctuary on Martha's Vineyard, where visitors can see osprey and other fish hawks, and Arcadia Wildlife Sanctuary in Massachussets, which features white-tailed deer, black bears, otters and beavers.

northern river otter

OBSERVING NATURE

song sparrow

Nature is always around us in some form, and not a day goes by when we do not see a plant or animal or notice the weather. In New England, the species and scenery are so abundantly gorgeous that we risk spoiling our senses. Wild beauty is ever present—even our neighborhoods and backyards host numerous species of plants and animals. Consider that city parks offer ample opportunity to revel in nature, listen to songbirds or the buzzing of insects, smell the perfume of flowers or the decadence of autumn ripeness, see the color of plants and birds, and watch the ongoing dramas and occupations of busy squirrels and courting nesting birds. On the coast, you can watch seabirds dive for fish or perhaps glimpse a humpback whale breech.

white-tailed deer

The Best Viewing Times

Many birds and mammals are most active at dawn and dusk, so the best times for viewing them are during these "wildlife hours," when animals emerge from their daytime hideouts or roosting sites. During winter, hunger may force some mammals to be more active during midday. Conversely, in warm seasons, some animals may become less active and less visible in the heat of the day.

Birding Basics

The Atlantic Flyway is an important migratory route, bringing birds to our area that are traveling between the Arctic and their wintering grounds to the south. Birding is an increasingly popular activity for many people, and there are scores of excellent books, online resources, clubs and organizations to learn from. When practised with patience and reserve, birding is a low-impact pastime and a ready source of mental and physical exercise. One must be patient, though, because birds are among the most highly mobile animals; they may be seen one moment and then vanish the next!

wood duck

pied-billed grebe

New England hosts many breeding birds and year-round residents, as well as large numbers of spring and autumn migrants. Approximately 345 bird species can be seen in the region on a regular basis, and nearly 500 species have been recorded in New England. The coastlines are wintering grounds for waterfowl, geese, loons and grebes. The Shepaug Dam in Southbury, Connecticut, is famous for the large concentrations of bald eagles that pass through during winter migration.

Even in winter, the mild climate of New England permits many bird species to overwinter along the coast, and Christmas bird counts tally up scores of species. Some people set up bird feeders in their backyards in winter and stock them through to late spring to help birds before the plants bloom or insects hatch. Be sure to keep bird feeders clean, especially nectar feeders, to prevent the spread of disease or spoilage that can make birds ill.

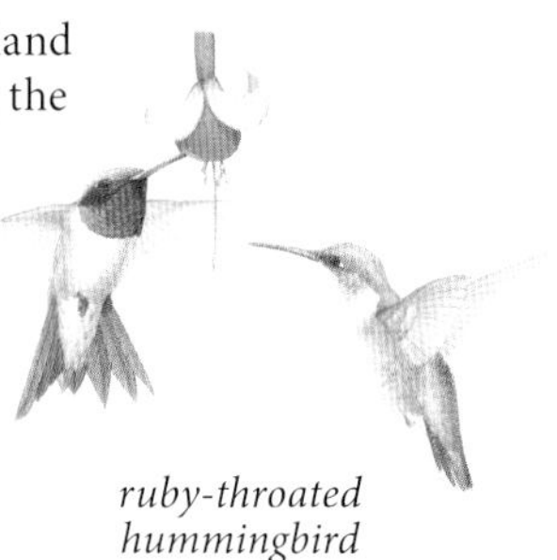

ruby-throated hummingbird

Naturescaping

Karner blue butterfly

Native plants in gardens and landscaping provide natural foods and shelter for birds, as well as for beneficial insects such as butterflies and bees, and even certain mammals. Flocks of waxwings have a keen eye for red mountain-ash berries, and hummingbirds enjoy columbine flowers. The cumulative effects of "naturescaping" in urban yards can be a significant step toward habitat conservation (especially when you consider that habitat is often lost in small amounts—a seismic line is cut in one area or a highway is built in another). Many good books and websites about attracting wildlife to your backyard are available. In contrast, learn how to keep your yard from attracting easily habituated wildlife such as coyotes and bears. Deal with garbage and compost responsibly, reconsider bird feeders that may lure bears, and do not leave pet food outside. When camping, be bear-wise with your food and toiletries, storing them in a manner that will not attract the keen noses and insatiable appetites of these animals.

winterberry

black bear

Whale Watching

Whale watching can be an organized activity, with boats taking groups of tourists out to known areas of high whale and dolphin sightings, but because many aquatic species frequent inshore waters, there can be random moments of fortune when you might see a whale or dolphin right from the shore. Although whale watching has strong merit for encouraging public awareness of and appreciation for marine mammals and the health of the oceans, it can disrupt cetacean behavior, so tour groups must be considerate and passive in the presence of these sensitive species. Encourage companies and fellow whale watchers to not harass the animals when trying get as close as possible for a photo op, and understand the decisions of tour organizers to keep a respectful distance.

humpback whale

Humans & Wildlife

Although more people have become conscious of the need to protect wildlife, human pressures have nevertheless damaged critical habitats, and some species experience frequent harassment. Modern wildlife viewing demands courtesy and common sense. Honor both the encounter and the animal by demonstrating a respect appropriate to the occasion. Here are some points to remember for ethical wildlife watching in the field:

- Stress is harmful to wildlife, so never chase or flush animals from cover or try to catch or touch them. Use binoculars and keep a respectful distance, for the animal's sake and often for your own. Amphibians are especially sensitive to being touched or held—sunscreen or insect repellent on your skin can poison the animal.

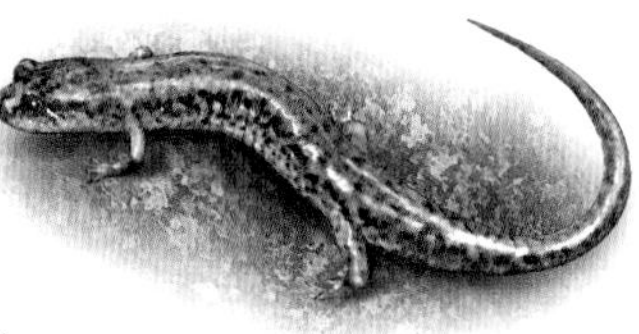

northern dusky salamander

- Leave the environment, including both flora and fauna, unchanged by your visit. Tread lightly and take home only pictures and memories. Do not pick wildflowers, and do not collect sea stars, sea urchins or seashells still occupied by the animal.
- Fishing is a great way to get in touch with nature, and many anglers appreciate the non-consumptive ethos of catch-and-release.
- Pets hinder wildlife viewing and may chase, injure or kill other animals, so control your pets or leave them at home.
- Take time to learn about wildlife and the behavior and sensitivity of each species.

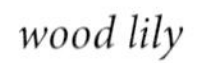

wood lily

ANIMALS

Animals are mammals, birds, reptiles, amphibians, fish and invertebrates, all of which belong to the Kingdom Animalia. They obtain energy by ingesting food that they hunt or gather. Mammals and birds are endothermic, meaning that their body temperature is internally regulated and will stay nearly constant regardless of the surrounding environmental temperature, unless the external temperature is extreme and persistent. Reptiles, amphibians, fish and invertebrates are ectothermic, meaning that they do not have the ability to regulate their own internal body temperature and tend to be the same temperature as their surroundings. Animals reproduce sexually, and they have a limited growth that is reached at sexual maturity. They also have diverse and complicated behaviors that are displayed in courtship, defense, parenting, playing, fighting, eating and hunting, as well as how they establish and recognize social hierarchies and how they deal with environmental stresses such as weather, change of season or availability of food and water. This guide includes the region's most common, wide-ranging, charismatic and historically significant animals. Diverse families such as rodents are represented by a few selected species.

red squirrel

barred owl

spotted salamander

Atlantic cod

green darner

MAMMALS

Mammals are the group to which human beings belong. In general, mammals are endothermic, bear live young (with the exception of the platypus), nurse their young and have hair or fur on their bodies. Typically, all mammals larger than rodents are sexually dimorphic, meaning that the male and the female differ in appearance, either by size or by other diagnostics such as antlers. Males are usually larger than females. Different groups of mammals include herbivores, carnivores, omnivores and insectivores. People often associate large mammals with wilderness, making these animals prominent symbols in Native American legends and stirring emotional connections with people in modern times.

Whales, Dolphins & Porpoises
pp. 48–53

Seals
pp. 54–55

Hoofed Mammals
p. 56

Cats
pp. 57–58

Bears
p. 58

Dogs
p. 59

Weasels & Skunks
pp. 60–62

Raccoon
p. 62

Rabbits & Hares
pp. 62–63

Beaver
p. 63

Porcupine
p. 64

Squirrels
pp. 64–65

Mice, Rats & Kin
pp. 66–68

Bats
pp. 69–70

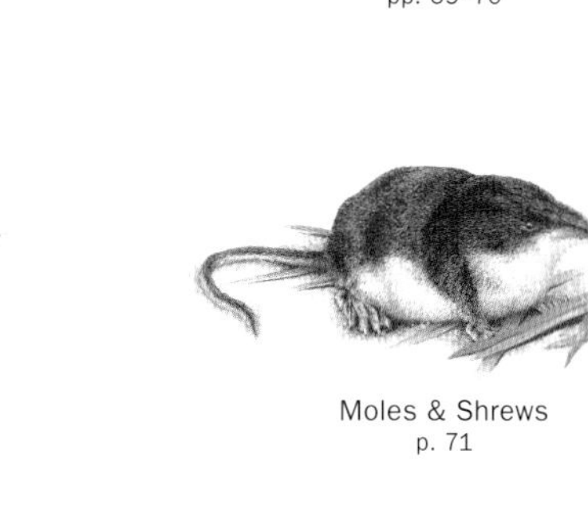

Opossum
p. 71

Moles & Shrews
p. 71

Blue Whale

Balaenoptera musculus

Length: to 110 ft; average 65–88 ft
Weight: to 150 tons; average 100–120 tons

Likely every account of the blue whale begins the same way: this is the largest animal ever to exist—it is even larger than the dinosaurs were. Despite its enormous size, this whale feeds almost exclusively on tiny krill—up to 5 million, or nearly 2 tons, per day—straining them through its baleen. It eats krill in our polar waters and migrates south to breed and calve. • This whale is critically endangered. **Where found:** offshore, but sometimes in shallow inshore waters; from the Arctic Circle to Panama, including the northwestern Gulf of Mexico. **Also known as:** sulfur-bottom whale (historically, because its belly was often colored yellow from diatoms accumulated in cold waters), great northern rorqual.

Fin Whale

Balaenoptera physalus

Length: to 85 ft; average 60–70 ft
Weight: 30–80 tons

When this long, sleek giant swims leisurely and gracefully along the surface of the water, its tall, narrow, dense blow reaches over 20 ft in height and is very noticeable on the horizon, but the whale does not show its flukes when beginning a dive. It is named for its recognizable and easily seen crescent-shaped dorsal fin. • The fin whale is found singly or in pairs but more often occurs in pods of 3 to 7 individuals, and on occasion several pods have been observed in a small area, creating concentrations of as many as 50 animals. • This whale is an exceptionally fast mover—it has been clocked at speeds over 20 mph in short bursts. It is a deep diver and is capable of breaching clear out of the water. **Where found:** inshore and offshore waters; from the Arctic Circle to the Greater Antilles, including the Gulf of Mexico.

Humpback Whale

Magaptera novaeangliae

Length: to 52 ft; average 38–45 ft
Weight: to 53 tons; average 23–30 tons

The haunting songs of the humpback last from a few minutes to a few hours and can endure as epic days-long concerts. They have inspired both scientists and artists and reach out to the imaginations of the many people who listen and wonder what this great creature is saying. • This rorqual employs a unique hunting strategy—it creates a bubble net to round up its prey into a tight cluster that the whale then ingests in a food-dense gulpful. **Where found:** along the coast along the continental shelf or island banks, sometimes in open offshore waters; from northern Iceland and western Greenland south to the West Indies, including the northern and eastern Gulf of Mexico.

Atlantic Minke Whale

Balaenoptera acutorostrata

Length: to 33 ft; average 25 ft
Weight: to 15 tons; average 5½–11 tons

The smallest of the rorquals, the minke whale is occasionally seen in our waters, but its seasonal distribution is governed by food availability. • The minke has been one of the more heavily hunted of the baleen whales since the 1980s, when populations of larger whale species had already collapsed. **Where found:** open offshore waters, sometimes in bays, inlets and estuaries; migrates seasonally between warm and cold waters; from the Arctic to the Lesser Antilles, including the eastern and northwestern Gulf of Mexico. **Also known as:** piked whale, sharp-headed finner, little finner, lesser finback, lesser rorqual.

Sei Whale

Balaenoptera borealis

Length: to 62 ft; average 39–52 ft
Weight: 15–30 tons

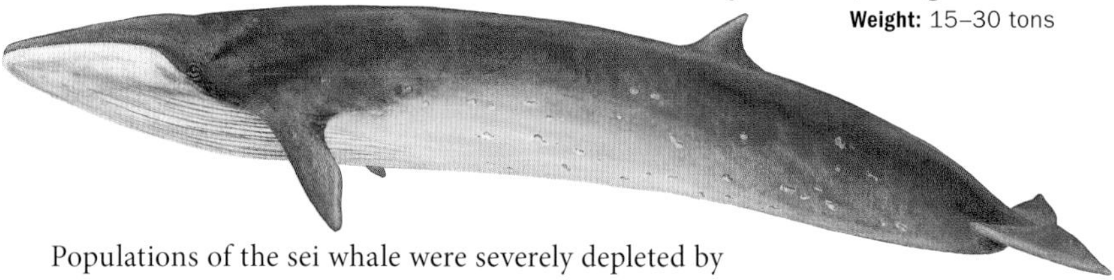

Populations of the sei whale were severely depleted by overhunting in the 1960s and '70s. Despite their overall small numbers, these whales can be locally abundant in "sei whale years." Typically seen singly or in small groups, they can occur in groups of up to 30 in areas with abundant food. • Although sei whales do not inhabit northern waters, they favor Subarctic feeding grounds in summer and migrate to warmer waters in winter. They eat fish, squid and crustaceans such as krill. **Where found:** throughout offshore temperate waters ranging as far north as the southern tip of Greenland. **Also known as:** sardine whale, pollack whale, coalfish whale, Japan finner, Rudolphi's rorqual.

North Atlantic Right Whale

Eubalaena glacialis

Length: to 59 ft; average 33–52 ft
Weight: to 117 tons; average 30–80 tons

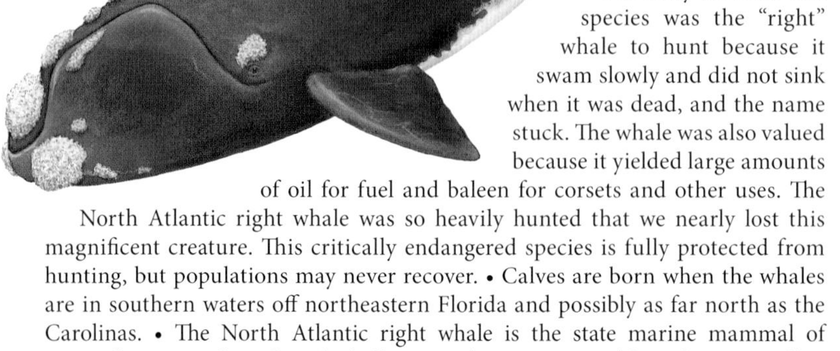

For early whalers, this species was the "right" whale to hunt because it swam slowly and did not sink when it was dead, and the name stuck. The whale was also valued because it yielded large amounts of oil for fuel and baleen for corsets and other uses. The North Atlantic right whale was so heavily hunted that we nearly lost this magnificent creature. This critically endangered species is fully protected from hunting, but populations may never recover. • Calves are born when the whales are in southern waters off northeastern Florida and possibly as far north as the Carolinas. • The North Atlantic right whale is the state marine mammal of Massachusetts. **Where found:** shallow nearshore waters and large bays, as well as offshore; from Iceland to eastern FL, occasionally into the southern Gulf of Mexico.

Sperm Whale

Physeter macrocephalus

Length: to 69 ft; average 48 ft
Weight: to 58 tons; average 35 tons

This whale's peculiar name comes from the oily fluid, called spermaceti, that fills its enormous head, which comprises a third of its total body length. This fluid has a couple of hypothesized functions: to regulate the whale's buoyancy as it dives, which can be to depths of 10,500 ft, and as a conduit through which the whale emits sounds for echolocation. • This is the only whale species that has a blow that sprays forward and to the left, owing to the orientation of its blowhole. • When executing a deep dive, a sperm whale first arches its back high above the surface of the water and then typically lifts its flukes into the air before slipping into the depths. • This whale is the state marine mammal of Connecticut. **Where found:** offshore waters all along the East Coast.

Long-finned Pilot Whale

Globicephala melas

Length: 12–20 ft
Weight: 2–3½ tons

Acrobatic pilot whales give great performances of some of the most amusing physical behaviors seen in whales: they spyhop (raise their heads straight up above the water's surface to take a look around), lobtail (raise their tail flukes above the water's surface) and slap their flukes on the water. All these great gestures may be a way of attracting attention in lieu of actually shouting out, "Hey! Look over here!" We can only speculate about why whales do the things they do, but they are fun to watch. Another thing we do not yet understand is why whales strand themselves on beaches, and this whale is frequently a victim to this phenomenon. • Squid are the favorite prey of these whales. **Where found:** offshore waters and bays, sometimes inshore in summer; from Iceland and Greenland south to NC.

Risso's Dolphin

Grampus griseus

Length: to 13 ft; average 8½–10 ft
Weight: to 1100 lb; average 880 lb

Risso's dolphins have the interesting social behavior of scratching and biting each other, leaving white scars all over their bodies—some older individuals are so scarred that they appear almost completely white. These dolphins can also become scarred from being stung by large squid, their preferred prey. • Although they are typically observed in groups of about a dozen, Risso's dolphins can occur in groups of several hundred, and they become quite engaged in play sessions of breaching, spyhopping, lobtailing and flipper and fluke slapping. **Where found:** deep offshore waters; from Atlantic Canada to the Lesser Antilles, including the northern and eastern Gulf of Mexico.

Short-beaked Common Dolphin

Delphinus delphis

Length: to 8½ ft; average 5½–6½ ft
Weight: to 300 lb; average 170 lb

Brilliant acrobatic feats accompany the thrill of having a group of these dolphins swim alongside your boat. They love to bow ride and can occur in very large groups of 50 up to 1000 individuals. A dolphin has the ability to rest one half of its brain at a time, allowing for a constant state of awareness. • The long-beaked common dolphin (*D. capensis*) is very similar both physically and behaviorally to the short-beaked, but does not range in our waters. **Where found:** offshore along the coast; from Atlantic Canada to northern South America.

Atlantic White-sided Dolphin

Lagenorhynchus acutus

Length: 6–9 ft; female larger than male
Weight: 365–440 lb

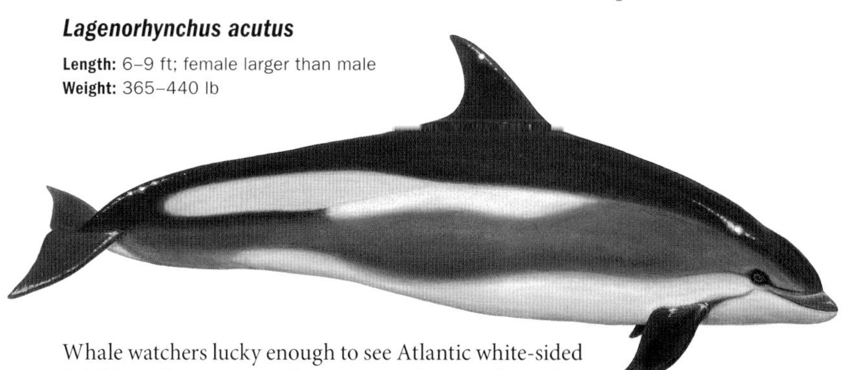

Whale watchers lucky enough to see Atlantic white-sided dolphins often get some bonus entertainment from these highly acrobatic animals, which breach, somersault, bow ride and seemingly get very excited at any opportunity to show off. Unlike humans, dolphins can focus their vision above and below water and often take a closer look at people by jumping alongside a boat or lifting their heads above the water's surface. **Where found:** open ocean; increased observations in coastal and sheltered waters, especially between islands and the mainland; from Greenland to New England. **Also known as:** lag, Atlantic striped dolphin, white-striped dolphin, hook-finned dolphin.

Harbor Porpoise

Phocoena phocoena

Length: 5½–6 ft
Weight: 125–145 lb

Although commonly seen because of its preference for inshore waters, the harbor porpoise is wary of boats and will not swim alongside them or bow ride. It will instead swim quietly along the surface of the water, feeding on octopus, squid and fish such as herring and doing its best to avoid large sharks and orcas (*Orcinus orca*), its main predators. **Where found:** Subarctic and cold-temperate inshore waters, in bays, harbors, estuaries and even at the mouths of rivers; in the Davis Strait and from southeastern Greenland to NC.

Harbor Seal

Phoca vitulina

Length: 4–5½ ft
Weight: 110–310 lb

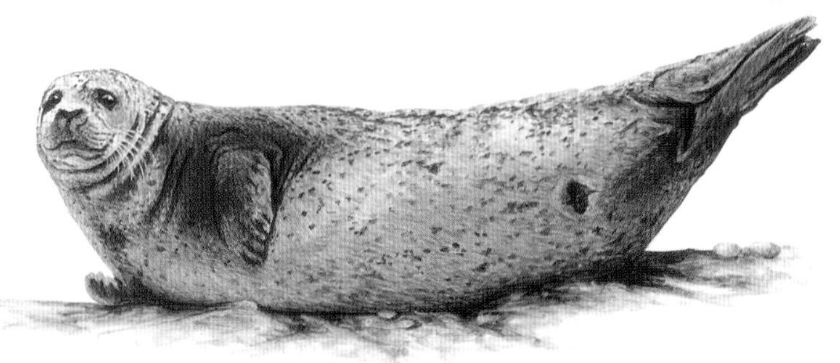

Year-round, large colonies of harbor seals can be observed either basking in the daytime or sleeping at night on rocky shores and islands. Oftentimes during the day, individuals can be seen bobbing vertically in the water. These seals are shy of humans but do occasionally pop their heads up beside a canoe or kayak to investigate, making a quick retreat thereafter. When they disappear below the surface, they are able dive to depths of over 300 ft—a feat accomplished by going without breathing for up to 30 minutes. **Where found:** bays, estuaries, intertidal sandbars, rocky shorelines and mouths of rivers along the coast; from Baffin I. and Hudson Bay coasts south to the Carolinas.

Gray Seal

Halichoerus grypus

Length: *Male:* to 8 ft; *Female:* rarely over 6½ ft
Weight: *Male:* 375–750 lb; *Female:* 220–440 lb

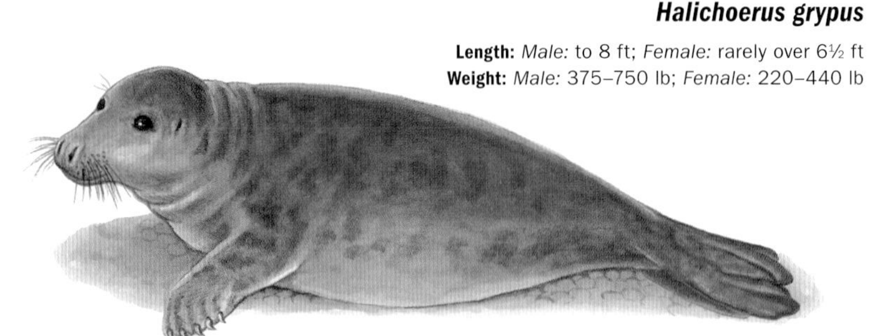

Gregarious gray seals haul out onto the shores of rocky coasts in large groups to breed and molt. After the winter breeding season, these seals disperse widely to feed in pelagic waters. Even pups, soon after being weaned, have been tracked 600 mi away from the shores of their birth. • These seals dive 100 to 230 ft to feed on fish, crustaceans and cephalopods, and have been recorded diving to depths of nearly 1000 ft and remaining submerged for up to 20 minutes. **Where found:** rocky shores; from Atlantic Canada to New England, with sightings as far south as VA. **Also known as:** horsehead seal.

Harp Seal

Phoca groenlandica

Length: 4½–6½ ft; average 5½ ft
Weight: average 285 lb

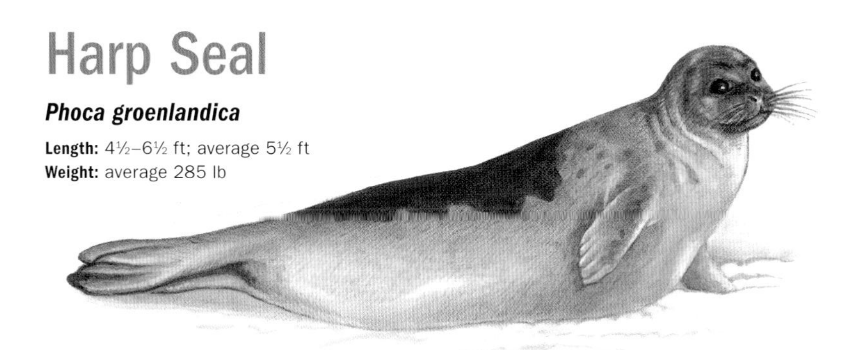

This high-endurance seal embarks upon annual migrations of up to 6000 mi and can to dive to 900 ft, holding its breath for up to 15 minutes. • Pups are born on the edge of the Arctic ice pack in February and are covered in white fur called lanugo. After nursing for 2 weeks, the pup grows from its birth weight of 12 lb to up to 100 lb, at which time the fat pup is left to fend for itself. Over the next couple of weeks, it drops half of its weight and molts its downy lanugo. Those that do not starve to death or fall prey to human hunters, polar bears or orcas eventually learn to fish and migrate north with the herd in summer. **Where found:** highly migratory in the North Atlantic from January to May, and the number of sightings and strandings has increased between ME and NJ, now considered the southern extent of this species' range. **Also known as:** *Pagophilus groenlandicus.*

Hooded Seal

Cystophora cristata

Length: 6–10 ft; average male 8 ft; average female 6½ ft
Weight: *Male:* 660 lb, maximum 880 lb; *Female:* 350 lb, maximum 500 lb

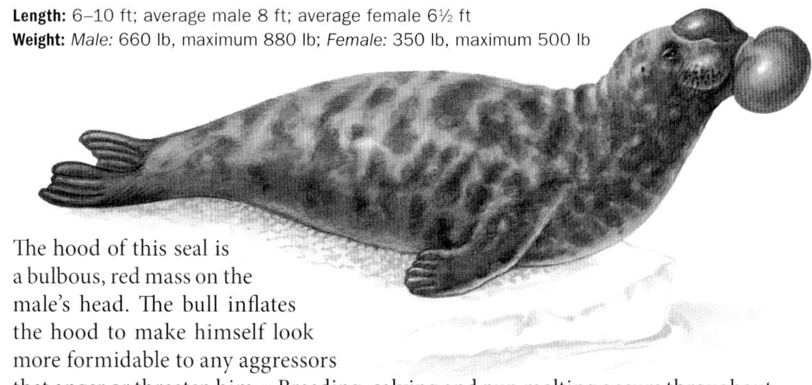

The hood of this seal is a bulbous, red mass on the male's head. The bull inflates the hood to make himself look more formidable to any aggressors that anger or threaten him. • Breeding, calving and pup molting occurs throughout the winter on the drifting pack ice. This seal is abundant in winter off the Grand Banks of Newfoundland, where there are large schools of fish to feed on so the seals can fatten up to survive the long cold season. In summer, the species disperses throughout the North Atlantic. • This seal can dive to depths of nearly 3300 ft and stay submerged for over 50 minutes. Individuals can live for 30 to 35 years. **Where found:** on the edge of drifting pack ice, in deep offshore waters of the North Atlantic; may stray into the Gulf of Maine during migration.

Moose

Alces alces

Length: 8–10 ft (including 3½–7½ in tail)
Shoulder height: 5½–7 ft
Weight: 500–1300 lb

The largest deer in the world, and state animal of Maine, Moose have been known to dive to depths of 13 ft to find aquatic plants rich in salts and minerals—and to escape those nasty biting insects! • Moose browse on trees and shrubs, and graze on grasses and forbs. • Bulls have large, wide antlers that can measure up to 5 ft across. A distinguishing dewlap, or "bell" (a long flap of fur-covered skin, hangs from the throat. **Where found:** near lakes and bogs; in riparian valleys, coniferous forests and willow and poplar groves; mostly in ME with dispersal south through New England; absent in VT, southeastern NH and northernmost MA.

White-tailed Deer

Odocoileus virginianus

Length: 4½–7 ft (including 8¼–14 in tail)
Shoulder height: 27–45 in
Weight: 110–440 lb

A wagging white tail disappearing into the forest is a common view of this deer. • When a mother deer is feeding, it leaves its scentless, spotted fawn behind among tall grasses or shrubs to hide it from potential predators. • A dense network of blood vessels covered by hair, called "velvet," covers the developing antlers of males in spring and summer. • The white-tailed deer is the state animal of New Hampshire. **Where found:** rolling country with open areas near cover; valleys and stream courses, woodlands, meadows and abandoned farmsteads with tangled shelterbelts; throughout New England. **Also known as:** Virginia deer.

Mountain Lion

Puma concolor

Length: 6–9 ft (including 20–35 in tail)
Shoulder height: 26–32 in
Weight: 65–190 lb

This secretive cat is seldom seen by people and has long been extirpated from New England, but occasionally track or scratch marks and rare sightings have been reported in Maine. • The mountain lion prefers to sit in a tree above an animal trail and pounce on its prey, which is mainly deer, but opportunities to take other prey—other ungulates, beavers, rabbits or birds—will not be passed up. **Where found:** in brushlands or open woodlands based on food availability; ME. **Also known as:** cougar, puma; *Felis concolor.*

Lynx

Lynx canadensis

Length: 31–40 in (including 3½–4¾ in tail)
Shoulder height: 18–24 in
Weight: 15–40 lb

With long legs and huge, well-furred paws, the lynx is uniquely adapted for catching snowshoe hares on snow. There is a very close predator-prey relationship between the lynx and the hare. Cyclical increases and decreases in hare populations, which are governed largely by food availability, cause lynx populations to follow similar trends—when hares are abundant, lynx kittens are more likely to survive and reproduce. • This feline's facial ruff, long, black ear tufts and short, black-tipped tail are distinctive features. The coat is gray to orange-brown. **Where found:** dense, old-growth coniferous forests with heavy undergrowth; rare in northern ME, NH and VT.

Bobcat

Lynx rufus

Length: 30–49 in
(including 5–6¾ in tail)
Shoulder height: 18–22 in
Weight: 15–29 lb

The nocturnal bobcat feeds on a wide range of prey, including rabbits, voles, mice, birds, reptiles and insects. Small but mighty, the bobcat is even capable of bringing down a deer by the throat if the opportunity presents itself. • This cat's atypically short, "bobbed" tail is well suited to the shrubby and forested areas in which it hunts, but the bobcat is highly adaptable and may even be seen close to residential areas. • Like most young cats, bobcat kittens are almost always at play. **Where found:** coniferous and deciduous forests, brushy areas and riparian areas with willow stands; VT, NH, ME, northern MA, northwestern CT and RI.

Black Bear

Ursus americanus

Length: *Male:* 4¼–6¼ ft;
Female: 4–5¼ ft
Shoulder height: 2–3.5 ft
Weight: *Male:* 250–880 lb;
Female: 90–500 lb

The black bear is primarily a forest dweller, with long claws well adapted to climbing trees and digging. It is omnivorous, eating plants, insects such as bees (and honey) and carrion. It sometimes even preys upon small rodents or young deer. This bear is prone to becoming habituated to humans by finding food in compost piles, garbage bins, granaries, bird feeders and the like. • Although variable in pelage in the West, eastern black bears almost always have the typical glossy, black fur with a tan muzzle, and many have a white "V" on the chest. **Where found:** mixed forests and shrub thickets with nut- and berry-producing plants; also swamps and suburban areas; VT (absent in the northwest), NH (absent in the southeast), northern and central ME, western and central MA and northwestern CT.

Coyote

Canis latrans

Length: 4–5 ft (including 12–15 in tail)
Shoulder height: 2–2¼ ft
Weight: 20–50 lb

Occasionally forming loose packs and joining in spirited yipping choruses, coyotes are intelligent and versatile hunter-scavengers, best described as opportunistic omnivores. • The size of an average dog, coyotes share many characteristics that we appreciate in domestic canines, but they are companions only to the wilderness and their fellow pack members. **Where found:** mixed and coniferous forests, meadows, agricultural lands and suburban areas; throughout New England. **Also known as:** brush wolf.

Red Fox

Vulpes vulpes

Length: 35–43 in (including 14–18 in tail)
Shoulder height: 15–18 in
Weight: 8–15 lb

The red fox is a talented and entertaining mouser with high-pouncing antics that are much more cat-like than canine. • This fox is typically a vivid reddish orange but can have darker color phases, with dark fur across the back and shoulders, or the coat can be almost entirely black with silver-tipped hairs. The tip of its elegant, bushy tail, however, is always white. **Where found:** prefers open, grassy habitats with brushy shelter, riparian areas and forest edges but avoids dense forests; throughout New England. **Also known as:** silver fox (referring to a color variation).

Gray Fox

Urocyon cinereoargenteus

Length: 11–17 in
Shoulder height: 14–15 in
Weight: 7½–13 lb

The mainly nocturnal gray fox prefers rocky, shrub-covered or forested terrain, and avoids populated areas, so it is rarely seen. Most remarkable is this fox's ability to climb trees—it is the only member of the dog family able to do so—to escape danger, pursue birds or rob egg-filled nests. • The gray fox's fur is shorter and denser than that of the red fox. **Where found:** open forests, shrublands and rocky areas; VT, NH, southern ME, MA (absent in the extreme south), CT (absent in the southeast) and northern RI.

American Marten

Martes americana

Length: 20–27 in (including 7–9 in tail)
Weight: 1–2½ lb

An expert climber with semi-retractable claws, this forest dweller is quick and agile enough to catch arboreal squirrels. Although it spends most of its time on the ground in search of rodent prey, the marten often dens in a tree hollow, where it raises its annual litter of 1 to 5 kits. • This animal is very elusive but sometimes falls victim to traplines, an ongoing threat even today. **Where found:** old-growth boreal and montane coniferous forests of spruce and fir with numerous dead trunks, branches and leaf cover; VT, NH and northern ME. **Also known as:** American sable, pine marten.

Fisher

Martes pennanti

Length: 31–47 in (including 12–16 in tail)
Weight: 4½–12 lb

Despite the name, fishers rarely consume fish but prey upon rodents, hares and birds, as well as eating berries, nuts and sometimes carrion. They will eat any animal they can overpower but are distinguished, along with mountain lions, for their ability to prey upon porcupines. • Fishers are extremely sensitive to any human disturbance and exist only in remote, forested wilderness, where they are top predators, quickly and nimbly maneuvering throughout the dense habitat. **Where found:** dense mixed and coniferous forests; absent from young, thinly treed, logged or burned forests; VT (absent in the southwest), NH, ME, central MA and northern CT.

Long-tailed Weasel

Mustela frenata

Length: 11–16½ in (including 5–11¼ in tail)
Weight: 3–14 oz

Following the tracks of the long-tailed weasel on a snow-covered meadow offers good insight into the curious and energetic nature of this little mammal. Constantly distracted from walking in a straight line, it continuously zigs and zags to investigate everything that catches its attention. • This weasel feeds on small rodents, birds, insects, reptiles, amphibians and occasionally fruits and berries. • Like other true weasels, it turns white in winter, but the tip of the tail remains black. **Where found:** aspen parklands, intermontane valleys and open forests; throughout New England.

Short-tailed Weasel

Mustela erminea

Length: 8–14 in (including 1½–3½ in tail)
Weight: 1½–3¾ oz

The short-tailed weasel is a voracious nocturnal hunter of mice and voles. Although relatively common, the short-tailed weasel will not linger for any admiring observers; a spontaneous encounter with this curious creature will reveal its extraordinary speed and agility as it quickly escapes from view. • This weasel's coat is white in winter, but the tail is black-tipped year-round. **Where found:** coniferous or mixed forests and grasslands; throughout New England. **Also known as:** ermine, stoat.

Mink

Neovison vison

Length: 18½–28 in (including 6–8 in tail)
Weight: 1½–3 lb

The mink's partially webbed feet make it an excellent swimmer, and it is capable of diving to depths of more than 10 ft in pursuit of fish. Its thick, dark brown to blackish, oily fur insulates its body from extremely cold waters. • The mink travels along established hunting routes, often along shorelines, rarely foregoing a prey opportunity. It stashes any surplus kills in temporary dens, typically dug into riverbanks, beneath rock piles or in evacuated muskrat lodges. **Where found:** shorelines of lakes, marshes and streams of forests and woods in foothills and on grasslands; throughout New England. **Also known as:** *Mustela vison.*

Northern River Otter

Lontra canadensis

Length: 3½–4½ ft (including 12–20 in tail)
Weight: 10–24 lb

The favorite sport of these frisky otters is sliding down riverbanks, wet, grassy hills and even snowy slopes in winter—look for their "slides" on the banks of rivers, lakes and ponds. When otters are not at play, they are engaged in the business of hunting. These swift swimmers mainly prey upon aquatic species such as crustaceans, turtles, frogs and fish, but they occasionally depredate bird nests and eat small rodents. **Where found:** fresh- and saltwater habitats; lakes, ponds and streams; also along the coast; VT, NH, ME, MA and northern CT and RI. **Also known as:** *Lutra canadensis.*

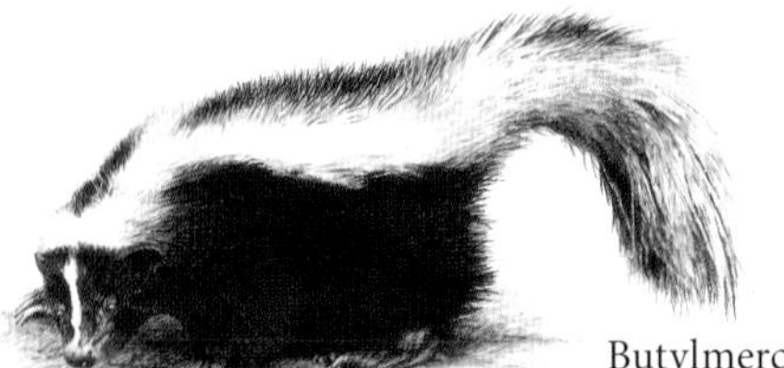

Striped Skunk

Mephitis mephitis

Length: 22–31 in (including 8–14 in tail)
Weight: 4–9 lb

Butylmercaptan is responsible for the stink of the striped skunk's musk, which is sprayed in self-defense. Only the great horned owl is undeterred by the skunk's odor and is one of this mammal's few predators. When undisturbed, the striped skunk is a quiet, reclusive omnivore, feeding on insects, worms, bird eggs, reptiles, amphibians, grains, green vegetation, berries and, rarely, small mammals and carrion. **Where found:** lower-elevation streamside woodlands, hardwood groves, semi-open areas, brushy grasslands and valleys; also urban areas; throughout New England.

Raccoon

Procyon lotor

Length: 26–39 in (including 7½–16 in tail)
Weight: 11–31 lb

Garbage containers are no match for the raccoon's curiosity, persistence and problem-solving abilities, making them and garden goldfish ponds prime targets for midnight food raids in urban areas. In this animal's natural habitat, an omnivorous diet of clams, frogs, fish, bird eggs and nestlings, berries, nuts and insects is more than ample. • The raccoon builds up its fat reserves during the warm months to sustain itself through the winter. **Where found:** lower-elevation riparian areas or edge habitats between forests and wetlands such as streams, lakes and ponds; throughout New England.

New England Cottontail

Sylvilagus transitionalis

Length: 10–15 in (including 1–2¼ in tail)
Weight: 1–2 lb

This endangered species is a rare sight, and this rabbit's secretive nature makes it doubly difficult to spot. New England cottontails hide out during the day in shallow burrows, called "forms," covered by impenetrable vegetation or in rock crevices to avoid their many predators. The adults do not camouflage white in winter, so they become even more reclusive but do not hibernate. • This species can be distinguished from the very similar eastern cottontail (*S. floridanus*) by its shorter ear length, slightly smaller body size, black spot between the ears, absence of a white spot on the forehead and a black line on the anterior edge of the ear. **Where found:** in brush, rocky areas and even buildings; isolated populations throughout New England except VT. **Also known as:** gray rabbit, brush rabbit, wood hare, cooney.

Snowshoe Hare

Lepus americanus

Length: 15–21 in (including 2 in tail)
Weight: 2¼–3¼ lb

Extremely well adapted for surviving harsh alpine winters, the snowshoe hare has large hind feet that allow it to move across deep snow without sinking, while the white pelage camouflages the animal. If detected by a predator, the hare explodes into a running zigzag pattern in its flight for cover, reaching speeds of up to 32 mph. • Populations of this hare, its winter food sources of willow and alder and its main predator, the lynx, are closely interrelated. **Where found:** brushy, second-growth forests, boreal and hardwood forests; VT, NH (absent in the southeast), ME (absent in the extreme south) and northeastern MA. **Also known as:** varying hare.

European Hare

Lepus europaeus

Length: 20–30 in (including 3–4 in tail)
Weight: 5½–14 lb

This species of hare was introduced from Europe about 100 years ago. Closely related to the native hares of western North America, it is the only hare that occurs in the East, and it is commonly seen wherever it ranges in New England. • Hares are larger than rabbits, have longer ears and distinctive, long, athletic legs. • This hare feeds on forbs in the summer, relying on twigs, bark and the buds of young trees in winter. **Where found:** fields and woodlands; southeastern corner of MA and central and western CT. **Also known as:** eastern hare, brown hare, eastern jackrabbit.

Beaver

Castor canadensis

Length: 3–4 ft (including 11–21 in tail)
Weight: 35–66 lb

The loud slap of a beaver's tail on water warns of intruders, and the tail is also an extremely effective propulsion device for swimming and diving (beavers can remain under water for 15 minutes). • The beaver's long, continuously growing incisors help the animal cut down trees in short order, and its strong jaws allow it to drag pieces of wood weighing up to 20 lb. **Where found:** lakes, ponds, marshes and slow-flowing rivers and streams with ample vegetation; throughout New England.

Porcupine

Erethizon dorsatum

Length: 21½–37 in (including 5½–9 in tail)
Weight: 7½–40 lb

Porcupines cannot actually throw their 30,000 or so quills but deliver them into the flesh of an attacker with a quick flick of the tail. • This excellent tree climber fills its vegetarian diet with forbs, shrubs and the sugary cambium of trees. An insatiable craving for salt occasionally drives it to gnaw on rubber tires, wooden ax handles, toilet seats and even hiking boots! • This slow-moving, nocturnal creature is a common road-kill victim. **Where found:** coniferous and mixed forests to grasslands; VT, NH, ME, western MA and extreme northeastern CT.

Woodchuck

Marmota monax

Length: 18–26 in (including 4–6 in tail)
Weight: 4–12 lb

Also known as "groundhog," this animal is rarely seen or even thought about until February 2, when everyone anticipates the sleepy creature emerging from its den to see its shadow. It would indeed be an early spring if the woodchuck stirred from its long slumber before February; you are unlikely to see one above ground before April or May. • The woodchuck's den is typically several feet deep, and abandoned dens are taken over by many other species, such as foxes. **Where found:** in or alongside their burrows in rock piles, ravines, open woodlands, pastures, meadows, under barns and in natural areas within city limits; throughout New England. **Also known as:** groundhog, marmot.

Eastern Gray Squirrel

Sciurus carolinensis

Length: 15–20 in (including 8¼–9½ in tail)
Weight: 14–25 oz

Originally found in large, mature forests, eastern gray squirrels have adapted to suburbia. Their large, rounded nests are made primarily of leaves and are often quite conspicuous in trees, though their winter den sites and birthing locales are in tree cavities. • These squirrels can locate their nut caches several months later, even if buried under snow. • In some areas, melanistic, or black, forms of this species predominate. Occasional albinos turn up, and these white squirrels often become local celebrities. **Where found:** mature deciduous or mixed forests with nut-bearing trees; common to abundant throughout New England. **Also known as:** black squirrel.

Red Squirrel

Tamiasciurus hudsonicus

Length: 11–14 in (including 4–6 in tail)
Weight: 6–11 oz

The red squirrel is a common visitor to backyards and town parks, generally causing a racket with its ongoing nattering and chattering—monologues directed at any passerby, either human or animal. It even mutters to itself while busily collecting food for its cache. • An adventurous diner, this squirrel will eat or store any available source of nutrition—pine cones, nuts, seeds, fungi, fruits and also animal protein such as eggs, nestling birds, baby mammals and carrion. The large caches keep the squirrel fed throughout the year, including winter, when it remains active. **Where found:** coniferous and mixed forests; throughout New England.

Southern Flying Squirrel

Glaucomys volans

Length: 8–10 in (including 4–7 in tail)
Weight: 1½–3 oz

Long flaps of skin, called the patagium, stretched between the fore and hind limbs and a broad, flattened tail allow the nocturnal southern flying squirrel to glide swiftly from tree to tree, with extreme glides covering distances up to 110 yards! • Flying squirrels play an important role in forest ecology because they dig up and eat truffles, spreading around the fruiting bodies of these beneficial ectomycorrhizal fungi. **Where found:** primarily old-growth, coniferous forests, but also aspen and cottonwood woodlands; VT, NH (absent in the north), southern ME, MA, CT and RI.

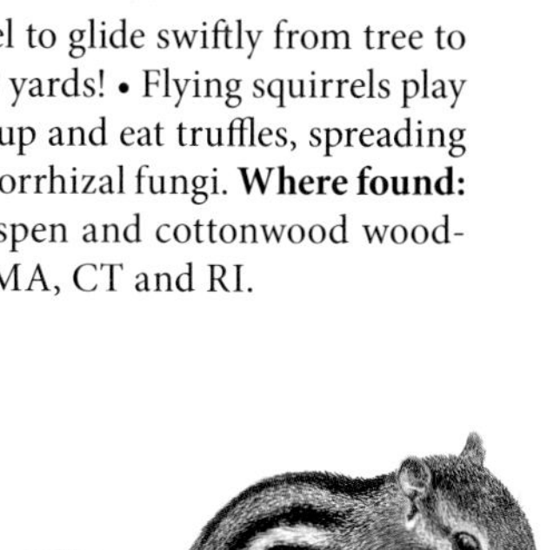

Eastern Chipmunk

Tamias striatus

Length: 9–12 in (including 2¾–4 in tail)
Weight: 2–5 oz

This common chipmunk of the eastern U.S. is fond of both city and country living—a natural inhabitant of the forest, it also makes itself at home in backyards and city parks. • The eastern chipmunk becomes quite cute and chubby after a summer of feasting on nuts, seeds, berries, fungi, insects, slugs and snails despite its active lifestyle. It needs this fat reserve to sustain itself throughout the winter, when it hibernates in its underground burrow. **Where found:** open, deciduous woodlands, forest edges, brushy areas, rocky outcroppings and treed urban areas; throughout New England.

Southern Bog Lemming

Synaptomys cooperi

Length: 4 ¾–6 in (including ½–1 in tail)
Weight: ¾–1¾ oz

The southern bog lemming is actually a species of vole, and where its range overlaps with that of the meadow vole, the lemming is outcompeted. When it finds sufficient habitat, it occupies itself by clearing paths through the grass, leaving neat piles of clippings—and plenty of droppings—along the route. Its strong, curved claws aid in digging elaborate winter runways and underground burrows, but the lemming may also use the abandoned burrows of other small mammals or build grassy aboveground nests. • Lemmings feed on grasses, sedges and clover, as well as fungi, mosses, roots and even algae. **Where found:** grassy meadows, shrub edges and open forests; throughout New England.

Meadow Vole

Microtus pennsylvanicus

Length: 5–7½ in (including 1–2 in tail)
Weight: 1–2¼ oz

Voles fulfill an important role as prey species for many predators, including birds of prey, snakes and carnivorous mammals. The meadow vole is likely one of the most abundant species, and it ranges across northern and central North America. • This vole is also active in winter, just below the snow. This subnivean habitat is insulated from the elements, contains insects and dried vegetation for food and conceals the vole from predators unless, like the fox, they have particularly good hearing and pounce through the snow layer to catch a winter's meal. **Where found:** grasslands, pastures, marshy areas and open woodlands; throughout New England.

Common Muskrat

Ondatra zibethicus

Length: 1½–2 ft (including 8–11 in tail)
Weight: 1¾–3½ lb

Although they share similar habitats and behaviors, the beaver and the common muskrat are not closely related. The muskrat also sports large incisors, which it uses to cut through a vast array of thick vegetation, particularly cattails and bulrushes. It makes a partially submerged den similar to that of a beaver, which provides a nesting spot for geese and ducks, as well as important shelter for other rodents when the muskrat moves house. **Where found:** low-elevation sloughs, lakes, marshes and streams with plenty of cattails, rushes and open water; throughout New England.

Brown Rat

Rattus norvegicus

Length: 13–18 in (including 5–9 in tail)
Weight: 7–17 oz

Native to Europe and Asia, the brown rat came to North America as a stowaway on ships in about 1775. This rodent is mainly associated with human settlements, feeding on cereal grains, fruits, vegetation and garbage, and basically making a nuisance of itself—an example of an introduced species becoming a reviled pest though it survives only in a non-native environment. • Captive-bred rats have aided scientific research in many fields. **Where found:** urban areas, farmyards and garbage dumps; throughout New England. **Also known as:** Norway rat, common rat, sewer rat, water rat.

Black Rat

Rattus rattus

Length: 13–18 in (including 6–10 in tail)
Weight: 4¼–12 oz

The black rat is an introduced species and causes a lot of ecological disturbance. It is extremely adaptable, easily habituating to urbanized areas with all its associated garbage to eat and buildings to use as shelter. • Rats carry a number of pathogens and are most famous for being a transmitter of the bubonic plague in the 14th century. Great attempts, some more successful than others, have been made to eradicate the black rat from New England, and North America in general. **Where found:** urbanized areas, shipyards and garbage dumps; southeastern NH, extreme southern ME, eastern MA, CT (absent in the northwest) and RI. **Also known as:** ship rat, roof rat, house rat.

House Mouse

Mus musculus

Length: 5–8 in (including 2½–4 in tail)
Weight: ½–1 oz

This familiar mouse can be found throughout most of North America. Like the brown rat, it arrived as a stowaway on ships from Europe, quickly spreading across the continent alongside early settlers. • The house mouse is nocturnal and may be responsible for gnawing the labels off the canned soup stored in your cupboards! • This mouse's pelage is brownish to blackish gray with gray undersides. **Where found:** usually associated with humans in both rural and urban settings, including houses, garages, farmyards, garbage dumps and granaries; throughout New England.

White-footed Mouse

Peromyscus leucopus

Length: 6–8 in (including 2½–4 in tail)
Weight: ¾–1 oz

The white-footed mouse is nearly impossible to distinguish from the deer mouse without a specimen in hand. When measurements are obtained, this mouse has a slightly shorter tail than the deer mouse. • This mouse is a strong swimmer and is frequently found colonizing islands in lakes. • This adaptable species is able to live in a wide variety of habitats, but it requires some form of canopy or shrub cover. **Where found:** shrublands and forests; throughout southern and central New England. **Also known as:** wood mouse.

Deer Mouse

Peromyscus maniculatus

Length: 5½ –8¼ in (including 2–4 in tail)
Weight: ¾–1¼ oz

The abundant deer mouse is a seed eater, but it will also consume insects, spiders, caterpillars, fungi, flowers and berries. It is in turn an important prey species for many other animals, so it must be a prolific breeder to maintain its population. • Although deer mice typically forage on the ground, they regularly climb into trees and shrubs to reach food. • A litter of 4 to 9 young leaves the nest after 3 to 5 weeks, and the young mice are sexually mature 1 to 2 weeks after that. Less than 5 percent survive a complete year. **Where found:** most dry habitats, grasslands, shrublands, forests and human settings; VT, NH, ME, MA, northern CT and northern RI.

Meadow Jumping Mouse

Zapus hudsonius

Length: 7–9½ in (including 4–6½ in tail)
Weight: ½–1 oz

Named jumping mice for a reason, this species is able to leap almost 6 ft in a single bound. This agility helps it to avoid predators. • This mouse feeds on fruits, seeds, herbs, fungi and roots, which it prefers to forage for at night, as it is nocturnal by nature. **Where found:** lush, humid areas near ponds, streams or marshes; also grasslands or woodlands; throughout New England.

Big Brown Bat

Eptesicus fuscus

Length: 3⅝–5½ in (including ⅞–2⅜ in tail)
Wingspan: 13 in (forearm 1⅝–2⅛ in)
Weight: 7/16–1 oz

An effective aerial hunter, the big brown bat uses ultrasonic echolocation (80,000 to 40,000 Hz) to detect flying insects up to 16 ft away. It flies above water, around streetlights and over agricultural areas hunting insects at dusk and dawn. • This bat is not abundant but is frequently encountered because of its tendency to roost in human-made structures. It has been known to change hibernation sites midwinter, a time when it is extremely rare to spot a bat. **Where found:** in and around human-made structures; occasionally roosts in hollow trees and rock crevices; throughout New England.

Eastern Pipistrelle

Pipistrellus subflavus

Length: 2¾–3½ in (including 1⅜–1⅝ in tail)
Wingspan: 8¼–10¼ in (forearm 1¼ in)
Weight: ¼–⅜ oz

Quite delicate, able to fit in a matchbox, with a weak erratic flight style, this pip of a pipistrelle is unable to fly in strong wind, yet it is stronger than its western counterpart. Some individuals even migrate several hundred miles in late summer and early fall to the caves where they hibernate for the winter. • Females are larger than males and give birth to twins. Lifespan records for this species are 15 years for males and 10 years for females. **Where found:** in caves in winter; in summer, roosts in trees, buildings and barns, and on cliffs; VT (absent in the northeast), southern NH, MA, CT and RI.

Eastern Red Bat

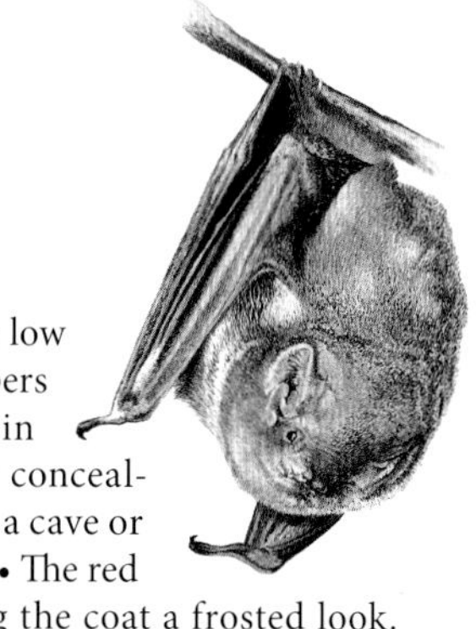

Lasiurus borealis

Length: 4–4¼ in (including 1¾–2½ in tail)
Wingspan: 11½–13 in (forearm 1½–1¾ in)
Weight: ¼–½ oz

The insectivorous, forest-dwelling eastern red bat hunts low to the ground, catching flying ants, moths, leaf hoppers and beetles. • Active at night, this bat usually roosts in a tree by day, preferring those with dense foliage for concealment, but it will also roost in the open or sometimes in a cave or tunnel. It is quite solitary and does not roost in colonies. • The red fur often has white tips, typically in the female, giving the coat a frosted look. **Where found:** deciduous forests; throughout New England in summer.

Hoary Bat

Lasiurus cinereus

Length: 4¼–6 in including 1½–2½ in tail
Wingspan: 16 in (forearm 1¾–2¼ in)
Weight: ½–1¼ oz

This large, beautiful bat roosts in trees, not caves or buildings, and wraps its wings around itself for protection against the elements, the frosty-colored fur blending in among the mosses and lichens. The hoary bat also roosts in orchards, but it is an insectivore and does not damage fruit crops. At night, it can be recognized by its large size and slow wingbeats over open terrain. **Where found:** in open areas and around lakes near coniferous and deciduous forests; VT, NH (absent in the southeast) and northern ME.

Little Brown Bat

Myotis lucifugus

Length: 2⅜–4 in (including 1–2⅛ in tail)
Wingspan: 9¾ in (forearm 1⅜ in–1⅝ in)
Weight: 3/16–5/16 oz

On warm, calm summer nights, the skies are filled with the shrill calls of bats, but the frequencies are beyond the range of our hearing. There are several species of mouse-eared bats (*Myotis* spp.) in our area—eastern small-footed bat (*M. leibii*), northern long-eared bat (*M. septentrionalis*) and Indiana bat (*M. sodalist*)—but they are generally indistinguishable from each other as they fly in dim light. **Where found:** roosts in buildings, barns, caves, rock crevices, hollow trees and under tree bark; hibernates in buildings, caves and mines; throughout New England. **Also known as:** little brown myotis.

Silver-haired Bat

Lasionycteris noctivagans

Length: 3½–4¼ in (including 1½–2 in tail)
Wingspan: 12 in (forearm 1½–1¾ in)
Weight: ½–1 oz

This bat takes flight at both dawn and dusk, embarking on feeding forays for moths and flies over open fields, water and treetops. • The silver-haired bat prefers to roost in trees. To conserve energy on cold days, it slows its metabolism—a state known as torpor. • Solitary in summer, this bat migrates south in winter and forms small colonies that hibernate in caves, mines or abandoned buildings. Females form nursery colonies in protected shelters such as tree cavities. **Where found:** roosts in cavities and crevices of old-growth trees but can adapt to parks, cities and farmlands; southern and central VT, southeastern and central NH, western and central MA, CT (absent in the south) and northeastern RI.

Virginia Opossum

Didelphis virginiana

Length: 27–33 in (including 12–14 in tail)
Weight: 2½–3½ lb

Contrary to most children's stories in which opossums are portrayed hanging by their prehensile tails, the Virginia opossum rarely assumes this posture, though it does climb and den in trees. It is a marsupial closely related to kangaroos and koalas. • This animal plays dead, a trick it is famous for, when is attacked in the hope that the predator will leave the opossum alone. This is where the expression "playing possum" comes from. However, playing dead is usually unsuccessful against cars, which are this slow-moving nocturnal creature's most common assailant. **Where found:** moist woodlands and brushy areas near watercourses; southern VT, southern NH, southern ME, MA, CT and RI.

Water Shrew

Sorex palustris

Length: 9 in (including 3 in tail)
Weight: ½ oz

Small rodents such as shrews and voles must reproduce rapidly and maintain large populations to sustain the high predation rates these animals suffer, being important prey species year-round for small carnivores such as foxes and weasels and birds of prey such as owls. • The water shrew is an excellent swimmer and diver. Its diet includes aquatic insects, small fish, tadpoles, slugs and snails. **Where found:** freshwater aquatic habitats, streams and lakes; throughout New England.

Star-nosed Mole

Condylura cristata

Length: 7¾ in (including 3 in tail)
Weight: 2 oz

The 22 finger-like tentacles surrounding this mole's nose, which are tactile and have enough dexterity and strength to manipulate objects, make this rarely seen little animal a star attraction. • The outward-facing front paws with long claws are ideal for digging tunnels through the moist soil in which this mole burrows. It is also an excellent swimmer, the paws working like paddles and the tail (which stores fat in the winter) working like a rudder. • The star-nosed mole feeds on insects, worms and aquatic invertebrates. **Where found:** swamps, meadows, marshes, lakes and streambanks; throughout New England.

BIRDS

Birds are the most diverse class of vertebrates. All birds are feathered but not all fly. Traits common to all birds are that they are two-legged, warm-blooded and lay hard-shelled eggs. Some migrate south in the colder winter months and return north in spring. For this reason, the diversity of bird species in a region varies with the seasons. Although some species can be seen year-round, northern climates dictate seasonal migration because few birds can adapt to the extreme changes from hot summer to frozen winter. Some birds change their local address to adapt to the seasons; for example, the common loon can be seen pretty much anywhere in the region when the weather is fine, but winters exclusively on milder coastal ocean waters, which do not freeze over in winter.

Wetland birds do not do well when lakes and ponds freeze and are therefore only fine-weather friends, most only seen in summer. Most of the ducks, herons, sandpipers, rails and bitterns fall into this category, as well as the osprey, which feeds on fish. Most of the raptors migrate south for the winter or find the northern extent of their winter range in New England. Many shorebirds breed in the Arctic and head south for the winter, passing through our region in migration. Some of our well-known winter birds include chickadees, downy woodpeckers, waxwings, nuthatches and snowy owls.

Spring brings scores of migrant waterfowl and colorful songbirds that breed in New England and other species such as shorebirds that continue on to Arctic breeding grounds. Even more migratory birds, such as Canada geese, pass through in fall, their numbers bolstered by the young of the year. Many species are in duller plumage in fall and winter.

Scores of migrating birds fly as far south as Central and South America. These neotropical migrants are of concern to biologists and conservationists because of habitat degradation and loss, collisions with human-made towers, pesticide use and other factors that threaten their survival. Education and an increasing appreciation for wildlife may encourage solutions to these problems.

Waterfowl
pp. 74–75
Grouse & Allies
p. 76
Diving Birds
pp. 77–78
Herons & Vultures
pp. 78–79
Birds of Prey
pp. 80–82
Rails
p. 83
Shorebirds
pp. 83–86
Gulls & Terns
p. 87
Doves & Cuckoos
p. 88
Owls
pp. 89–90
Nightjars
p. 91
Swifts, Hummingbirds & Kingfishers
pp. 91–92
Woodpeckers
pp. 92–94
Flycatchers
pp. 94–95
Shrikes & Vireos
pp. 95–96
Jays & Ravens
p. 96
Larks & Swallows
p. 97
Chickadees, Nuthatches & Wrens
p. 98
Kinglets & Thrushes
pp. 99–100
Mimics & Waxwings
p. 101
Wood-warblers
pp. 102–103
Sparrows
pp. 104–105
Tanagers, Grosbeaks & Buntings
pp. 105–106
Blackbirds & Allies
p. 107
Finch-like Birds
p. 108

Canada Goose

Branta canadensis

Length: 35–45 in
Wingspan: 4½–5½ ft

Canada geese mate for life and are devoted parents to their 2 to 11 goslings. • Wild geese can be aggressive when defending their young or competing for food. Hissing sounds and low, outstretched necks are signs that you should give these birds some space. • Geese graze on aquatic grasses and sprouts, and you can spot them tipping up to grab for aquatic roots and tubers. • The Canada goose was split into 2 species in 2004; the smaller subspecies has been renamed the cackling goose (*B. hutchinsii*). **Where found:** near water bodies and in parks, marshes and croplands; year-round throughout all but northernmost New England.

Wood Duck

Aix sponsa

Length: 15–20 in
Wingspan: 29–31 in

A forest-dweller, the wood duck is equipped with sharp claws for perching on branches and nesting in tree cavities, which may be as high as 20 to 30 ft. Shortly after hatching, the ducklings jump out of their nest cavity, but, like downy ping-pong balls, they bounce upon landing and are seldom injured. • A female often returns to the same nest site each year; being familiar with potential threats at established sites may help her improve her brood's survival rate. **Where found:** swamps, ponds, marshes and lakeshores with wooded edges; summer resident throughout New England.

American Black Duck

Anas rubripes

Length: 23 in
Wingspan: 33–37 in

These common ducks are seen year-round, typically in pairs throughout winter after pair bonds are established in September. They often mingle with mallards (*A. platyrhychos*), with which they frequently interbreed, and the offspring show the coloration and features of both parents. • These ducks eat primarily plant matter throughout summer but feed on invertebrates in winter to obtain heat-generating protein. **Where found:** fresh water, flooded fields, croplands and coastal bays; throughout New England in summer; year-round on the coast.

Blue-winged Teal

Anas discors

Length: 14–16 in
Wingspan: 23 in

Speedy on the wing and able to execute sharp twists and turns, the blue-winged teal lurks in the dense vegetation of marshes and is easily overlooked. • After breeding, males often undertake a partial migration before molting into duller "eclipse" plumage. • Dabbling ducks such as teals have small feet set near the center of their bodies. Other ducks dive underwater to feed and are propelled by large feet set farther back. **Where found:** shallow lake edges, wetlands and estuaries; prefers short, dense emergent vegetation; common migrant and summer resident throughout New England; nesters are more common northward.

Ring-necked Duck

Aythya collaris

Length: 14–18 in
Wingspan: 25 in

"Ring-billed duck" might be a better name for this species because the ring around the bill stands out more than the faint cinnamon band encircling the drake's neck. • Large flocks of this abundant migrant often collect on roadside borrow ponds and reservoirs. • Whereas most diving ducks require a sprint across the water to become airborne, these ducks practically leap into the air, more like dabbling ducks. • The females are much less showy and can be an identification challenge. Fortunately, hens are nearly always with drakes, an excellent clue to their identity. **Where found:** ponds with lily pads and other surface vegetation, swamps, marshes, borrow ponds and lakes; common migrant because New England is the transition between the species' northern summer and southern winter ranges.

Common Merganser

Mergus merganser

Length: 22–27 in
Wingspan: 34 in

To take off, the common merganser must run along the surface of the water, beating its heavy wings to gain sufficient lift, but once up and away, it flies arrow-straight and low over the water. • This large duck will nest in a tree cavity, occasionally on the ground, on a cliff ledge or in a large nest box, usually close to water. In winter, any source of open water with a fish-filled shoal will support good numbers of these skilled divers. **Where found:** large rivers and deep lakes; year-round throughout most of New England; only in the south in winter.

Ring-necked Pheasant

Phasianus colchicus

Length: *Male* 30–36 in; *Female:* 20–26 in
Wingspan: *Male:* 31 in; *Female:* 28 in

Since being introduced in the late 1800s, this Asian bird has endured many pressures. Ring-necked pheasant populations have had to be continually replenished by hatchery-raised young, not only because this species is hunted, but also because of diminished habitat, intensive farming practices and our harsh winters. Unlike native grouse, this pheasant lacks feathered legs and feet for insulation and cannot survive on native plants, depending instead on grain and corn crops. **Where found:** shrubby grasslands, urban parks, woodlots, hayfields and croplands; year-round resident, with patchy distribution in northwestern New England.

Ruffed Grouse

Bonasa umbellus

Length: 15–19 in
Wingspan: 22 in

A low, booming sound echoing through the forest in spring is most likely being made by a male ruffed grouse "drumming" to proclaim his territory. Every spring, and occasionally in fall, the male grouse struts along a fallen log with his tail fanned and his neck feathers ruffed, beating the air periodically with accelerating wing strokes. • In winter, scales grow out along the sides of the ruffed grouse's feet, creating temporary "snowshoes." **Where found:** hardwood and mixed forests, riparian woodlands; young, second-growth stands with birch and aspen; year-round throughout New England.

Wild Turkey

Meleagris gallopavo

Length: 3–3½ ft
Wingspan: 4–5½ ft

The once common wild turkey suffered habitat loss and overhunting in the early 20th century. Today, efforts at restoration have re-established the species in many areas. • This charismatic bird is the only widely domesticated native North American animal—the wild ancestors of most other domestic animals came from Europe. **Where found:** deciduous, mixed and riparian woodlands; occasionally eats waste grain and corn in late fall and winter; year-round resident, with patchy distribution throughout New England.

Common Loon

Gavia immer

Length: 28–35 in
Wingspan: 4–5 ft

When the haunting call of the common loon pierces a still evening, cottagers know that summer has begun. This loon actually has several different calls; individuals have a laughing distress call, separated pairs seem to wail *Where aaare you?* and groups give soft, cohesive hoots as they fly. • The loon has solid bones that reduce its buoyancy and allow it to dive to depths of 180 feet. **Where found:** *Breeding:* large lakes and rivers, often with vegetated islands or even muskrat lodges to nest on; coastal waters; ME and slightly south. *Winter:* ocean bays and headlands; all along the coast.

Pied-billed Grebe

Podilymbus podiceps

Length: 12–15 in
Wingspan: 22½ in

Despite being very rare in winter, when the larger, more interesting-looking horned grebe (*Podiceps auritus*) and red-necked grebe (*Podiceps grisegena*) can be seen on the Atlantic coast, the pied-billed grebe is nonetheless our most common and only nesting grebe. It builds a floating nest in the middle of a pond so it can watch for predators. If a threat is present, the grebe will cover its eggs with vegetation and then slip into the water with only its eyes and nostrils above the surface. **Where found:** ponds, marshes and backwaters with sparse emergent vegetation; summer resident throughout New England; year-round on Cape Cod. **Also known as:** hell-diver.

Northern Gannet

Morus bassanus

Length: 3 ft
Wingspan: 6 ft

If you are boating offshore, keep your eyes open for these amazing, skydiving birds. From over 100 ft in the air, northern gannets tuck in their wings and plunge torpedo-style into the water in pursuit of fish. They have reinforced skulls to cushion the impact. • Gannets mate for life and pairs perform elaborate bonding rituals during nesting that involve much preening, bowing and sky pointing as well as raising their wings and spreading their tails. **Where found:** coastal and open waters in winter. **Also known as:** solan goose (in Europe).

Double-crested Cormorant

Phalacrocorax auritus

Length: 26–32 in
Wingspan: 4¼ ft

The double-crested cormorant looks like a bird but smells and swims like a fish. With a long, rudder-like tail, excellent underwater vision, sealed nostrils for diving and "wettable" feathers that lack oil glands, this bird has mastered the underwater world. After a dive, a cormorant often perches with its wings partially spread, drying out its feathers. • The male's ear tufts are only visible in breeding season. **Where found:** large lakes and large, meandering rivers; nests in colonies on platforms of sticks and guano on islands or in trees; summer resident throughout New England; year-round on Cape Cod. **Also known as:** shag (in Europe).

American Bittern

Botaurus lentiginosus

Length: 24–28 in
Wingspan: 3½ ft

When an American bittern hears or sees you approach, it stands completely still with its bill pointing skyward, its vertically streaked, brown plumage blending in with the reeds and rushes. You are more likely to hear a bittern than spot one; in spring, the marshlands resonate with its deep, booming mating call. **Where found:** marshes, wetlands and lake edges with reeds, rushes and sedges; summer breeding resident throughout New England.

Great Blue Heron

Ardea herodias

Length: 4½ ft
Wingspan: 6 ft

The long-legged great blue heron has a stealthy, often motionless hunting strategy. It waits for a fish or frog to approach, spears the prey with its bill, then flips its catch into the air and swallows it whole. This heron usually hunts near water, but it also stalks fields and meadows in search of rodents. • Great blue herons settle in communal treetop nests called rookeries, and nest width can reach 4 ft. **Where found:** forages along the edges of rivers, lakes and marshes; also in fields and wet meadows; summer breeder throughout New England; year-round along the Gulf of Maine.

Great Egret

Ardea alba

Length: 3–3½ ft
Wingspan: 4 ft

The plumes of great egrets and snowy egrets (*Egretta thula*) were used to decorate hats in the early 20th century. An ounce of egret feathers cost as much as $32—more than an ounce of gold at the time—and, as a result, egrets began to disappear. Some of the first conservation legislation in North America was enacted to outlaw the hunting of these magnificent birds. • The great egret is the symbol for the National Audubon Society, one of the oldest conservation organizations in the United States. **Where found:** marshes, open riverbanks, irrigation canals and lakeshores; just into ME, with pockets in northern VT; the eastern fringe of New England marks the northern extent of this bird's breeding range.

Green Heron

Butorides virescens

Length: 18 in
Wingspan: 26 in

The intelligent green heron uses bait to catch fish—it drops small debris, such as bits of vegetation or a feather, onto the water's surface to attract its prey. Standing still among the weedy wetland vegetation, the heron goes unnoticed by the fish until the bird strikes. This heron is also a skilled frog hunter. • The metallic green feathers are inconspicuous until the light hits them at the right angle, making them shimmer. **Where found:** freshwater marshes, lakes and streams with plenty of vegetation; summer breeder throughout New England except northern ME.

Black-crowned Night-heron

Nycticorax nycticorax

Length: 23–26 in
Wingspan: 3½ ft

When dusk's long shadows shroud the marshes, black-crowned night-herons arrive to hunt in the marshy waters. These herons crouch motionless, using their large, light-sensitive eyes to spot prey lurking in the shallows. Look for them in summer, between dawn and dusk, as they fly between nesting and feeding areas. **Where found:** shallow cattail and bulrush marshes, lakeshores and along slow-flowing rivers; summer breeder along the coast with some populations found inland to the far west of the New England states.

Turkey Vulture

Cathartes aura

Length: 25–31 in
Wingspan: 5½–6 ft

Turkey vultures are playful, social birds, and groups live and sleep together in large trees, or roosts. Some roost sites in North America are over a century old and have been used by the same family of vultures for several generations. • No other bird uses updrafts and thermals in flight as well as the turkey vulture. Pilots have reported seeing vultures soaring at 20,000 ft. **Where found:** usually flies over open country, shorelines or roads, rarely over forests; summer resident throughout New England; year-round increasingly northward from Cape Cod.

Osprey

Pandion haliaetus

Length: 22–25 in
Wingspan: 5½–6 ft

While hunting for fish, this large, powerful raptor hovers in the air before hurling itself in a dramatic headfirst dive. An instant before striking the water, it rights itself and thrusts its feet forward to grasp its quarry. • Ospreys build bulky nests on high, artificial structures such as communication towers and utility poles or on buoys and channel markers over water, where the pair tends to 2 to 3 chicks. **Where found:** lakes and slow-flowing rivers and streams; estuaries and bays in migration; widespread summer resident.

Bald Eagle

Haliaeetus leucocephalus

Length: 30–43 in
Wingspan: 5½–8 ft

While soaring high in the air, a bald eagle can spot fish swimming underwater and small rodents scurrying through the grass. • This eagle does not mature until its fourth or fifth year—only then does it develop the characteristic white head and tail plumage. • Bald eagles mate for life and renew their pair bonds by adding sticks to the same nest each year. Nests can be up to 16 ft in diameter and are the largest of any North American bird. **Where found:** coastal areas, estuaries, large lakes, river valleys and farmlands; year-round except northern ME; rare in summer in VT.

Northern Harrier

Circus cyaneus

Length: 16–24 in
Wingspan: 3½–4 ft

The spring courtship flight of the northern harrier is spectacular. The male climbs almost vertically in the air, then stalls and plummets in a reckless dive toward the ground. At the last second, he saves himself with a hairpin turn that sends him skyward again. • Britain's Royal Air Force named the Harrier aircraft after this raptor because of the bird's impressive maneuverability. **Where found:** open country including fields, wet meadows, cattail marshes, bogs and croplands; nests on the ground, usually in tall vegetation; in summer in the north; year-round in the south; rare or absent in central New England.

Sharp-shinned Hawk

Accipiter striatus

Length: *Male:* 10–12 in; *Female:* 12–14 in
Wingspan: *Male:* 20–24 in; *Female:* 24–28 in

After a successful hunt, this small hawk often perches on a favorite "plucking post," holding its meal in its razor-sharp talons. It preys almost exclusively on small birds. • Short, rounded wings and a long, rudder-like tail allow this hawk to maneuver through the forest at high speed. • As it ages, the sharp-shinned hawk's bright yellow eyes become red. **Where found:** dense to semi-open coniferous forests and large woodlots; occasionally along rivers and in urban areas; may visit backyard bird feeders to prey on songbirds in winter; year-round resident; absent or rare in winter in western New England.

Northern Goshawk

Accipiter gentilis

Length: 21–26 in
Wingspan: 3½–4 ft

This forest raptor navigates through the trees in swift pursuit of its prey, which includes birds and small mammals. • The northern goshawk will aggressively protect its nest from any perceived threats from predators, or even innocent passersby, with aerial, dive-bombing assaults accompanied by a deafening attack screech. **Where found:** mature woodlands; forest edges, parkland and farmland in winter; year-round throughout New England.

Red-shouldered Hawk

Buteo lineatus

Length: 15–19 in
Wingspan: 3½ ft

This hawk is typically seen perched on fence posts and power lines watching for prey, which includes small birds and mammals, reptiles, amphibians and large insects. In the air, its slow, regular wingbeats, white underwings with black, pointed wing tips and single, broad, white band on the dark tail help identify it. **Where found:** moist, mixed woodlands near water; throughout New England in summer; year-round in the south.

Red-tailed Hawk

Buteo jamaicensis

Length: *Male:* 18–23 in; *Female:* 20–25 in
Wingspan: 4–5 ft

Spend a summer afternoon in the country and you will likely see a red-tailed hawk perched on a fence post or soaring on a thermal. • Courting red-tails will sometimes dive at one another, lock talons and tumble toward the earth, breaking away at the last second to avoid crashing into the ground. • The red-tailed hawk's piercing call is often paired with the image of an eagle in TV commercials and movies. **Where found:** open country with some trees; also roadsides and woodlots; often flies above cities; throughout New England in summer; year-round closer to the coast.

American Kestrel

Falco sparverius

Length: 7½–8 in
Wingspan: 20–24 in

The colorful American kestrel, formerly known as "sparrow hawk," is not shy of human activity and is adaptable to habitat change. This small falcon has benefited from the grassy roadway margins that provide habitat for grasshoppers, which make up most of its diet, and other small prey such as mice. • Kestrels will shelter in tree cavities but also use nest boxes meant for sparrows. **Where found:** along rural roadways, perched on poles and telephone wires; agricultural fields, grasslands, riparian woodlands, woodlots, forest edges, bogs, roadside ditches and grassy highway medians; summer resident throughout New England; year-round in the southern Gulf of Maine and western VT.

Virginia Rail

Rallus limicola

Length: 9½ in
Wingspan: 13 in

Although it is secretive like all rails, the Virginia rail likes to sing. In breeding season, which is when the Virginia rail is found in our region, its repertoire includes a territorial song—a two-phrase *tik-tik, tik-tik-tik* or *kid kid kidick kidick*—as well as a *tik tik tik turrr*, which may have another purpose. Year-round, this bird's call is a descending, accelerating series of notes that has been described as a raspy *oink*. **Where found:** among sedges and reeds in wet grasslands, wetlands and coastal and inland marshes; throughout New England in summer.

Sora

Porzana carolina

Length: 8–10 in
Wingspan: 14 in

The sora has a small body and large, chicken-like feet. Even without webbed feet, this unique creature swims quite well over short distances. • Two rising *or-Ah or-Ah* whistles followed by a strange, descending whinny indicate that a sora is nearby. This secretive bird is hard to spot because it prefers to remain hidden in dense marshland, but it will occasionally venture into the shallows to search for aquatic insects and mollusks. **Where found:** wetlands with abundant emergent cattails, bulrushes, sedges and grasses; also grain fields; throughout New England in summer; in saltwater marshes during migration.

Piping Plover

Charadrius melodus

Length: 7½ in
Wingspan: 18 in

The piping plover is one of those cute little birds that runs back and forth on beaches, chasing and being chased by the waves. Though it looks like a great game that they are playing for the sheer joy of it, they are actually running as fast as they can to catch tiny prey such as aquatic worms, crustaceans and insects that is thrown ashore by the surf. **Where found:** sandy beaches, lakeshores and dunes; summer breeder along the Gulf of Maine, from central ME south.

Charadrius vociferus

Length: 9–11 in
Wingspan: 24 in

The killdeer is a gifted actor, well known for its "broken wing" distraction display. When an intruder wanders too close to its ground nest, the killdeer utters piteous cries while dragging a wing and stumbling about as if injured. Most predators take the bait and follow, and once the killdeer has lured the predator far away from its nest, it miraculously recovers from the injury and flies off with a loud call. **Where found:** open, wet meadows, lakeshores, sandy beaches, mudflats, gravel streambeds and golf courses; summer breeder throughout New England; year-round from Cape Cod south.

American Oystercatcher

Haematopus palliatus

Length: 18½ in
Wingspan: 35 in

The bright orange bill sets this shorebird aside from all the rest. • Although it may catch the odd oyster, the mainstay of this bird's diet is small clams. It is a shoreline grazer that eats almost any small invertebrate it can find. • Hunting and egg collecting in the 1800s completely extirpated this bird from New England; with protection from the Migratory Bird Treaty Act, the oystercatcher's range now extends northward to its historical habitat. **Where found:** coastal beaches and mudflats; breeding range has expanded northward to ME.

Spotted Sandpiper

Actitis macularius

Length: 7–8 in
Wingspan: 15 in

The female spotted sandpiper diligently defends her territory, mates, lays her eggs and leaves the male to tend the clutch. Only about one percent of birds display this unusual breeding strategy, which is known as "polyandry." She may mate with several different males, lay up to 4 clutches and produce 20 eggs in one summer. **Where found:** shorelines, gravel beaches, drainage ditches, swamps and sewage lagoons; occasionally cultivated fields; throughout New England in summer.

Willet

Tringa semipalmata

Length: 14–16 in
Wingspan: 25–26 in

This shorebird spends its summers on our southern beaches, probing the mud and sand for invertebrates and occasionally reminding us of its presence by calling out its name—*will-will-willet*—in sharp, quick notes. It is occasionally seen perched on fence posts. • At the first hint of winter, the willet is one of the first birds to high-tail it to South America. **Where found:** flooded fields, pastures, wetlands, marshes, mudflats and beaches; southern coastal New England in summer.

Upland Sandpiper

Bartramia longicauda

Length: 12 in
Wingspan: 17–20 in

Unlike most other sandpipers, this species is not a shorebird and prefers open grasslands and fields. Often just its long neck and head are seen poking above the grass. These birds sometimes stand on fence posts or even telephone poles, as if to gain a higher perspective. • Upland sandpipers have a distinctive call, a series of descending whistles. • This species is fairly common in midwestern North America, but populations are scattered in the East and thought to be declining. **Where found:** prairies, fields and airports; scattered throughout New England in summer.

Red Knot

Calidris canutus

Length: 10½ in
Wingspan: 23 in

After nesting on the tundra, this little bird makes an astonishing migration to South America—a distance of approximately 16,700 mi. This species is capable of flying nonstop for up to 8 days and can cover up to 5000 mi without resting. When it does rest, a major stopping point is along the mid-Atlantic coast, namely at Cape Cod and Delaware Bay, to gorge on horseshoe crab eggs. The exploitative overharvesting of these eggs for commercial fertilizer has caused a severe crash in this bird's population. **Where found:** beaches; Cape Cod and possibly other beaches along the coast in spring.

Sanderling

Calidris alba

Length: 8 in
Wingspan:; *W* 17 in

The sanderling chases the waves in and out, snatching up aquatic invertebrates before they are swept back into the water. On shores where wave action is limited, it resorts to probing mudflats for a meal of mollusks and insects. • To keep warm, a sanderling will seek the company of other roosting shorebirds. It will also stand with one leg tucked up, a posture that conserves body heat. **Where found:** sandy and muddy shorelines, cobble and pebble beaches, spits, lakeshores, marshes and reservoirs; winter resident only in the very south of the Gulf of Maine; otherwise only seen in migration.

Wilson's Snipe

Gallinago delicata

Length: 11 in
Wingspan: 18 in

When flushed from cover, snipes perform a series of aerial zigzags to confuse predators. Hunters who were skilled enough to shoot snipes became known as "snipers," a term later adopted by the military. • Courting snipes make an eerie, winnowing sound, like a rapidly hooting owl. The sound is produced by the male's specialized outer tail feathers, which vibrate rapidly in the air as he performs daring, headfirst dives high above a wetland. **Where found:** cattail and bulrush marshes, sedge meadows, poorly drained floodplains, bogs and fens; also willow and dogwood tangles; local breeder; may overwinter in southern New England in mild years.

American Woodcock

Scolopax minor

Length: 11 in
Wingspan: 18 in

Though classified as a shorebird, the American woodcock does not live on the shore but in thickets and woods, searching for earthworms during the night. Earthworms comprise approximately 60 percent of this bird's diet, the rest being other small invertebrates along with a few seeds. **Where found:** moist woodlands, bogs, thickets and open forests; local breeder; may overwinter in southern New England in mild years. **Also known as:** timberdoodle, bog-sucker, mudsnipe.

Herring Gull

Larus argentatus

Length: 22–25 in
Wingspan: 4 ft

The voracious appetite of this gull as it scavenges beaches for dead fish, crustaceans and any other carrion benefits us by helping keep the beaches clean. However, this gull is not widely appreciated for stealing meals from fishermen, eating fish placed on fields for fertilizer and, in particular, for its habit of dropping shellfish from high in the air to crack open the shells, often denting car roofs. • The herring gull is one of the most abundant gulls in our region. **Where found:** coastlines, rivers and lakes; throughout New England year-round; offshore in winter.

Great Black-backed Gull

Larus marinus

Length: 29–31 in
Wingspan: 5½ ft

A non-discriminating scavenger, aggressive predator and ruthless food thief, stealing meals from other birds, the great black-backed gull has a diverse diet of fish, small mammals, the chicks of other seabirds and garbage. • This gull builds its nest on a mat of vegetation on the ground, but it may also be found in colonies on rocky ledges. It is gregarious in winter, when it flocks with other gull species. **Where found:** coastlines, large lakes, urban areas and garbage dumps; throughout New England year-round.

Common Tern

Sterna hirundo

Length: 12–14½ in
Wingspan: 30 in

This colony nester is a gregarious presence on our coastlines and wetlands in summer. It lays its eggs in a scrape or on a platform of vegetation on the ground, a precarious location if on a heavily trafficked beach—always watch your step in spring. • This tern's breeding plumage shows a dark cap and red bill, whereas nonbreeding juveniles have a pale bill and a thinning of the black cap at the front of the head, giving the appearance of a receding hairline. • Terns dive like little torpedoes into the water to catch fish and other small aquatic animals. **Where found:** lakes, islands, marshes and coastlines; summer breeder throughout New England.

Rock Pigeon

Columba livia

Length: 12–13 in
Wingspan: 28 in (male is typically larger)

The rock pigeon is likely the descendant of a Eurasian bird that was first domesticated in about 4500 BC. European settlers introduced the species to North America in the 17th century, and today this bird is familiar to almost everyone. • Both Caesar and Napoleon used rock pigeons as message couriers. • No other "wild" bird varies as much in coloration, a result of semi-domestication and extensive inbreeding over time. **Where found:** urban areas, railroad yards and agricultural areas; high cliffs often provide habitat in the wild; throughout New England year-round. **Also known as:** rock dove.

Mourning Dove

Zenaida macroura

Length: 11–13 in
Wingspan: 18 in

One of the most abundant native birds in North America, this dove's numbers and range have increased as human development has created more open habitats and food sources such as waste grain and bird feeders. • The mourning dove's soft cooing is often confused with the sound of a hooting owl. • The female lays only 2 eggs a time but may produce up to 6 broods each year—more than any other native bird. **Where found:** open and riparian woodlands, forest edges, agricultural and suburban areas and open parks; summer breeder; year-round in all but northern New England.

Yellow-billed Cuckoo

Coccyzus americanus

Length: 11–13 in
Wingspan: 18 in

The insectivorous yellow-billed cuckoo enjoys munching on caterpillars, particularly spiny tent caterpillars. When its stomach lining becomes packed with spines, it has the bizarre and revolting ability to regurgitate the entire lining and grow a replacement. • The cuckoo sings its name, *cu-cu-cu cu-cu-cu*, which superstition says predicts rain. • The black-billed cuckoo (*C. erythropthalmus*) also ranges along the eastern seaboard. **Where found:** forest edges, thickets, woodlands, scrublands and along streams; summer breeder, but absent from northern New England.

Barn Owl

Tyto alba

Length: 12½–18 in
Wingspan: 3¾ ft

People and barn owls have a mutually beneficial relationship—we provide roosting and nesting structures such as barns and open hunting habitat such as croplands, and in return, this dedicated hunter keeps rodent populations down. Its tolerance of humans makes it one of the most likely owls to encounter. **Where found:** roosts and nests in cliffs, hollow trees, barns, mineshafts, caves and bridges; hunts in open areas such as agricultural fields, pastures, lawns, marshy meadows, open beach edges and open streamside areas; throughout southern New England.

Great Horned Owl

Bubo virginianus

Length: 18–25 in
Wingspan: 3–5 ft

This highly adaptable and superbly camouflaged hunter has sharp hearing and powerful vision that allow it to hunt by night and day. The leading edge of the flight feathers is fringed rather than smooth, which interrupts airflow over the wing and allows the owl to fly noiselessly. • The great horned owl has a poor sense of smell, which might explain why it is the only consistent predator of skunks. **Where found:** fragmented forests, fields, riparian woodlands, suburban parks and wooded edges of landfills; throughout New England year-round.

Snowy Owl

Bubo scandiacus

Length: 23 in
Wingspan: 4½ ft

There are few more beautiful winter sights than that of a snowy owl swooping over a frosty landscape on a moonlit night. We are graced with this owl's presence for a few months each year. • Feathered to the toes, the snowy owl can endure temperatures that send other owls to the woods to seek shelter. It is active day and night, hunting small rodents, especially lemmings, as well as sea and water birds. **Where found:** perches on the ground, fence posts, low stumps and buildings; winter resident along the coast.

Barred Owl

Strix varia

Length: 21 in
Wingspan: 3½ ft

Our most common owl, the barred owl hoots a distinctive, rhythmic call, described as *Who cooks for you, who cooks for you all?* • It is recognizable for the distinct, dark rings on its facial disk, but more interesting to note are the dark, nearly completely black eyes. Only the barn owl has these same dark eyes; all the rest of our owls have yellow eyes. • The barred owl nests in tree cavities and is dependent upon old-growth forests for habitat. **Where found:** old-growth, mixed woodlands, dense coniferous forests and swampy areas; throughout New England year-round.

Long-eared Owl

Asio otus

Length: 15 in
Wingspan: 3 ft

A friend of the farmer but a terror to rats and mice, the long-eared owl is credited both for its diet, of which 80 to 90 percent is made up of injurious rodents, and for its distaste for domestic poultry. It hunts by night, and by day it roosts deep in the seclusion of the forest. • The long "ears" are really just tufts of feathers. • To scare off an intruder, this owl expands its air sacs, puffs its feathers and spreads its wings. **Where found:** forest and woodland edges, open fields and riparian stands; summer breeder; year-round in southern New England.

Northern Saw-whet Owl

Aegolius acadicus

Length: 8 in
Wingspan: 16½ in

A nocturnal owl, the saw-whet is difficult to observe and is more frequently heard—it has various calls that sound like whistles, screeches and barks. The name "saw-whet" refers to one of this owl's calls, which is similar to the metallic sound of a saw being sharpened. • The saw-whet owl nests in hollow trees, often reusing the nest of a northern flicker, or sometimes in a nest box. By day, it roosts in a tree in dense forest. **Where found:** coniferous or mixedwood forests, swamps and tamarack bogs; throughout New England year-round.

Common Nighthawk

Chordeiles minor

Length: 8–10 in
Wingspan: 23–26 in

The common nighthawk, like all nightjars, has adapted to catch insects in midair—its large, gaping mouth is surrounded by feather shafts that funnel insects into its bill. This bird can eat more than 2600 insects in one day, including mosquitoes, black flies and flying ants. • In an energetic courting display, the male nighthawk dives, then swerves skyward, making a hollow booming sound with its wings. **Where found:** *Breeding:* forest openings, bogs, rocky outcroppings and gravel rooftops. *In migration:* near water or any area with large numbers of flying insects.

Whip-poor-will

Caprilmulgus vociferous

Length: 9–10 in
Wingspan: 16–20 in

Few birds are easier to hear, yet harder to see, than the whip-poor-will. When at rest on a lichen-speckled limb or leafy forest floor, it blends perfectly into the background, but its loud, oft-repeated song is delivered incessantly and is a near-perfect rendition of the bird's name. One bird was documented singing over 28,000 songs in a single night! • These ground-nesting birds time their egg laying to the lunar cycle so that hatching occurs during a full moon, when their moth prey is readily captured. **Where found:** open deciduous and pine woodlands, often along forest edges; breeds sparingly throughout New England, but populations are in decline.

Chimney Swift

Chaetura pelagica

Length: 5–5½ in
Wingspan: 14 in

Chimney swifts are most at home on the wing—feeding, drinking, bathing, nest material collection and mating are all done in flight. • Unable to perch like most birds, they prop themselves against a vertical surface using their stiff tails for support. Most swifts nest in chimneys, and during migration, large numbers funnel in *en masse* at dusk. • Chimney swifts feed solely on insects and migrate to South America for the winter. **Where found:** forages above cities and towns; roosts and nests in chimneys or tree cavities; summer breeder throughout New England.

Ruby-throated Hummingbird

Archilochus colubris

Length: 3½–4 in
Wingspan: 4½ in

Several dozen tiny wingbeats per second allow this aerial extremist to maneuver forward and backward and even hover like a helicopter. At full tilt, this nickel-weight speedster has a heart rate of over 1000 beats per minute. • Sugarwater or nectar feeders can attract dozens of ruby-throated hummingbirds, which will joust with other hummers for access. • The female lays 2 jellybean-sized eggs within a nest the size of half a walnut shell, woven with spiderwebs and shingled in lichen. **Where found:** open, mixed woodlands, wetlands, gardens and backyards; summer breeder throughout New England.

Belted Kingfisher

Megaceryle alcyon

Length: 11–14 in
Wingspan: 20–21 in

From a bare-branch perch over a productive pool, a belted kingfisher will plunge headfirst into the water, snatch up a fish or frog, flip it into the air, and then swallow it headfirst. Nestlings are able to swallow small fish whole when they are only 5 days old. • With a reddish band across her belly, the female kingfisher is more colorful than her mate. **Where found:** rivers, large streams, lakes, marshes and beaver ponds, especially near exposed soil banks, gravel pits or bluffs; summer breeder; year-round in southern New England. **Also known as:** *Ceryle alcyon*.

Red-bellied Woodpecker

Melanerpes carolinus

Length: 9–10½ in
Wingspan: 16 in

These large woodpeckers are common and conspicuous. Frequent visitors to backyard bird feeders, these loud, aggressive birds are near the top of the pecking order. More of a southern species, red-bellies are actively expanding northward into our region. • The red "belly" of this species is faint and can only be seen up close and under good conditions. **Where found:** mature, deciduous woodlands and occasionally wooded residential areas; year-round in southern New England, but absent in the north.

Downy Woodpecker

Picoides pubescens

Length: 6–7 in
Wingspan: 12 in

A bird feeder well stocked with peanut butter and sunflower seeds may attract a pair of downy woodpeckers to your backyard. These approachable little birds are more tolerant of human activity than are most other species, and they visit feeders more often than the larger, more aggressive hairy woodpeckers (*P. villosus*). • The downy woodpecker's white outer tail feathers have several dark spots, whereas the hairy's are pure white. **Where found:** any wooded environment, especially deciduous and mixed forests and areas with tall, deciduous shrubs; year-round throughout New England.

Black-backed Woodpecker

Picoides arcticus

Length: 9½ in
Wingspan: 17 in

Rather than knocking holes in trees, and perhaps to avoid rattling its skull too much, the black-backed woodpecker tends to flake bark off old trees in search of larvae and insects hiding beneath. It requires old-growth forest habitat to find trees full of invertebrates as well as hollows in which to nest. It is also attracted to burned areas. **Where found:** coniferous, old-growth forests; year-round resident in northern New England, but absent in the south.

Northern Flicker

Colaptes auratus

Length: 12–13 in
Wingspan: 20 in

The northern flicker scours the ground and tree trunks in search of invertebrates, particularly ants, which it squashes and then uses to preen itself. The formic acid in the ants' bodies kills small parasites on the bird's skin and feathers. • There are 2 races of northern flicker: the yellow-shafted flicker of eastern North America has yellow underwings and undertail coverts, whereas those of the red-shafted flicker of the west are reddish. **Where found:** open woodlands, forest edges, fields, meadows, beaver ponds and other wetlands; summer breeder; year-round in southern New England.

Pileated Woodpecker

Dryocopus pileatus

Length: 16–19 in
Wingspan: 27 in

This crow-sized bird, the sixth-largest woodpecker in the world, is an unforgettable sight if you are fortunate enough to see one. Despite its size, noisy wood-pecking habits and maniacal breeding calls, it is quite elusive. Large, distinctively oval-shaped nest holes reveal its presence, as do trees that look as if someone has taken an ax to them. • Wood ducks, American kestrels, owls and even flying squirrels nest in abandoned pileated woodpecker nest holes. **Where found:** large, mature forests; throughout New England year-round.

Eastern Wood-pewee

Contopus virens

Length: 6–6½ in
Wingspan: 10 in

One of the most common breeding birds of our deciduous forests, the eastern wood-pewee is named for its plaintive, whistled *pee-ah-wee* song. In fact, because the pewee sings incessantly, it is easier to detect it by song than to spot it in the dense shade of its wooded haunts. • Eastern wood-pewees engage in "yo-yo" flights, darting from a perch in the forest understory, grabbing an insect in midair and then returning to the same perch. **Where found:** open to dense, mixed and deciduous woodlands; summer breeder throughout New England.

Alder Flycatcher

Empidonax alnorum

Length: 5–6 in
Wingspan: 8 in

The alder flycatcher forages for insects by catching them in midair. It is constantly on the move, never seeming to rest as it flits from shrub to shrub, catching a morsel on each pass. • This bird's nest is made of grasses and affixed to a low shrub. It adorns its nest with plant down or long grass stems, which do not seem to serve any purpose other than exterior decoration. **Where found:** brushy habitats near bogs, swamps and wetlands; also birch and alder thickets; summer breeder throughout New England, but rare around Cape Cod.

Eastern Phoebe

Sayornis phoebe

Length: 6½–7 in
Wingspan: 10–11 in

Eastern phoebes often nest on building ledges, bridge trestles and under the eaves of barns and sheds and consequently are close to people. Their loud, emphatic *fee-bee!* song is a familiar sound. • Most flycatchers are not very tolerant of cold and typically migrate to the tropics in winter, where a good supply of flying insects is assured. But the tough eastern phoebe routinely attempts to overwinter as far north as the southern Great Lakes; migrants return by March. **Where found:** open deciduous woodlands, forest edges and clearings; often near bridges, culverts and other such structures; summer breeder throughout New England.

Eastern Kingbird

Tyrannus tyrannus

Length: 8½ in
Wingspan: 15 in

As its scientific name suggests, the eastern kingbird is somewhat of a tyrant among birds, harassing and mobbing crows, hawks and even humans that enter its territory. It is no friend of insects, either, for which this bird has a voracious appetite. • You will often see kingbirds perched on fencelines or utility wires along roadsides. **Where found:** fields and agricultural landscapes, woodland clearings and near water; summer breeder throughout New England.

Northern Shrike

Lanius excubitor

Length: 10 in
Wingspan: 14–15 in

One of the most vicious predators in the bird world, the northern shrike relies on its sharp, hooked bill to catch and kill small birds and rodents, which it spots from treetop perches. Its habit of impaling its prey on thorns and barbs for later consumption has earned it the name "butcher bird." Shrikes are the world's only true carnivorous songbirds. • Northern shrikes visit our region each winter in unpredictable and highly variable numbers. **Where found:** semi-open country, scrub and low-elevation orchards, farmlands and ranches; winter resident throughout New England.

Red-eyed Vireo

Vireo olivaceus

Length: 6 in
Wingspan: 10 in

One of the most common breeding birds in our area, the red-eyed vireo is difficult to spot high in the canopy where it prefers to forage. • Virtuoso male vireos have an impressive repertoire of songs and a record 21,000 tallied in a single day, with dozens of phrases expressed each minute. Most of the songs are likely improvised, one-time performances for lucky listeners. **Where found:** deciduous or mixed woodlands; summer breeder throughout New England. **Also known as:** preacher bird.

Blue Jay

Cyanocitta cristata

Length: 11 in
Wingspan: 16 in

Blue jays can be quite aggressive when competing for sunflower seeds and peanuts at backyard feeders, rarely hesitating to drive away smaller birds, squirrels or even cats. • Blue jays cache nuts and are very important to the forest ecosystem. In fall, one jay might bury hundreds of acorns, later forgetting where many were hidden and thus planting scads of oaks. • Blue jays have been proven to live up to 15 years. **Where found:** all types of habitats, from dense forests to suburbia; throughout New England year-round.

Common Raven

Corvus corax

Length: 22 in
Wingspan: 4 ft

The common raven soars with a wingspan comparable to that of a hawk, traveling along coastlines, over deserts, along mountain ridges and even over the Arctic tundra. Few birds occupy such a large natural range. • From producing complex vocalizations to playfully sliding down snowbanks, this raucous bird exhibits behaviors that many people once thought of as exclusively human. • All corvids are extremely intelligent, with some rivaling chimpanzees in problem-solving tests. **Where found:** coniferous and mixed forests and woodlands; also townsites, campgrounds and landfills; throughout New England year-round.

Horned Lark

Eremophila alpestris

Length: 7–7½ in
Wingspan: 12 in

One way to distinguish a horned lark from a sparrow is by its methods of locomotion: horned larks walk, but sparrows hop. • This bird has a dark tail that contrasts with its light brown body and belly, and it has 2 unique black "horns." This feature will help you to spot the horned lark in its open-country habitat. • In spring, male larks perform impressive, high-speed, plummeting courtship dives. **Where found:** short-grass habitats, farmlands and roadsides in summer; prefers agricultural fields and beaches in winter; year-round throughout New England, but possibly absent in winter in northern ME.

Tree Swallow

Tachycineta bicolor

Length: 5½–6 in
Wingspan: 13 in

An early bird of spring and one of the last to leave in fall, tree swallows spend a large part of the year in our region. They are common near old-growth forests, where they find cavities to nest in, but they will also happily take up residence in nest boxes or under barn eaves. • Both parents share the duties of nest building and caring for the nestlings, tirelessly flying to and fro, collecting building materials, catching insects and feeding the hungry babies. **Where found:** old-growth woodlands, near water; summer breeder throughout New England.

Barn Swallow

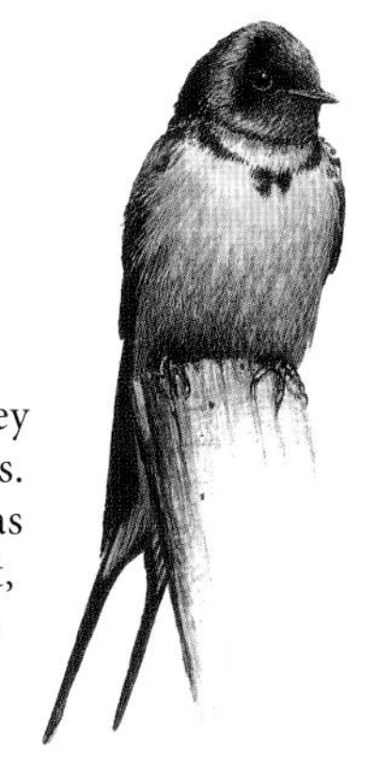

Hirundo rustica

Length: 6½–7½ in
Wingspan: 15 in

Barn swallows are a familiar sight around farmsteads, where they build their mud nests under the eaves of barns and other buildings. It is now almost unheard of for them to nest in natural sites such as cliffs, to which they once were restricted. • The males have elegant, long, forked tails and beautiful coloring. **Where found:** open landscapes, especially in rural and agricultural areas, often near water; summer breeder throughout New England.

Black-capped Chickadee

Poecile atricapillus

Length: 5–6 in
Wingspan: 8 in

A common visitor to backyard feeders, chickadees join the company of kinglets, nuthatches and small woodpeckers. In spring and fall, they join mixed flocks of vireos and warblers. • The calling out of its name, *chick-a-dee-dee-dee*, is this bird's most distinctive sound, but it also sings a slow, whistled *swee-tee* or *fee-bee*. • The black-capped chickadee is the state bird of both Maine and Massachusetts. **Where found:** deciduous and mixed forests, riparian woodlands and wooded urban parks; also backyard feeders; year-round throughout New England.

White-breasted Nuthatch

Sitta carolinensis

Length: 5½–6 in
Wingspan: 11 in

The white-breasted nuthatch has a somewhat dizzying view of the world as it moves down tree trunks head-first, cleaning up any seeds, insects and nuts that woodpeckers have overlooked. They are attracted to backyard bird feeders filled with suet or peanut butter. • Nuthatches excavate a cavity nest or use an abandoned woodpecker nest and smear the entrance with sap to keep away ants and other insects that can transmit fungal infections or parasitize nestlings. **Where found:** deciduous and mixed woodlands; year-round throughout New England.

Winter Wren

Troglodytes hiemalis

Length: 4 in
Wingspan: 5½ in

Called "winter wren" because it passes the winter days in the southeastern United States, it should be called "summer wren" in New England. • This tiny bird boldly lays claim to its territory with its call and distinctive, melodious song, which it can sustain for 10 seconds, using up to 113 tones. • Although the male contributes to raising the family, defending the nest and finding food for the nestlings, he sleeps elsewhere at night, in an unfinished nest. **Where found:** lowland forests and thickets; prefers wet forests; summer breeder; year-round in southern New England. **Also known as:** Jenny wren; *T. troglodytes*.

Golden-crowned Kinglet

Regulus satrapa

Length: 4 in
Wingspan: 7 in

The dainty golden-crowned kinglet is not much bigger than a hummingbird, and when it gleans the forest canopy for insects, berries and sap, it is prone to unique hazards such as perishing on the burrs of burdock plants. • This songbird's perpetual motion and chronic wing flicking can help identify it from a distance. **Where found:** at the tops of spruces, pines and firs in mature coniferous forests; moves to coastal forests, riparian areas and sometimes urban parks and gardens in migration and winter; year-round throughout New England except the extreme southeast, where it only occurs in winter.

Eastern Bluebird

Sialia sialis

Length: 7 in
Wingspan: 11½ in

It is a treasured occasion when an eastern bluebird takes up residence in a nest box on your property. Nest boxes placed on fence posts have greatly bolstered bluebird populations. • The male displays gorgeous deep blue and contrasting warm rufous plumage, and it sings a soft, pleasing, warbling song. The female is duller in color, and young birds are heavily spotted below, revealing this species' relationship to the thrushes. **Where found:** agricultural fields and pastures, orchards, fencelines, meadows, open woodlands and forest clearings and edges; summer breeder throughout New England; year-round in the south.

Veery

Catharus fuscescens

Length: 7 in
Wingspan: 11 in

At twilight, this woodland songster begins its summer's night song, which is composed of downward spirals of flute-like notes. It spends the summer in our region, nesting on damp ground or on very low branches, but in fall, it migrates to spend the winter in South America. **Where found:** moist, dense, deciduous woodlands with a heavy understory, streamside thickets and riparian woodlands; summer breeder throughout New England.

Hermit Thrush

Catharus guttatus

Length: 6–7 in
Wingspan: 11½ in

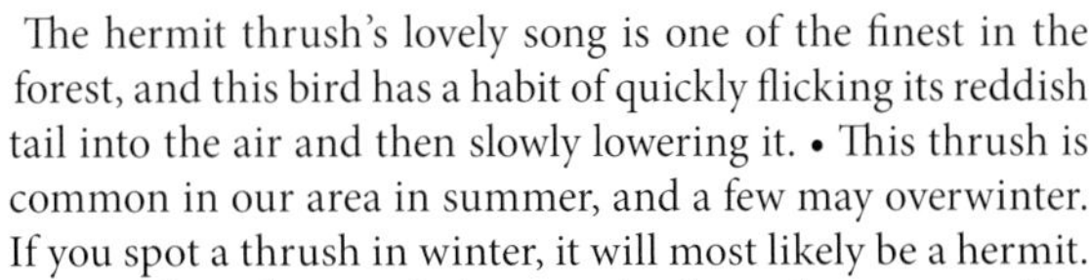

The hermit thrush's lovely song is one of the finest in the forest, and this bird has a habit of quickly flicking its reddish tail into the air and then slowly lowering it. • This thrush is common in our area in summer, and a few may overwinter. If you spot a thrush in winter, it will most likely be a hermit. Perhaps this tendency to not follow along with the rest of its kin is how it earned its reclusive name. • The hermit thrush is the state bird of Vermont. **Where found:** forests and edge habitats; summer breeder throughout New England; eastern RI marks the northern limit of its winter range.

Wood Thrush

Hylocichla mustelina

Length: 8 in
Wingspan: 13 in

The clear, flute-like, whistled song of the wood thrush is one of the most beautiful and characteristic melodies of the eastern deciduous forest. A split syrinx, or vocal organ, enables the wood thrush to sing 2 notes simultaneously and thus create harmonies and hauntingly ethereal songs that delight listeners. • Still common but on the decline, the wood thrush faces loss of habitat and other threats, both here and in its Central American wintering habitat. **Where found:** moist, mature and preferably undisturbed deciduous woodlands and mixed forests; summer breeder throughout New England.

American Robin

Turdus migratorius

Length: 10 in
Wingspan: 17 in

The American robin is a familiar and common sight on lawns as it searches for worms. In winter, it switches to fruit trees, which can attract flocks to feed. • American robins build cup-shaped nests of grass, moss and mud. The female incubates 4 light blue eggs and raises up to 3 broods per year. The male cares for the fledglings from the first brood while the female incubates the second clutch of eggs. • The American robin is Connecticut's state bird. **Where found:** residential lawns and gardens, pastures, urban parks, broken forests, bogs and river shorelines; winters near fruit-bearing trees and springs; summer breeder throughout New England; year-round along the coast.

Gray Catbird

Dumetella carolinensis

Length: 8½ in
Wingspan: 11 in

A gray catbird in full song issues a nonstop, squeaky barrage of warbling notes interspersed with poor imitations of other birds' songs. Occasionally it lets go with loud, cat-like meows that might even fool a feline. • The female catbird is one of the few birds that can recognize and remove a brown-headed cowbird egg sneakily laid in her nest. **Where found:** dense thickets, brambles, shrubby areas and hedgerows, often near water; summer breeder throughout New England; year-round around Cape Cod.

Northern Mockingbird

Mimus polyglottos

Length: 10 in
Wingspan: 14 in

Masters of mimicry, mockingbirds can have a vocal repertoire of over 400 different song types. They imitate a wide array of sounds flawlessly, rivaling other birds at singing their own songs, mocking crows, and surprising and confusing humans with wolf-whistles, fire engine sirens and the backup beeps of garbage trucks. Male mockingbirds calling out for a mate have been known to sing through the night, to the frustration of anyone trying to sleep. **Where found:** hedges, fencerows and suburban parks and gardens; year-round in all but northern New England.

Cedar Waxwing

Bombycilla cedrorum

Length: 7 in
Wingspan: 12 in

With its black mask and slick hairdo, the cedar waxwing has a heroic look. • To court a mate, the gentlemanly male hops toward a female and offers her a berry. The female will accept the berry and hop away, then stop and hop back toward the male to offer him the berry in return. **Where found:** *Breeding:* hardwood and mixed forests, woodland edges, fruit orchards, young pine plantations and among conifers in riparian hardwood stands. *In migration* and *winter:* open woodlands and brush, often near water, residential areas and any habitat with nearby berry trees. Throughout New England.

Ovenbird

Seiurus aurocapilla

Length: 6 in
Wingspan: 9½ in

The ovenbird gets its name from the shape of its nest, which resembles an old-fashioned Dutch oven. • Finding an expertly concealed nest on the forest floor is nearly impossible, but these birds are easy to identify by sound. Issuing a loud *tea-CHER tea-CHER tea-CHER* song that ascends in volume, ovenbirds are conspicuous singers. • Unlike most other warblers, ovenbirds are primarily ground feeders and walk about poking through leaf litter for food. **Where found:** undisturbed, mature forests, often with little understory; summer breeder throughout New England. **Also known as:** teacher bird.

Black-and-white Warbler

Mniotilta varia

Length: 5½ in
Wingspan: 8½ in

In a habit unique to warblers but typical of nuthatches, the black-and-white warbler forages by creeping along branches and up and down tree trunks searching for insects in bark crevices. • This bird's song is reminiscent of a squeaky wheel, but it also has a dull *chip* call and a high-pitched flight note. **Where found:** mature and second-growth, deciduous and coniferous forests; summer breeder throughout New England.

American Redstart

Setophaga ruticilla

Length: 5 in
Wingspan: 8½ in

This bird's Latin American name, *candelita*, meaning "little torch," perfectly describes the American redstart. Not only are the male's bright orange patches the color of a glowing flame, but the bird never ceases to flicker, rhythmically swaying its tail and flashing its orange wings, even when perched. • By flashing the bright orange or yellow spots in its plumage, the redstart flushes insects from the foliage. A broad bill and the rictal bristles around its mouth help it capture prey. **Where found:** dense, shrubby understory in deciduous woodlands, often near water; summer breeder throughout New England. **Also known as:** butterfly bird.

Common Yellowthroat

Geothlypis trichas

Length: 5 in
Wingspan: 7 in

This skulker's loud *witchity witchity witchity* song bursting from the cattails gives it away. These little masked bandits are probably our most common breeding warblers, reaching peak numbers in wetlands and damp, overgrown fields. Females can be difficult to identify but share the male's big-headed, slender-bodied, long-legged dimensions. • Surprisingly hardy, common yellowthroats occasionally linger well into winter in milder years. **Where found:** wetlands, riparian areas and wet, overgrown meadows; common and widespread throughout New England during summer and migration.

Yellow Warbler

Setophaga petechia

Length: 5 in
Wingspan: 8 in

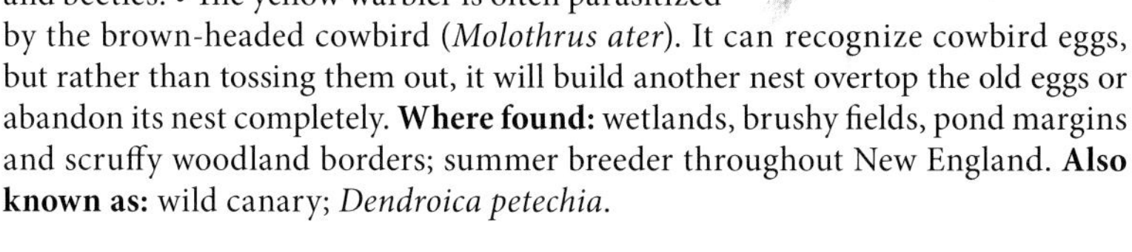

Showy, bright yellow and common in summer, the yellow warbler is a delight. It is also a useful bird to have around because it feeds on caterpillars, aphids and beetles. • The yellow warbler is often parasitized by the brown-headed cowbird (*Molothrus ater*). It can recognize cowbird eggs, but rather than tossing them out, it will build another nest overtop the old eggs or abandon its nest completely. **Where found:** wetlands, brushy fields, pond margins and scruffy woodland borders; summer breeder throughout New England. **Also known as:** wild canary; *Dendroica petechia.*

Black-throated Blue Warbler

Setophaga caerulescens

Length: 5 in
Wingspan: 8½ in

When foraging, the shy and inconspicuous black-throated blue warbler prefers to work deliberately and methodically over a small area, snatching up insects among branches and foliage. • This bird's song is a slow, husky *I am so lay-zeee* that rises slowly throughout. • The female's plain plumage looks nothing like that of her male counterpart. **Where found:** mature deciduous and mixed woodlands; summer breeder throughout New England, but rare to absent in RI. **Also known as:** *Dendroica caerulescens.*

Chipping Sparrow

Spizella passerina

Length: 5–6 in
Wingspan: 8½ in

Although you may spot the relatively tame chipping sparrow singing from a high perch, it commonly nests at eye level, so you can easily watch its breeding and nest-building rituals. • This bird's song is very similar to that of the dark-eyed junco but slightly faster, drier and with a less musical series of notes. **Where found:** *Breeding:* grassy woodlands and clearings in dry forests. *In migration* and *winter:* open grasslands with brushy cover, scrublands and residential woodlots; also backyard feeders. Summer breeder throughout New England, overwinters in the south.

Savannah Sparrow

Passerculus sandwichensis

Length: 5½ in
Wingspan: 8 in

The savannah sparrow is inconspicuous in plumage and song, but it is one of our most common sparrows. You will typically observe it clinging to a swaying weed stalk. • This bird forages on the ground in search of seeds and insects but tends to fly directly to a raised perch if disturbed. **Where found:** in a wide variety of habitats, including grasslands, grassy beach dunes, farmlands and marshes; summer breeder throughout New England. **Also known as:** gray bird.

Song Sparrow

Melospiza melodia

Length: 6–7 in
Wingspan: 8 in

Although its plumage is unremarkable, the well-named song sparrow is among the great singers of the bird world. By the time a young male is only a few months old, he has already created a courtship tune of his own, having learned the basics of melody and rhythm from his father and rival males. • The presence of a well-stocked backyard feeder may be a fair trade for a sweet song in the dead of winter. **Where found:** hardwood brush in forests and open country, near water or in lush vegetation in riparian willows, marshy habitats and residential areas; summer breeder throughout New England; year-round in the south.

White-throated Sparrow

Zonotrichia albicollis

Length: 6–7 in
Wingspan: 8½ in

White-throated sparrows sing a distinctive song—a clear, whistled *poor Sam Peabody Peabody Peabody*—in a somewhat mournful minor key. • White-throats have 2 color morphs. One has black and white stripes on the head, whereas the other has brown and tan stripes. These color morphs should not be misinterpreted as a difference between males and females. **Where found:** coniferous and mixed forests; summer breeder in northern New England; year-round in the south; in RI in winter only.

Dark-eyed Junco

Junco hyemalis

Length: 6–7 in
Wingspan: 9 in

Juncos usually congregate in sheltering conifers and at backyard bird feeders—with such amenities at their disposal, more and more are appearing in urban areas. • There are 5 closely related dark-eyed junco subspecies in North America that differ in coloration and range. The slate-colored junco occurs in our area. **Where found:** shrubby woodland borders and backyard feeders; year-round throughout New England, except winter only along the southern coast of the Gulf of Maine. **Also known as:** black snowbird.

Scarlet Tanager

Piranga olivacaea

Length: 7 in
Wingspan: 11½ in

Almost shocking in appearance, the male scarlet tanager glows neon red, its scarlet body contrasting with shiny, black wings and tail. • These tanagers spend most of their time high in the forest canopy, so knowing their song helps tremendously in locating them. Their tune is a raspy, whistled series of phrases that sounds like an American robin with a sore throat. • Most tanagers winter in the jungles of South America. **Where found:** dense, mature forests; summer breeder throughout New England.

Northern Cardinal

Cardinalis cardinalis

Length: 8½ in
Wingspan: 12 in

One of the most familiar eastern North American birds, the northern cardinal is the state bird of seven states. • This species is named for the color of its plumage, which matches the red robes of Roman Catholic cardinals. • Cardinals maintain strong pair bonds. Some couples sing to each other year-round, whereas others join loose flocks, re-establishing pair bonds in spring during a "courtship feeding"—the male offers a seed to the female, which she then accepts and eats. **Where found:** woodland edges, thickets, backyards and parks; year-round throughout New England, except northern ME.

Rose-breasted Grosbeak

Pheucticus ludovicianus

Length: 7–8½ in
Wingspan: 12½ in

The rose-breasted grosbeak's call note is a squeaky sound reminiscent of a sneaker on a basketball court. Listen for grosbeaks to find them—they remain high in leafy canopies and are rather sluggish. • The male has beautiful, black-and-white plumage and a bold, inverted "V" of crimson pink on his breast. The female looks like a big sparrow and is unusual among songbirds because she also sings. **Where found:** deciduous and mixed forests; summer breeder throughout New England.

Indigo Bunting

Passerina cyanea

Length: 5½ in
Wingspan: 8 in

These abundant birds often sing from roadside wires and look like small blackbirds, but catch one in good light and the vivid electric-blue males will knock your socks off. They look every inch like a tropical exotic, which they are. Indigo buntings spend most of their time in the Caribbean and Central America. • Males are persistent singers, vocalizing throughout the hottest summer days. The females look like plain, brown sparrows. **Where found:** deciduous forests, woodland edges, agricultural areas with fencerows, orchards and shrubby fields; summer breeder throughout New England, except the northern tip of ME.

Red-winged Blackbird

Agelaius phoeniceus

Length: 7½–9 in
Wingspan: 13 in

The male red-winged blackbird wears his bright red shoulders like armor—together with his short, raspy song, they are key in defending his territory from rivals. Nearly every cattail marsh worthy of note in our region hosts this bird. • The female's cryptic coloration allows her to sit inconspicuously on her nest, blending in perfectly among the cattails or shoreline bushes. **Where found:** cattail marshes, wet meadows and ditches, croplands and shoreline shrubs; summer breeder throughout New England; year-round in the south.

Eastern Meadowlark

Sturnella magna

Length: 9–9½ in
Wingspan: 14 in

The clear, ringing, whistled song of the eastern meadowlark sounds like *spring of the year!* • From above, the meadowlark's muted, somber hues of speckled brown blend in with the vegetation. • When flushed, meadowlarks reveal conspicuous, white outer tail feathers and fly with distinctive stiff, shallow wingbeats. **Where found:** grassy meadows, roadsides, pastures, old fields and croplands; summer resident throughout New England; year-round along the extreme southern Gulf of Maine.

Common Grackle

Quiscalus quiscula

Length: 11–13½ in
Wingspan: 17 in

The common grackle is a species of blackbird. It is not popular among birders because of its aggressive bullying at feeders or with farmers thanks to its habit of pulling up new corn shoots. • The male's iridescent plumage gleams in sunlight. • Grackles form enormous roosts in fall and winter with other blackbirds and European starlings (*Sturnus vulgaris*). **Where found:** nearly all habitats, especially in open to semi-open areas; summer breeder throughout New England; year-round in the south and along the Gulf of Maine.

Purple Finch

Carpodacus purpureus

Length: 5–6 in
Wingspan: 10 in

Male purple finches are more raspberry red than purple. They are often confused with house finches (*C. mexicanus*), but the latter is more reddish and is prominently streaked below. Female purple finches have a bolder eyeline and facial pattern than do female house finches. • Purple finches are attracted to sunflower seeds, and large numbers can be lured to feeders in winter. • The purple finch is the state bird of New Hampshire. **Where found:** coniferous and mixed forests; throughout New England year-round.

American Goldfinch

Spinus tristis

Length: 4½–5 in
Wingspan: 9 in

Like vibrant rays of sunshine, American goldfinches cheerily flutter over weedy fields, gardens and along roadsides, perching on late-summer thistle heads or poking through dandelion patches in search of seeds. It is hard to miss their jubilant *po-ta-to-chip* call and distinctive, undulating flight style. **Where found:** weedy fields, woodland edges, meadows, riparian areas, parks and gardens; throughout New England year-round. **Also known as:** willow goldfinch; *Carduelis tristis.*

House Sparrow

Passer domesticus

Length: 6–6½ in
Wingspan: 9½ in

This abundant and conspicuous bird was introduced to North America in the 1850s as part of a plan to control insects that were damaging grain and cereal crops. But, as it turns out, the house sparrow is largely vegetarian! • This bird will usurp the territory and nests of native birds such as bluebirds, swallows and finches, and it has a high reproductive output of 4 clutches per year, with up to 8 young per clutch. **Where found:** townsites, urban and suburban areas, farmyards and agricultural areas, railroad yards and other developed areas; throughout New England year-round.

AMPHIBIANS & REPTILES

Amphibians and reptiles are commonly referred to as "cold blooded," but this term is misleading. Although these animals lack the ability to generate their own internal body heat, they are not necessarily cold blooded. Amphibians and reptiles are ectothermic, or poikilothermic, meaning that the temperature of the surrounding environment governs their body temperature. These animals obtain heat from sunlight, warm rocks and logs, and warmed earth. In cold regions, reptiles and amphibians hibernate through winter, and some reptile species aestivate (are dormant during hot or dry periods) in summer in hot regions. Both reptiles and amphibians molt (shed their skins) as they grow.

Amphibians are smooth skinned and most live in moist habitats. They are represented by the salamanders, frogs and toads. These species typically lay eggs without shells in jelly-like masses in water. The eggs hatch into gilled larvae (the larvae of frogs and toads are called tadpoles), which later metamorphose into adults with lungs and legs. Amphibians can regenerate their skin and sometimes even entire limbs. Males and females often differ in size and color, and males may have other specialized features when sexually mature, such as the vocal sacs present in many frogs and toads.

Reptiles are vertebrates with scaly skin. In this guide, the representatives are turtles and snakes. Most reptiles bury their eggs in loose soil, but some snakes give birth to live young. Reptiles do not have a larval stage.

Salamanders
pp. 110–111

Toads & Frogs
pp. 112–114

Turtles
pp. 115–117

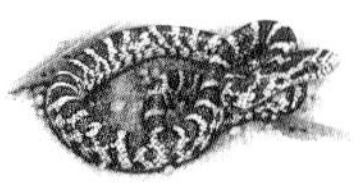

Snakes
pp. 118–120

Red-spotted Newt

Notophthalmus viridescens

Length: *Adult:* 3–5½ in; *Eft:* 1½–3 in

Like all amphibians, the newt morphs through several life stages. The larva hatches from an egg (the female lays up to 400 singly on submerged vegetation) after 1 to 2 months, but at the end of summer, rather than morphing into an adult newt, the larva develops into a terrestrial, nonbreeding eft, a stage that can last up to 4 years. The eft seeks shelter under logs and in rock crevices, but when it wanders through moist leaf litter, its vibrant red skin announces its toxicity to predators. When the eft returns to the water to morph into a mature breeding adult, a stage that can last another decade, its red skin dulls to green or brown with just a few red spots. **Where found:** moist forests; throughout New England. **Also known as:** eastern newt.

Blue-spotted Salamander

Ambystoma laterale

Length: 3–5 in

The best time to observe this salamander is in spring when it emerges from underground, sometimes in the hundreds, to breed in ponds and wetlands. It is rarely seen again until late summer, particularly on rainy evenings, when newly transformed young emerge from their breeding ponds and migrate to terrestrial habitats. **Where found:** mixed woodlands and continuous forests; wetlands or lakes during breeding; throughout New England but rare and threatened in the south.

Spotted Salamander

Ambystoma maculatum

Length: 6–10 in

Look into the depths of clear, shallow ponds that are void of fish in spring, and you may see this salamander walking about the bottom in search of a mate. The bright yellow spots make identification easy. You may also see several clumps of up to 250 eggs or a single, large mass of eggs laid by the female spotted salamander attached to underwater vegetation. The remainder of the adult's life is spent under debris and loose soil in the forest. **Where found:** forested areas surrounding ponds; hardwood and mixed coniferous-deciduous forests; throughout New England.

Northern Two-lined Salamander

Eurycea bislineata

Length: 2½–5 in

The 2 lines that give this salamander its name are made up of many closely adjacent black spots, but a more distinctive identifying mark is the bold, yellow coloration between the 2 lines that runs the entire length of the animal—half of which is tail. • This salamander's long tail helps it navigate the currents of the fast-flowing streams along which it lives. **Where found:** cool, moist, forested areas alongside fast-moving streams; throughout New England.

Red-backed Salamander

Plethodon cinereus

Length: 2½–5 in

This salamander is lungless; instead of breathing with lungs, it breathes through its thin, moist skin. It belongs to a family of salamanders called Plethodontidae, which means "many teeth." • The red-backed salamander is abundant in almost any wooded environment, including woodlots, making it probably the most frequently encountered salamander in New England. **Where found:** damp, mature deciduous or mixed forests, beneath coarse, woody ground litter and fallen, rotting logs; throughout New England.

Northern Dusky Salamander

Desmognathus fuscus

Length: 2½–4½ in

This salamander is reclusive, but if you start turning over stones and logs near clean woodland streams, you may discover one. Its back legs are unusually long in relation to its front legs, which may be what allows this amphibian to run and jump and quickly escape you once you find it. If you manage to corner it long enough to get a good look, you may notice the pale facial line that also identifies this species. **Where found:** wooded streams, springs and seeps; throughout New England.

American Toad

Anaxyrus americanus

Length: 2½–4½ in

Touching a toad will not give you warts, but the American toad does have a way of discouraging unwanted affection—when handled, it may urinate on you! Despite this danger, children like to catch this large, reddish olive or brown toad. A more passive way of enjoying this amphibian is listening to its distinctive, long and loud croaking in spring. **Where found:** fields, woodlands, gardens and lawns; throughout New England.

Fowler's Toad

Anaxyrus fowleri

Length: 2½–4 in

Fowler's toad is similar in appearance to the American toad, and they do sometimes interbreed. Important field marks for this species include the marbled pattern, 3 or more warts in larger individuals, dark blotches and a pale, unmarked belly, often with a single spot. Another diagnostic that sets it apart from the American toad is its call. Breeding male Fowler's toads let off an explosive, nasal *waaaahhh!* that sounds like a short scream. **Where found:** sandy beaches, meadows and forests; from southern VT and NH to the coast almost to ME and south throughout the rest of New England.

American Bullfrog

Lithobates catesbeianus

Length: 6 in or longer

Bullfrogs are very large, weighing from 2 to 30 oz or more, and long-lived, with an average lifespan of 7 to 9 years. There are records of individuals in captivity living up to 16 years. • Bullfrogs are predatory and will eat anything they can swallow, including other species of frogs, certain snakes, fish and even small birds and mammals. • The bullfrog's call is described as a deep monotone *jug-o-rum more rum*. **Where found:** warm, still, shallow, vegetated waters of lakes, ponds, rivers and bogs; throughout New England. **Also known as:** *Rana catesbeiana*.

Gray Treefrog

Hyla versicolor

Length: 2½ in

Many people who hear this diminutive tree dweller may think that the coarse trilling sound coming from high in the trees is a bird. The gray treefrog is arboreal and has surface-gripping toe pads that give it a Spiderman-like climbing ability. • Gray treefrogs can change color like chameleons to perfectly match their background, morphing from a rather bright gray-green to a dull pearly gray. **Where found:** woodlands near water; hibernates under soil or leaves; throughout New England except northern ME.

Northern Spring Peeper

Pseudacris crucifer

Length: to 1 in

A grand chorus erupts from these tiny voices announcing the arrival of spring. Spring peepers will repeat their high-pitched *peep* up to 4000 times per hour! They sing most zealously from late afternoon through the night. These little frogs do not limit their operatic season to springtime but will continue throughout summer and fall, until the snow flies. **Where found:** almost any shrubby or forested natural area near water; throughout New England.

Wood Frog

Lithobates sylvaticus

Length: 2–3 in

This hardy animal is famous for being able to survive being completely frozen! The frog's body produces complex sugars and proteins to draw water out of cells to prevent them from rupturing when frozen. The animal hibernates underground through winter, thaws out in spring and takes to still, icy ponds in search of heart-warming romance. **Where found:** moist woodlands, grasslands and most still water bodies; throughout New England. **Also known as:** *Rana sylvatica*.

Northern Leopard Frog

Lithobates pipiens

Length: 1½–4 in

Once a widespread and abundant frog, this species suffered dramatic declines in the 1970s that it still has not recovered from in parts of its range. Much of the decline was attributed to water pollution from pesticides and herbicides, but it is unknown why this species suffered more than others. **Where found:** damp forests and wetlands; historically, throughout New England; extirpated in developed areas of CT, MA and RI, but may be recovering. **Also known as:** *Rana pipiens.*

Pickerel Frog

Lithobates palustris

Length: 2–3½ in

Somewhat similar in appearance to the northern leopard frog, this species differs in its rectangular spots, overall brownish rather than green color and the bright yellow coloration on the lower belly and under the hind legs. Also, the pickerel frog inhabits cooler, moving waters rather than the warm, marshy habitats of the leopard frog. • This frog's toxic skin secretions cause many predators to avoid it and may be potent enough to kill other frogs kept in the same aquarium. **Where found:** brooks, streams, fens and springs; throughout New England, but declining. **Also known as:** *Rana palustris.*

Green Frog

Lithobates clamitans

Length: 3–4 in

This is the most likely frog you will catch anywhere in New England, though a big, fat individual could be easily mistaken for an American bullfrog. Unlike the deep, croaking *jug-o-rum* of the American bullfrog, however, the green frog's call is best described as a banjo-like twang. • As with bullfrogs, the tympanic membrane—the large, round disk behind the eye—is much larger than the eye on males, but about the same size as the eye in females. **Where found:** near ponds, lakes and other permanent water bodies; throughout New England. **Also known as:** *Rana clamitans.*

Common Snapping Turtle

Chelydra serpentina

Length: 8–18½ in

This large, freshwater turtle spends most of its existence wallowing in the mud or walking along lake or pond bottoms eating weeds and scavenging for carrion. The female only comes on land in late spring to dig a nest in which to lay her 25 to 50 eggs. Snapping turtles do not mate until at least 15 years of age. • This species' reputation for biting off toes is greatly exaggerated, but they do snap, so be wary. **Where found:** soft, muddy bottoms of ponds and brackish water with plenty of vegetation; throughout New England.

Common Musk Turtle

Sternotherus odoratus

Length: 3–5½ in

Aggressive and feisty, this little turtle won't hesitate to bite and can extend its rubbery neck backward nearly to its hind legs. Its name comes from its offensive strategy of expelling a nasty, smelly, yellowish liquid from glands under its shell when threatened. • This turtle walks along the bottom of ponds in search of aquatic invertebrates and carrion or basks at the water's surface. • A captive musk turtle was recorded as living for 55 years. **Where found:** still, shallow water bodies; throughout New England. **Also known as:** stink pot.

Painted Turtle

Chrysemys picta

Length: 4–10 in

The bright yellow belly, red markings along the edge of the shell and distinct yellow stripes on the head are excellent diagnostics for identifying this striking turtle. • This reptile supplements its mainly vegetarian diet with invertebrates, amphibian larvae and small fish. **Where found:** shallow, muddy-bottomed water bodies with abundant plant growth; logs, cattail mats and open banks on sloughs, ponds, lakes and marshes and along sluggish rivers with oxbows; throughout New England.

Blanding's Turtle

Emydoidea blandingii

Length: 6–10 in

You can often get a great close-up view of most pond turtles with binoculars as they bask on logs. This species can be identified from afar by its high, domed shell and distinctive bright yellow throat. • The tall, top-heavy shell makes Blanding's turtle a poor swimmer. It prefers to walk along pond bottoms, feeding on aquatic invertebrates and vegetation. **Where found:** ponds, marshes, lake margins with aquatic vegetation and sometimes swampy woods; from southern NH to ME and eastern MA.

Spotted Turtle

Clemmys guttata

Length: 4–5 in

This small, secretive turtle is a common inhabitant of peatlands, where people tend not to wander. It forages out of sight under bog mats or sedge duff. If luck brings one across your path, you can admire its striking coloration with those distinctive spots. • Spotted turtles hibernate communally in groups of over a dozen in favored burrows known as hibernacula. Development and the filling in of wetlands and peatlands has resulted in significant habitat loss and great reductions in populations of this charming little turtle. **Where found:** peatlands, bogs, fens, wet prairies and sometimes beaver ponds and wetlands; throughout New England.

Wood Turtle

Glyptemys insculpta

Length: 6–10 in

This mini-tortoise stomps its feet on the ground to encourage earthworms to the surface so it can eat them. It is a pretty smart move and shows this turtle lives up to its sage looks and demeanor. Although considered a sprinter among turtles, its top speed of about ¼ mph (about 22 feet per minute) is not fast enough to outrun poachers; this species has been overharvested by collectors in the past, which, coupled with habitat loss, has caused a decline in its population. **Where found:** woods, forests and wetlands; hibernates in water; throughout New England. **Also known as:** *Clemmys insculpta*.

Eastern Box Turtle

Terrapene carolina

Length: 5–8 in

This turtle is sometimes seen near or on roads attempting to cross—if you find one, you can help it by placing it safely on the side it was heading for. A box turtle "boxes itself in" by pulling in its limbs and head, then tightly closing its shell, but it is no match for a vehicle. The lower shell, or plastron, is hinged and can be brought up securely against the domed carapace to exclude predators. • If this turtle survives road crossings, predators and poachers, it can live well over 100 years. **Where found:** varied habitats from wooded wetlands to fields; hibernates in soil; southern New England.

Loggerhead Sea Turtle

Caretta caretta

Length: 3 ft

The loggerhead is named for its obviously large head, which can be up to 1 foot in diameter, though such historical measurements have not been matched by any of this reptile's contemporaries observed by researchers. • Loggerheads range throughout the Atlantic Ocean. They do not nest in New England, but juveniles (aged 7–12 years) occur offshore and occasionally wash up on Cape Cod beaches. • Loggerheads do not reach breeding age until they are approximately 35 years old, a very slow reproductive rate when survival to this age is rare. **Where found:** inshore, neritic; Gulf of Maine.

Green Sea Turtle

Chelonia mydas

Length: 3 ft

Green sea turtles are seen only rarely in our waters. They spend most of their lives in warmer climes, but young turtles are sometimes found in summer in New England water. • These turtles are estimated to reach breeding age at the earliest at 20 years and possibly not until they are 50 years old. • Unlike other sea turtles, which are omnivorous, this species is strictly herbivorous, which is believed to make their flesh green. **Where found:** nearshore to offshore; Gulf of Maine.

Eastern Garter Snake

Thamnophis sirtalis

Length: 33–39 in

Swift both on land and in water, the eastern garter snake is an efficient hunter of amphibians, fish, small mammals, slugs and leeches. It is a harmless and well-known snake, famous for its large hibernacula. • Several subspecies exist across the country with variable coloration; the New England subspecies is brown or gray, with a poorly defined spinal stripe and alternating dark marks on the back. **Where found:** wetlands, forests, fields and urban areas; throughout New England.

Ribbon Snake

Thamnophis sauritus

Length: 18–26 in

Stunning in looks and graceful of movement, the sleek-bodied ribbon snake is among our most beautiful reptiles. Its blackish body is adorned with 3 bright yellow stripes running from head to tail, and it has a crescent-moon-shaped marking in front of each eye. Although similar to a garter snake, the ribbon snake is more slender and has a whip-like quality. • Ribbon snakes are often found in or near water, basking on logs or hunting for prey. **Where found:** wet meadows, wetlands, weedy lakeshores and creeks; VT, NH and southwestern ME, south throughout the rest of New England.

Northern Water Snake

Nerodia sipedon

Length: 25–45 in

Although not aquatic, the northern water snake is almost always found near water. This species bites fiercely and expels an unpleasant musk from glands near the end of its tail. • The northern water snake has a thick body, and the body color ranges from gray to brown, with darker bands near the head, followed by alternating back and side blotches. • This snake preys on small vertebrates such as frogs and fish, as well as various invertebrates. **Where found:** near or in water; hibernates underground; from northwestern VT through southern NH, ME and the rest of New England.

Red-bellied Snake

Storeria occipitomaculata

Length: to 16 in

This diminutive snake is not much larger than the worms it feeds upon. Its preferred prey species are the worms and slugs that it finds under logs and other forest debris in the woodlands in which it lives. • The red-bellied snake is named for the color of its belly, which can be red, orange or yellow. The rest of its body is brown, gray or black, with one to several dark or light dorsal stripes. **Where found:** open woodlands, forest edges and meadows, typically under boards, logs or other debris; throughout New England except northern ME and southern CT and RI.

Northern Ring-necked Snake

Diadophis punctatus

Length: 10–24 in (average less than 18 in)

Despite its outstanding good looks, this snake is shy and prefers to hide beneath rocks, logs, bark, wooden planks or leaf debris. If it is discovered and threatened, this harmless, pencil-thin snake will show its brightly colored underside by coiling its tail upward like a fiery corkscrew, hide its head beneath its body and emit a pungent musk. • This snake's preferred prey is the red-backed salamander. **Where found:** wooded areas and nearby meadows; throughout New England.

Eastern Milk Snake

Lampropeltis triangulum

Length: 24–36 in (occasionally to 50 in)

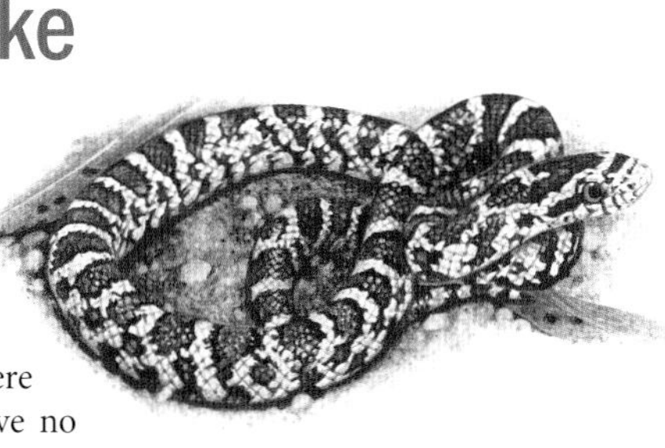

Much folklore surrounds the behaviors of this snake, including how it got its name. Because milk snakes frequently enter barns, it was assumed that they were milking the cows, though to date we have no evidence of this activity! When milk snakes enter barns and old buildings, they are hunting mice and rats, benefitting the farmer rather than stealing his milk. Milk snakes also eat frogs, bird eggs and invertebrates. • A pale "Y" or "V" marking on the head and the bold body pattern identify this snake. **Where found:** forests, meadows, edge habitats and agricultural areas; from northwestern VT through southern NH, ME and the rest of New England.

Black Rat Snake

Elaphe obsoleta

Length: 3¾–6¼ ft (exceptional individuals reach 8¼ ft)

A fully grown black rat snake is an impressive sight. It may look intimidating, but, like most other snakes, it is not normally aggressive and is somewhat of a gentle giant unless you are a rat. Rat snakes prey on rodents as well as many other small animals, including birds, amphibians and other snakes. They are excellent climbers, often taking to trees to raid bird nests and commonly holing up in tree cavities. **Where found:** variable habitats from flat farmland to rocky hillsides; southwestern New England.

Eastern Racer

Coluber constrictor

Length: 30–60 in

The eastern racer relies on speed to catch prey and escape danger—at full tilt, this snake can briefly hit 12 mph. On the ground, it moves with its head held high for a better view of the terrain. It will also climb shrubs to find birds and insects. • When alarmed, the racer will sometimes vibrate its tail rapidly, creating a rattlesnake-like buzz. **Where found:** open forests and edges, wooded hills, grassy ditches, fields, wetlands and riparian areas; southern New England.

Timber Rattlesnake

Crotalus horridus

Length: 36–60 in

Generally unappreciated by humans, the timber rattlesnake plays an important ecological role, preying upon rodents and other small mammals. • A rattlesnake bite is painful but rarely lethal to an adult unless left untreated for several hours. • The only other pit viper species in our region is the copperhead (*Agkistrodon contortrix*). It occurs only in southern New England and is also endangered. **Where found:** second-growth deciduous or coniferous forests, rocky outcroppings, steep ledges, rock slides, dry ridges, abandoned buildings and old stone walls; parts of VT, southern NH, MA and CT but declining; thought to be extirpated in the rest of New England, so report any sightings to authorities.

FISH

Fish are ectothermic vertebrates that live in the water, have streamlined bodies covered in scales and possess fins and gills. A fundamental feature of fish is the serially repeated set of vertebrae and segmented muscles that allow the animal to move from side to side, propelling it through the water. A varying number of fins, depending on the species, further aid the fish to swim and navigate. Most fish are oviparous and lay eggs that are fertilized externally. Spawning is an intense time for fish, often involving extraordinary risks. Eggs are either produced in vast quantities and scattered, or they are laid in a spawning nest (called a "redd") under rocks or logs. All these methods are designed to keep the eggs healthy and surrounded by clean, oxygen-rich water. Parental care may be present in the defense of such a nest or territory.

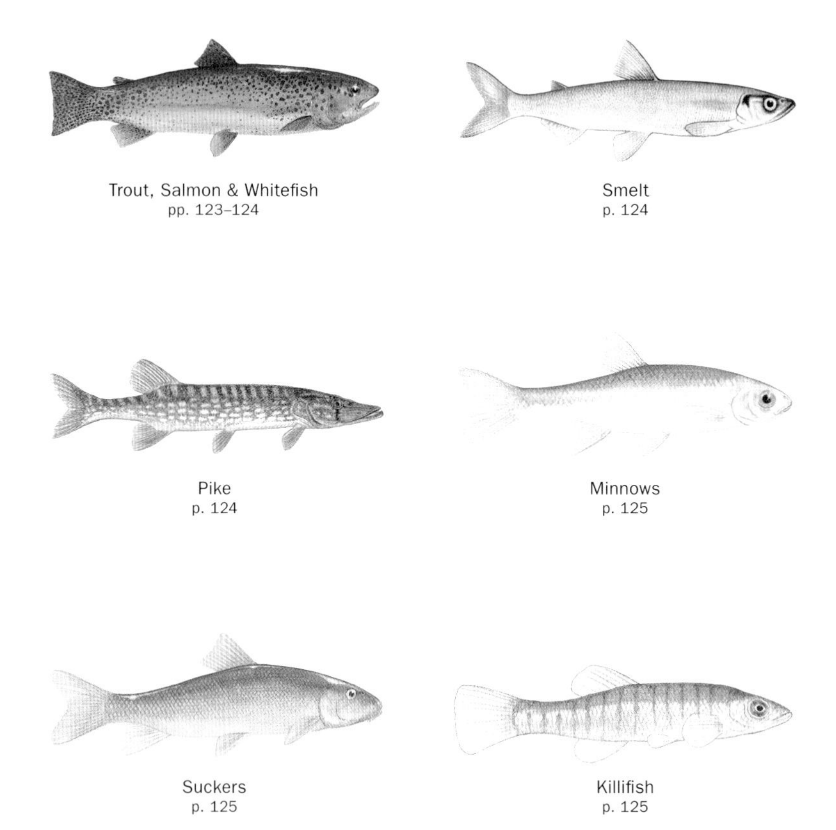

Trout, Salmon & Whitefish
pp. 123–124

Smelt
p. 124

Pike
p. 124

Minnows
p. 125

Suckers
p. 125

Killifish
p. 125

Sculpins
p. 126

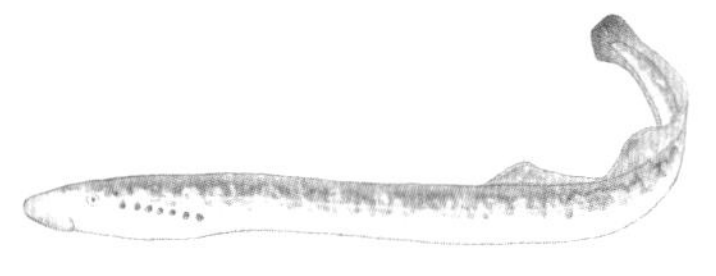

Eels & Lampreys
p. 126

Sturgeons
p. 127

Cod
p. 127

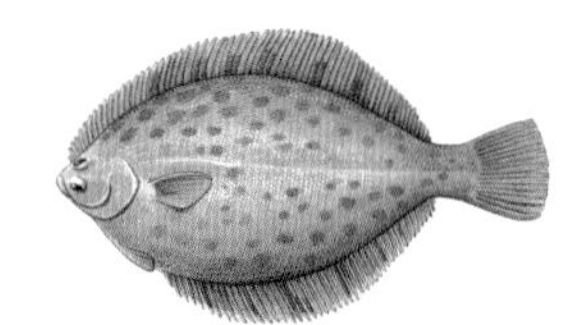

Flounders
p. 128

Mackerels & Tunas
p. 128

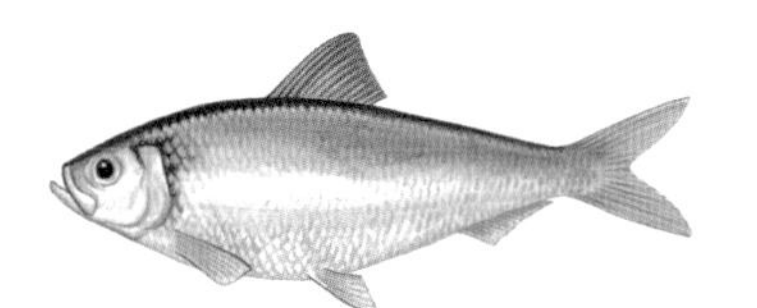

Alewife
p. 129

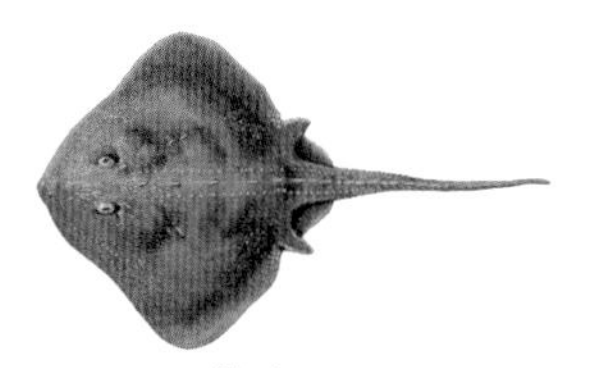

Skates
p. 129

Sharks
p. 129

Rainbow Trout

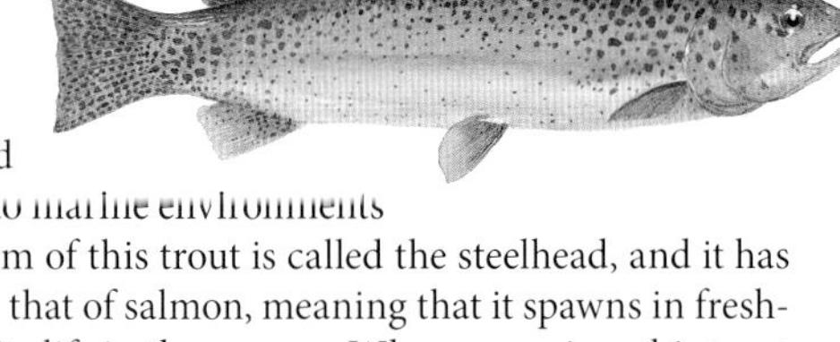

Oncorhynchus mykiss

Length: 7½–18 in

This Pacific native was introduced to lakes for angling and accidently to marine environments through aquaculture. The latter form of this trout is called the steelhead, and it has an anadromous life cycle similar to that of salmon, meaning that it spawns in freshwater but spends the remainder of its life in the ocean. • When spawning, this trout shows the colors of its namesake, with a greenish to bluish back, silvery sides and belly that are often tinged with yellow and green and a reddish lateral line. **Where found:** lakes and coastal rivers; throughout New England. **Also known as:** steelhead.

Atlantic Salmon

Salmo salar

Length: to 5 ft

Instinct draws the salmon back to its freshwater spawning grounds after up to 4 years in the ocean. After surpassing all obstacles, including predators and an arduous upstream swim, the female salmon lays her eggs and the male fertilizes them before they both expire in the shallow waters of their birthplace. Only the fittest survive to return to the ocean. • Some populations are landlocked and are appreciated as Maine's state fish. • **Where found:** open sea close to coasts; deep, cold lakes if landlocked; spawns in clear, oxygen-rich, flowing waters; throughout New England. **Also known as:** summer or fall salmon; parr, smolt, grilse and kelt during specific life stages.

Brook Trout

Salvelinus fontinalis

Length: to 8 in

Colorful and feisty, the brook trout is a is a type of char and is one of the most sought-after game fish. It has a freshwater, or resident, form as well as a sea-run, or anadromous, form. The resident form is smaller and darker than the sea-run. • Unlike salmon, sea-run "brookies" stay near the coast, moving in and out of river estuaries. During spawning runs, they race up their home rivers to the headwaters, lay and fertilize their eggs, and then return to the sea. **Where found:** lakes, coastlines, freshwater streams and river estuaries; throughout New England. **Also known as:** brookie, brook char, speckled trout, coaster trout, sea trout.

Lake Whitefish

Coregonus clupeaformis

Length: 16–20 in

The lake whitefish is what biologists call a "plastic species," which means that the species changes its behavior, food habits and appearance in different habitats. One of the best identifiers for the different forms is the number of gillrakers. Fish that live in more open water develop extended gillrakers that are better for filtering plankton. Lake whitefish caught closer to the surface tend to have higher gillraker counts than those that nibble food from the lake bottom. **Where found:** cool, deep water at the bottom of larger lakes; occasionally in rivers; throughout New England. **Also known as:** humpback whitefish, eastern whitefish.

Rainbow Smelt

Osmerus mordax

Length: to 8 in

The commercial smelt industry originated on the Atlantic coast, but the rainbow smelt was one of the first fish to be experimented with as a gillnet fishery on the Great Lakes, starting in 1948, where it flourished. Sport fishing for smelt is also popular, as is ice fishing on several small lakes where there are landlocked smelt populations. **Where found:** all along the coast in cool, deep, offshore waters; landlocked populations are found in various lakes, particularly in NH and ME. **Also known as:** American smelt.

Chain Pickerel

Esox niger

Length: 24 in (large males may exceed this length)

If you canoe, watch for adult chain pickerel hanging motionless among the reeds or along the edges of a dense aquatic plant bed. This carnivorous fish lies in wait for prey—other fish, ducklings or shorebirds—then attacks with a quick stab of its long snout, clamping down on its victim with heavily toothed jaws. A popular sport fish, it is also competes with the fishermen for other fish. • Northern pike (*E. lucius*) and muskellunge, or "muskies" (*E. masquinongy*), as well hybrids of the two known as tiger muskies, can also be found in New England waters. **Where found:** warm, clear vegetated lakes and slow-flowing rivers and streams in northern New England. **Also known as:** jackfish, pike, water wolf.

Emerald Shiner

Notropis atherinoides

Length: 2–5 in

This baitfish is abundant in larger rivers and lakes and is important to many predators, both aquatic and avian. Its populations fluctuate greatly, influencing the populations of many other fish species in the process. • These minnows spend much of their time in open water feeding on plankton, which they follow up to the surface at dusk. In fall, large schools of these little gems gather near shorelines and docks. **Where found:** open water of lakes, large rivers and shallow lakeshores in spring and fall; throughout New England. **Also known as:** lake shiner, common shiner, buckeye shiner.

White Sucker

Catostomus commersoni

Length: 10–24 in

This generalist species lives in habitats ranging from cold streams to warm, even polluted, waters. It avoids rapid currents and feeds in shallow areas. • During the spring spawning season, mating white suckers splash and jostle in streams or shallow lakeshores. Suckers migrate upstream shortly after the ice breaks up, providing an important food for other fish, eagles and bears. Once hatched, the fry provide critical food for other young fish. **Where found:** varied habitats; prefers shallow lakes and rivers with sandy or gravel substrate; tolerant of turbidity and stagnant water; throughout New England. **Also known as:** common sucker, mud sucker, brook sucker.

Banded Killifish

Fundulus diaphanus

Length: 2–5 in

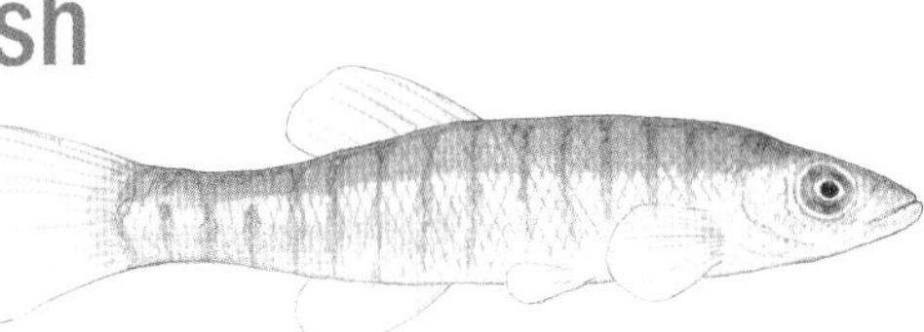

These small, schooling fish provide important food for mudpuppies (*Necturus* spp.), birds and larger fish, including bass and pike. They are named for the vertical stripes or bands that run along their bodies. • Their scientific name is derived from the Latin *fundus*, meaning "bottom," and the Greek *diaphanus*, for "transparent." • Killifish are members of the topminnow family, so named because these species typically forage at or near the water's surface, where they can easily be observed. **Where found:** shallows of warmer lakes and slow-moving rivers; throughout New England.

Mottled Sculpin

Cottus bairdii

Length: 3–6 in

The sculpin is famous for its looks—it is so ugly that it is beautiful. Bulging eyes, fat, wide lips, rough-textured skin with mottled coloration and several dorsal spines add up to one visually impressive fish. • When stressed, this fish expands its gills and emits a low-pitched, humming sound. **Where found:** shallow coastal waters with sandy bottoms; spawns in bays, estuaries and saltwater sloughs; some adults move to deep water in non-spawning seasons; throughout New England.

American Eel

Anguilla rostrata

Length: *Male:* 16–40 in; *Female:* may exceed 36 in

Eels are catadromous fishes—when they reach maturity, they migrate from fresh water to the ocean to spawn. However, some eels stay in coastal or estuarine waters until maturation or migrate periodically between river and estuary. Some remain in fresh water from 5 to 20 years, though up to 80 years has been reported. • The environment influences eel gender—crowding or poor conditions result in more males; in larger rivers, most eels become female. **Where found:** coastal waters, estuaries, rivers and open ocean; throughout New England.

Sea Lamprey

Petromyzon marinus

Length: to 36 in

Lampreys look eel-like, but they are not eels. Lampreys lack jaws and instead have a prominent sucking disc filled with large, hooked teeth. They also have several gill openings and lack pectoral fins, and instead of a backbone or cartilage, they have a primitive pliable notochord. They are parasitic, latching onto host fish to feed on blood and tissue. Strangely, some adults are non-parasitic and will go without food until they spawn and die. • Lamprey larvae live in silt and mud on the ocean floor for up to 5 years. **Where found:** rivers, estuaries, along coasts and in open waters; throughout New England.

Atlantic Sturgeon

Acipenser oxyrinchus oxyrinchus

Length: to 14 ft

Sturgeons are among the oldest fish species in the world, and individuals are themselves long-lived, reaching up to 60 years of age, by which time they can weigh around 800 lbs. They are coveted for their caviar—it is the European sturgeon or giant beluga (*Huso huso*) of the Adriatic, Black and Caspian seas that is most prized for this delicacy, leading to poaching of this now-endangered species. • Distinctive features of the Atlantic sturgeon are the 5 scutes (large, bony shields) and long nose. • The short-nosed sturgeon (*A. brevirostrum*) is also found in the Gulf of Maine. **Where found:** rivers and ocean; Gulf of Maine. **Also known as:** sea sturgeon.

Burbot

Lota lota

Length: 12–40 in

The burbot is the only member of the cod family confined to fresh water. • The single chin barbel and the pectoral fins contain taste buds. As these fish grow, they satisfy their ravenous appetite for whitefish and suckers by eating larger fish instead of increased numbers of smaller ones, sometimes swallowing fish almost as big as themselves. • Once considered by anglers to be a "trash" fish, the burbot is gaining popularity among sport fishers. **Where found:** bottom of cold lakes and rivers; abundant in northern New England. **Also known as:** freshwater cod, eelpout, ling, lawyer, loche.

Atlantic Cod

Gadus morhua

Length: to 6 ft

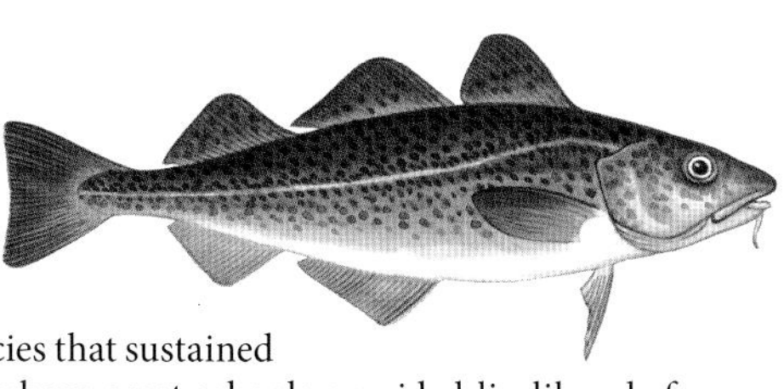

Stories will ever abound about the Atlantic cod, which was a critical species that sustained the Atlantic marine ecosystem and whose great schools provided livelihoods for Atlantic fisher folk. Whether we ever see the return of such numbers is doubtful, and the trickle effects of impacts to wild species that rely on the Atlantic cod for food are yet to be seen. • The maximum mature size of this fish is another thing perhaps lost—once recorded at weights over 200 lbs, today this fish is rarely seen at half that size. • The Atlantic cod is the state fish of Massachusetts. **Where found:** in deep waters on or near the bottom of the continental shelf; from western Greenland south to NC, but most abundant (historically) from Labrador to NY.

Winter Flounder

Pseudopleuronectes americanus

Length: 25 in

Masters of disguise, flounders lie flat and partially buried in sand on the ocean floor and change their pigmentation and patterns to exactly match the sand and pebbles around them. • Young flounders actually look like normal fish, but the left eye slowly moves to the right (in some species it is the right eye that moves to the left), and the fish remains on one side of its body at rest and while swimming for the rest of its adult life. **Where found:** sandy bottoms in shallow coastal waters in winter; from Atlantic Canada south to GA. **Also known as:** blackback flounder, lemon sole.

Atlantic Mackerel

Scomber scombrus

Length: to 22 in

Traveling in large schools, this fish is migratory in habit and is an abundant and important species for commercial fisheries. Often harvested as a baitfish or feed for fish farms, this small fish is more sustainable than larger fish species for feeding fish-hungry nations, and it is higher in omega fatty acids and lower in bio-accumulated toxins. • The chub mackerel (*S. japonicus*) is another of the 23 North American mackerel species and is present from Nova Scotia to Florida. **Where found:** open waters in temperate regions; from Newfoundland to Cape Hatteras.

Atlantic Bluefin Tuna

Thunnus thynnus thynnus

Length: to 10 ft

The Atlantic bluefin tuna is warm blooded, which is rare among fish, and can therefore maintain its body temperature in cold water and during deep dives (to 3500 ft). This allows the bluefin to range into northern Canadian waters during summer and fall. • Since sushi became popular outside Japan, the global demand for this premium fish has led to overharvesting and to concerns for the sustainability of this fishery and, more importantly, for the survival of this species. • The tuna's natural predators include sharks and whales. • The bluefin is a large species and can weigh up to 1000 lb. **Where found:** throughout the Atlantic Ocean.

Alewife

Alosa pseudoharengus

Length: less than 12 in

The alewife and a closely related species, the blueback herring (*A. aestivalis*), are commonly referred to interchangeably as gaspereau in Atlantic Canada and as river herring along the Atlantic coast of the United States. The term "alewife" can represent either species because both have a somewhat similar appearance and biology; fishermen make no distinction between them. Historically, they were used as baitfish, but now they are commercially valuable. • Both species are anadromous, returning from the sea to natal rivers to spawn. **Where found:** rivers and ocean; throughout New England. **Also known as:** river herring (U.S.), gaspereau (Canada).

Thorny Skate

Amblyraja radiata

Length: 3 ft

Skates and rays are species of shark but are more reminiscent of birds as they gently flap their "wings" while swimming in their watery sky. Skates stay close to the ocean floor, searching for crustaceans, fish and shellfish prey, and keep their eyes looking skyward for predators such as larger sharks. • Leathery "mermaid purses," 4 to 6 in long, are skate egg cases, in which 1 to 2 baby skates develop. • Unfortunately, skates are slow-growing fish unable to tolerate overfishing, and skate meat is often sold as giant scallops, merely cookie-cutter stamps of meat from the flat flanks of the skate. **Where found:** over hard and soft bottoms, mainly offshore, at depths of 60–4600 ft; from western Greenland to SC.

Porbeagle Shark

Lamna nasus

Length: 12 ft

The porbeagle shark is potentially dangerous to humans because of its size (500 lb), but conflicts are extremely rare; this big fish prefers to feed on smaller fish such as herring, mackerel, flounder and cod, as well as squid and other sharks. • The porbeagle is an endangered species, but it is still commercially and recreationally hunted in the Atlantic and caught as bycatch by commercial fisheries. • Porbeagle sharks prefer deep, cold water and have the ability to thermoregulate, which is rare in fish, to maintain body temperature. **Where found:** continental shelf and open water but does occur inshore; from Newfoundland to NJ.

INVERTEBRATES

More than 95 percent of all animal species are invertebrates, and there are thousands of invertebrate species in our region. The few mentioned in this guide are frequently encountered and easily recognizable. Invertebrates can be found in a variety of habitats and are an important part of most ecosystems. They provide food for birds, amphibians, shrews, bats and other insects, and they also play an important role in the pollination of plants as well as aiding in the decay process.

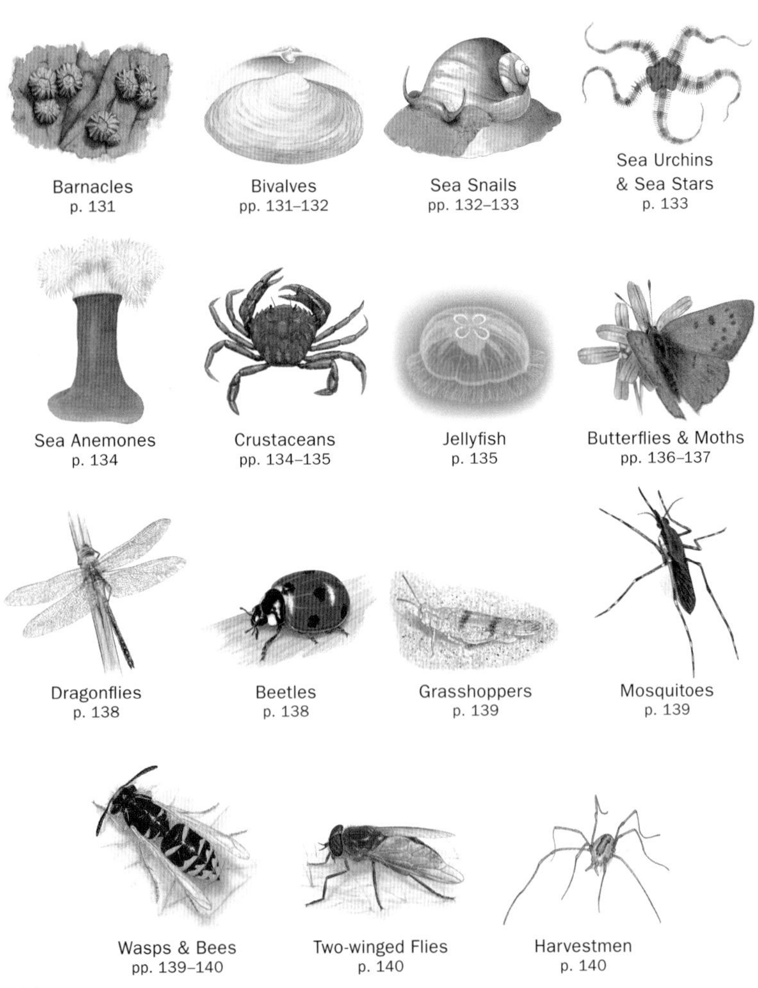

Barnacles
p. 131

Bivalves
pp. 131–132

Sea Snails
pp. 132–133

Sea Urchins & Sea Stars
p. 133

Sea Anemones
p. 134

Crustaceans
pp. 134–135

Jellyfish
p. 135

Butterflies & Moths
pp. 136–137

Dragonflies
p. 138

Beetles
p. 138

Grasshoppers
p. 139

Mosquitoes
p. 139

Wasps & Bees
pp. 139–140

Two-winged Flies
p. 140

Harvestmen
p. 140

Acorn Barnacle

***Balanus* spp.**

Diameter: to 4 in

We typically see this barnacle closed, but when it feeds, though rarely and sometimes not for months at a time, long, feathery plumes reach out from the top of the barnacle's shell to filter bits of organic matter from the water. • This barnacle is intolerant of exposure and must remain almost continuously covered by water or it will become desiccated. • Capable of sexual reproduction, yet immobile, this animal has the largest penis-to-body size ratio of all animals, necessary so that it can reach its mate. **Where found:** rocky shores and exposed coasts; lower intertidal zone with continuous water cover; subtidal zone to depths of 300 ft.

Softshell Clam

Mya arenaria

Length: 2–2¾ in

Frequently the clam of choice at a clambake, this bivalve is also a major food source for many shorebirds, invertebrates and fish. Beyond its role as a meal, it also serves a valuable function in filtering and cleaning water sources, and does so to such an effective degree that it is often used as a water-quality control tool by agencies enforcing pollution standards. • This clam's white to pale gray shell varies in color depending on the minerals in the sand into which it burrows. **Where found:** brackish waters and estuaries; burrows to depths of 12 in; typically in upper to lower intertidal zones but also in deep water to 620 ft. **Where found:** from Labrador to Cape Hatteras. **Also known as:** eastern softshell clam, long-necked clam, sand gaper, nannynose, steamer clam; *M. hemphillii.*

Blue Mussel

Mytilus edulis

Length: 1¼–4 in

Great colonies of blue mussels can be seen covering rocks, wooden pilings or anything solid and stationary to which they can anchor themselves. • In clean waters, these mussels are popular edible shellfish. Blue mussels are common and widespread, found also on the west coast and even in Europe, where they are commercially farmed and are much more commonly eaten than in North America, though their popularity here is increasing. **Where found:** near the low tide line; along the coast from the Arctic to SC. **Also known as:** edible mussel.

American Oyster

Crassostrea virginica

Length: 2–10 in

More than half of the oysters harvested in the U.S. and Canada are American oysters, a common species along the eastern seaboard and particularly important as a commercial fishery and a popular culinary delicacy. • This shellfish has prolific reproductive abilities—a female spawns 10 to 20 million eggs on average, and a large female may spawn up to 100 million. • An oyster changes gender throughout its life cycle, with larger, older individuals remaining female. **Where found:** on hard or soft substrates in low-salinity waters on the ocean floor at depths of 10–40 ft; from the Gulf of St. Lawrence to FL and the Gulf of Mexico. **Also known as:** eastern oyster.

Atlantic Deep-sea Scallop

Placopecten magellanicus

Diameter: to 8 in

Because it inhabits deep waters (to 250 ft, though as shallow as 6½ ft in estuaries and bays)), you are unlikely to see this scallop in the wild, but you will likely find it in fish markets and restaurants. You might also find its almost circular, somewhat two-toned shell (with the upper, rounded valve ranging from yellow to purplish and the lower, flat valve being white) washed up on the beach. **Where found:** sandy or gravelly ocean floors at depths of 12–400 ft; from Labrador to NC. **Also known as:** giant scallop, ocean scallop, smooth scallop.

Northern Moon Snail

Euspira heros

Length: 4½ in

This snail's shell is named after the moon, and a full one at that—the shell is quite spherical, almost as wide (3½ in) as it is long, and pale gray to white in color. There are typically 5 convex whorls. • When the animal is disturbed, it retracts into its shell and closes a sort of trap door, called an operculum. • If you find a little round fort, or collar, of sand, you will have discovered the "egg collar" where this snail has laid its eggs. **Where found:** sandy beaches and ocean bottoms at the low tide line to depths of 1200 ft or greater; from Labrador to NC. **Also known as:** moon shell; *Lunatia heros.*

Common Periwinkle

Littorina littorea

Length: 1 in

Hundreds of these little snails can be seen grazing on algae on the surface of rocks, seaweed or even the shells of other mollusks. • A periwinkle can remain out of the water for long periods of time without becoming desiccated by closing off the entrance to its shell with a tightly fitting trap door called an operculum. • This little snail was introduced from Europe, where it is a hugely popular food item. **Where found:** on rocks, other shellfish or seaweed at low to high tide lines; from Labrador to MD. **Also known as:** rough periwinkle, smooth periwinkle.

Green Sea Urchin

Strongylocentrotus droebachiensis

Diameter: 3¼ in

Be careful when wading in the calm waters of protected bays—you risk stepping on this abundant sea urchin, a very painful experience that may leave broken spines imbedded in your foot. • The sea urchin's round shell, called a test, is about 1½ in tall in the center, with the spines being a maximum of about a third of this height. When the animal dies, the spines fall off, and the empty test can be found on shore; the bumps on the shell are where the spines once attached. **Where found:** rocky shores and kelp beds, from the low tide line to depths of 3800 ft; from the Arctic to NJ.

Daisy Brittle Star

Ophiopholis aculeata

Width: to 4 in

This common sea star is usually reddish in color, but can sometimes have dark markings or variable coloration. • The daisy brittle star feeds mainly on bivalves, wrapping its 5 to 7 long (up to 3 in) arms around them and forcing them out of their shells. Its own predators include other sea stars, mollusks and crustaceans. The brittle star's escape strategy is to detach whichever arm may be in the predator's grasp or even in curious human hands, hence the name "brittle star." **Where found:** hidden within or beneath rocks in tidal pools, burrowed in the sand and mud; also in lower intertidal zones; from Labrador and Newfoundland south to Cape Cod.

Frilled Anemone

Metridium senile

Height: 12 in
Width (crown): 1–2 in

Ornately beautiful when its multitude (from hundreds to thousands, increasing with the size of the animal) of tentacles dance in the currents, this anemone looks like no more than a blob of jelly when the tentacles are retracted. • If this animal finds itself out of water at low tide, it will cover itself with a layer of sand. • In deep, subtidal waters this anemone can grow to 20 in tall and 10 in wide. • The frilled anemone is typically white, but other pale colors, including yellow, pink, orange, red, gray, brown and olive green, occur. **Where found:** adheres to rocks, artificial structures and shells along sandy, muddy or rocky shorelines where there are medium to strong currents, from the low-tide line to depths of 540 ft; all along the Atlantic shoreline.

Horseshoe Crab

Limulus polyphemus

Length: to 24 in
Width: to 12 in

The long, spiny tail of the horseshoe crab looks dangerous, but it is not used for defense—the animal uses it to right itself if it gets flipped upside down in the surf. These living fossils are not true crabs but are more closely related to spiders. • Horseshoe crabs are seen ashore in great numbers during their spring mating season. The female will lay 200 to 300 eggs in a hole in the sand above the low-tide line, where the male fertilizes them. **Where found:** muddy or sandy ocean bottoms; from near low-tide line to depths of 75 ft; from the Gulf of Maine to the Gulf of Mexico.

Green Crab

Carcinus maenas

Width: 3 in

Introduced from Europe, this small scavenger is probably the most common little seashore crab you will encounter. It was accidentally introduced to our shores and to other parts of the world by stowing away on ships. It has flourished in its new habitats and become a pest, forcing local shellfish and other organisms out of house and home. **Where found:** in tidal pools, mud banks and wetlands, from open shores to brackish water; all along the Atlantic coast. **Also known as:** European crab.

Northern Shrimp

Pandalus borealis

Length: to 7 in

Commercial trawling for this deep-water shrimp at depths of 65 to 4400 ft, usually on soft, muddy bottoms, feeds the demand for this crustacean. It is served in restaurants as "prawns" and sold in most large supermarkets. • This shrimp's red color camouflages it in deep water, where red wavelengths of light cannot reach, thus rendering the northern shrimp nearly invisible. **Where found:** deep ocean waters; from the Arctic to Cape Cod. **Also known as:** Maine shrimp, boreal shrimp, red shrimp, pink shrimp, deep-water prawn, deep-sea prawn.

North American Lobster

Homarus americanus

Length: 34 in

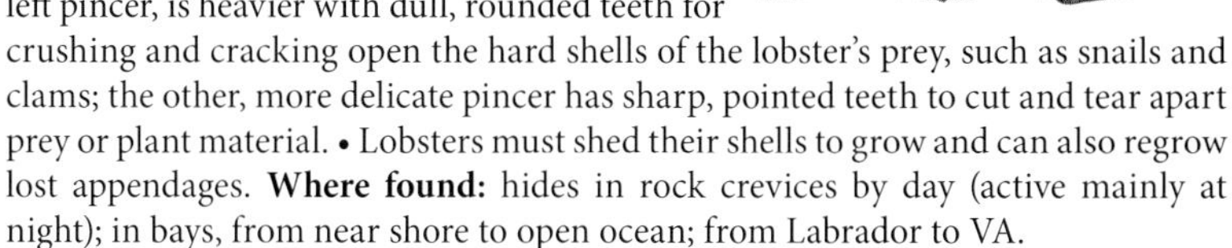

The lobster turns red when cooked, but it is otherwise greenish, or rarely yellow or blue. • The 2 pincers serve different purposes: one, typically the left pincer, is heavier with dull, rounded teeth for crushing and cracking open the hard shells of the lobster's prey, such as snails and clams; the other, more delicate pincer has sharp, pointed teeth to cut and tear apart prey or plant material. • Lobsters must shed their shells to grow and can also regrow lost appendages. **Where found:** hides in rock crevices by day (active mainly at night); in bays, from near shore to open ocean; from Labrador to VA.

Moon Jellyfish

Aurelia aurita

Diameter: 16 in

This ethereal whitish to translucent medusa is a favorite food of the leatherback sea turtle but not liked by swimmers and snorkelers—the animal can deliver a painful sting, and it also releases polyps in the water that are difficult to see but easily felt. The sting may cause a slight rash or itching for several hours. • The moon jellyfish has 8 lobes fringed by numerous short tentacles and 4 long, oral arms with frilly margins. **Where found:** floats near the water's surface just offshore; often washes up on beaches during high tide or after a storm; throughout the Atlantic Ocean. **Also known as:** moon jelly.

Cabbage White

Pieris rapae

Wingspan: 1–2 in

This diminutive butterfly flits about the garden looking pretty, but its caterpillar is the bane of gardeners, who find holes bored in their vegetables by this hungry juvenile. • Butterflies need heat to fuel their wings, which is why they are often seen sunning themselves with their wings spread. The dark bases of this butterfly's wings help absorb solar heat and transfer it to the flight muscles, while the white wing surfaces reflect light inward to heat the butterfly's body. **Where found:** any open habitat, especially gardens and agricultural fields; avoids dense forests; throughout New England.

Eastern Black Swallowtail

Papilio polyxenes

Wingspan: 3–8½ in

This gorgeous black butterfly is, lucky for us, one of the most common to frequent our backyard gardens. • The variably colored caterpillar, which is typically white and green with black bands and yellow spots, has an orange osmeterium (a type of gland) that looks like a forked snake tongue. The organ not only deters predators upon sight, but also omits a foul odour if the caterpillar is threatened. **Where found:** open fields, meadows, backyards and roadsides; throughout New England.

Monarch

Danaus plexippus

Wingspan: 3–4 in

The state butterfly of Vermont, the regal monarch is a well-known and widely distributed butterfly, famous for its incredible migrations. Millions of monarchs overwinter as adults in Mexico, and with the arrival of warmer temperatures, adults migrate northward, laying eggs in patches of milkweed plants. These eggs quickly develop into adults, which continue the migration north to our region. • Toxic compounds in the milkweeds on which this insect feeds make it unpalatable to birds, and the birds remember the coloration of the monarch to avoid it in the future. **Where found:** milkweed patches and flower meadows; throughout New England.

American Copper

Lycaena phlaeas

Wingspan: 1–1½ in

There are dozens of copper species across the United States. All of them, including the species in New England, have a coloration that combines orange and brown, and sometimes purple, giving a coppery luster to this butterfly's wings. • These butterflies attempt to be inconspicuous and stay low to the ground, but they do appear in residential gardens to sip from the flowers. In good years, they can produce 2 generations, the second being more abundant. **Where found:** open or disturbed sites including pastures, landfills, vacant lots, road edges and old fields; throughout New England.

Karner Blue Butterfly

Plebejus melissa samuelis

Wingspan: about ½ in

These beautiful little butterflies live as adults for a mere 1 to 2 weeks but produce 2 generations per summer. The females only lay their eggs on or near lupines, the host plant for the caterpillar, but the butterflies dine on the nectar of several flower species. • The Karner blue is the state butterfly of New Hampshire and is a federally listed endangered species. **Where found:** sandy pine barrens, lakeshore dunes, prairies and open areas with sandy soil and lupines; once ranged from MN to ME but now has only small populations in patchy distribution. **Also known as:** *Lycaeides melissa samuelis.*

Luna Moth

***Actias* spp.**

Wingspan: 3¼–4½ in

The beautiful, green wings of this large moth camouflage it against leaves of trees, particularly birch trees. These moths are hard to find because of this disguise, and also because they are nocturnal and short lived—the adult lifespan is only about 1 week. The adult does not have a mouth and lives solely to reproduce. • This moth is considered an endangered species; populations have plummeted as a result of pollution and pesticide use. **Where found:** deciduous forests; throughout New England.

Green Darner

Anax junius

Length: to 3 in

This gorgeous dragonfly is an agile and effective hunter, and one that we like to see in abundance because it feasts on our most irritating insects, mosquitoes and blackflies. The aquatic larvae also do their share of pest control, feasting on the larvae of mosquitoes and other insects. • The male darner is mostly blue with a green thorax; the female is green with a gray or brown abdomen. • This migratory insect spends the summer in our region. **Where found:** near ponds and lakes; throughout New England.

Firefly

Photuris pennsylvanica

Length: about ½ in

At night, fireflies seem like fairies dancing in the forest. They light up in a beautiful, sparkling courtship dance, using the time-honored strategy of attracting a mate with something shiny and sparkly! • The insects can control the chemical reaction that causes their abdomens to glow a bright yellow-green. The larvae also glow and are known as "glow worms." • Fireflies belong to the beetle family and hatch from eggs as larvae. **Where found:** deciduous forests; throughout New England.

Seven-spot Ladybug

Coccinella septempunctata

Length: ⅜–½ in

There are several ladybug species, all distinguishable from each other by size, number of spots and coloration. Some ladybugs are not even red. They emerge from their pupae and do not change their size or number of spots as they age. • Ladybugs feed ravenously on aphids, which is why this particularly voracious species was introduced from Europe. It has spread throughout North America, outcompeting many of our native ladybugs. • The seven-spot ladybug is the state insect of New Hampshire and Maine. **Where found:** open areas, hilltops and urban gardens in spring and fall; throughout New England.

Seaside Grasshopper

Trimerotropis maritima

Length: 1–1¾ in

The male seaside grasshopper courts a mate by flashing his colorful hindwings (they are otherwise cryptically colored to blend into the sand upon which these insects live) and beats, or crepitates, them to create a buzzing sound, like a finger being run along the teeth of a comb. When the female allows the male closer, he produces softer chirps by rubbing his hind leg on his front wing and making rapid movements with his hind legs. Only the eggs, laid into the sand, survive the winter. **Where found:** sandy areas, beaches, dunes, sandy pine barrens, riverine sand bars and disturbed sandy sites; along the Atlantic coast south from southern ME. **Also known as:** sand grasshopper, citrus-winged grasshopper.

Saltmarsh Mosquito

Aedes sollicitans

Length: ¼ in

At twilight, these vampires emerge from their daytime stupor in search of blood. If you cross their path, which is pretty much any damp ground, you risk waking a sleeping female that will immediately attack, indifferent to the daylight. • These mosquitoes are a vector for several pathogens in domestic animals such as dogs and horses. • The female lays her eggs individually, particularly on grasses in salt marshes, but also in wastewater, dredging and tailings ponds. **Where found:** damp soil and grass, swamps and salt marshes; within 5 mi of the coast along the entire Gulf of Maine. **Also known as:** *Culex sollicitans, Ochlerotatus sollicitans.*

Eastern Yellow Jacket

Vespula maculifrons

Length: ½–¾ in

These predators kill a variety of other insects and sometimes feed on nectar at flowers. They are attracted to sweets such as fruit, juices and sodas. • Big and boldly striped in black and yellow, these ill-tempered hornets nest in ground burrows, often those made by small mammals. • Yellow jackets also build amazing paper nests that are often even more elaborate than those of the true paper wasps (*Polistes* spp.). **Where found:** nearly ubiquitous in open areas; throughout New England. **Also known as:** hornet.

Honey Bee

Apis mellifera

Length: ½ in (queen is almost twice the size of workers)

Honey bees were brought to North America by European settlers and escaped into the wild. • A hive typically consists of about 80,000 bees—a queen, a handful of male drones and many sterile, female worker bees. The queen bee may live up to 8 years and can lay over 1500 eggs per day. • Recent declines in populations of all bee species worldwide have raised concern for these invaluable pollinators. • The honey bee is the state insect of Maine. **Where found:** clearings and meadows wherever there are flowering plants; naturalized throughout New England. **Also known as:** European honey bee.

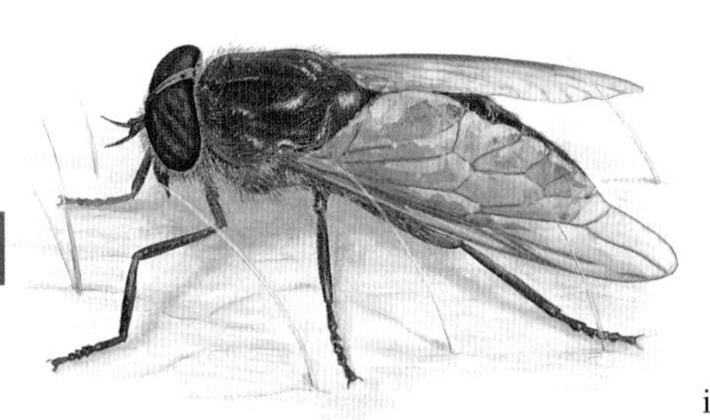

Horsefly

Tabanus americanus

Length: ¾–1⅛ in

Horseflies are known for their nasty bite, which can bleed for several minutes because of anticoagulants in the flies' saliva. They are strongly associated with wet habitats, where they lay eggs in masses attached to plants overhanging fresh water. When the larvae hatch, they fall into the water and overwinter in the muddy bottom. **Where found:** swamps, salt marshes and ponds; from Newfoundland to FL.

Eastern Daddy Longlegs

***Leiobunum* spp.**

Length: ¼–⅜ in (body)

Daddy longlegs have tiny bodies and very long, thin legs up to 40 times longer than the body. These arachnids are not actually spiders, which are in the order Araneae; they are harvestmen and belong to the order Opiliones. Daddy longlegs do not make webs, and they feed on decaying vegetable and animal matter. **Where found:** open areas on foliage, tree trunks and shady walls on buildings; throughout New England. **Also known as:** harvestman.

PLANTS

Plants belong to the Kingdom Plantae. They are autotrophic, which means they produce their own food from inorganic materials through a process called photosynthesis. Plants are the basis of all food webs. They supply oxygen to the atmosphere, modify climate and create and hold soil in place. Plants disperse their seeds and pollen through carriers such as wind, water and animals. Fossil fuels come from ancient deposits of organic matter—largely plants. In this book, plants are separated into 3 categories: trees; shrubs and vines; and herbs, grasses, ferns and seaweeds.

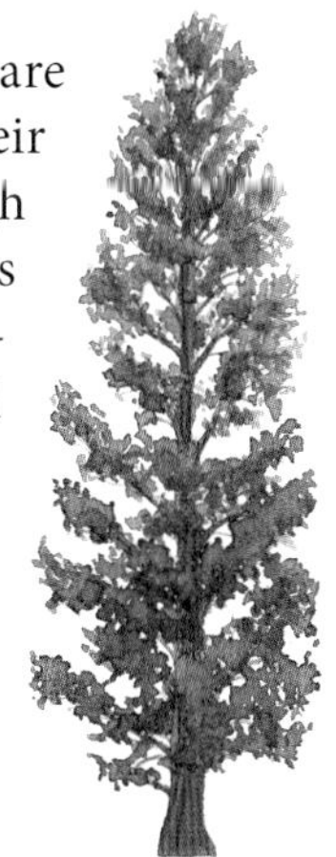

eastern red-cedar

red oak *staghorn sumac* *black raspberry*

false Solomon's-seal *rush* *ostrich fern* *sugar kelp*

TREES

Trees are long-lived, woody plants that are normally taller than 16 feet. There are 2 types of trees: coniferous and broadleaf. Conifers, or cone-bearers, have needles or small, scale-like leaves. Most conifers are evergreens, but some, such as larches (*Larix* spp.), shed their leaves in winter. Most broadleaf trees lose their leaves in fall and are often called deciduous trees (deciduous means "falling off" in Latin). Some exceptions include rhododendrons and several hollies.

A single tree can provide a home or a food source for many different animals. Tree roots bind soil and play host to a multitude of beneficial fungi, and even support certain semi-parasitic plants such as Indian-pipe (*Monotropa uniflora*). Trunks provide a substrate for numerous species of mosses and lichens, which in turn are used by many animals for shelter and nesting material. Tree cavities are used by everything from owls to squirrels to snakes. Leafy canopies support an amazing diversity of life. Myriad birds depend on mature trees, as do scores of insects. Both the seed cones of coniferous trees and the fruits of deciduous trees are consumed by all manner of wildlife.

A group of trees can provide a windbreak, camouflage or shelter, and can hold down soil, thus preventing erosion. Streamside (riparian) woodlands are vital to protecting water quality. Their dense root layers filter out sediments and other contaminants that would otherwise enter watercourses. It is no mystery why the healthiest rivers are those buffered by abundant, undisturbed woodlands. There are many types of forest communities, and their species composition is largely dictated by the type of soil on which they occur. To a large extent, the types of trees within a forest determine what other species of plants and animals are present. Old-growth forest is critical habitat for many species that use the fallen or hollowed-out trees as nesting or denning sites. Many species of invertebrates live within or under the bark, providing food for birds. Fallen, decomposing logs provide habitat for snakes, salamanders, mosses, fungi and invertebrates. The logs eventually completely degrade into nutrient-rich soil to perpetuate the continued growth of plant life and keep organic matter in the ecosystem. Large forests retain carbon dioxide, an important preventive factor of global warming. One giant old-growth tree can extract 15 pounds of airborne pollutants annually and put back 30 pounds of oxygen. Responsibly managed forests can also sustain an industry that provides wood products and jobs.

Tree heights provided in the following accounts reflect the usual size and shape of each species, but trees can reach greater heights in ideal conditions. Conifers have both pollen cones (male) and seed cones (female), but only mature seed cones are described. They are useful in identifying conifers because they are found year-round on the tree or on the ground nearby. Leaf, cone and fruit measurements and descriptions are given for mature plants only.

Red Spruce

Picea rubens

Height: 50–80 ft
Needles: ½–1 in long, shiny, yellow-green, curved, 4-sided
Seed cones: 1–1½ in long, oval, brown or reddish brown when mature, hanging at branch tips

The needles of red spruce give a bottlebrush look to the stems of this tree. • The cones hang near the top of the tree and drop in fall, so are not present in winter. • The needles are yellowish green, but the dark brown bark has a reddish hue, giving this spruce its common name. • Spruce species are valuable for pulp wood; red spruce is also popular for lumber. **Where found:** prefers open, well-drained sites; growth is stunted in wet habitats; from New England south in the mountains to western NC, at elevations of 4500–6500 ft.

Eastern Hemlock

Tsuga canadensis

Height: 65–100 ft, occasionally to 150 ft
Needles: ¼–½ in long, flat, flexible, blunt, unequal, in 2 opposite rows
Seed cones: ½–¾ in long, brown and dry, hanging at ends of twigs

These trees can live for 600 years, with some living for a millennium; there were once pure stands of eastern hemlocks, with trunks reaching 3 ft in diameter. Some of these ancient trees can still be found in old-growth Acadian forests. • The brittle wood separates along annual rings, making it easy to split, but it often "pops" and sparks when burned. The wood also has hard knots and frequently twists, but it remains a popular lumber for outdoor products such as lawn furniture because it is rot resistant. • Eastern hemlock provides an abundant food supply and dense cover for many animals, including white-tailed deer, snowshoe hares, seed-eating birds and ruffed grouse. **Where found:** cool, sandy, moist sites, ravines and riparian areas; from New England south through the mountains to northern AL, at elevations to 3000 ft.

Eastern White Pine

Pinus strobus

Height: 65–100 ft, formerly to 150 ft or more
Needles: 2–6 in long, slender, flexible, soft, 3-sided, in bundles of 5
Seed cones: 4–8 in long, brown, woody, cylindrical

The airy, graceful eastern white pine is the largest North American conifer and once occurred in vast virgin stands that were estimated to contain 900 billion board-feet of lumber. When European settlers arrived, the trees were rapidly cut down to make everything from ship masts to matchsticks. • The cone and tassel of the eastern white pine together are the state tree and flower of Maine. • This valuable tree provides food and shelter for many species of wildlife, including chickadees, red squirrels and porcupines. • The scientific name *strobus* means "gum-yielding" or "pitchy tree" in Latin and "cone" in Greek. **Where found:** from dry sand, rocky ridges and gravelly soils to sphagnum bogs and humid sites with well-drained soil; from New England south to northern GA, at elevations from near sea level to 2000 ft.

Red Pine

Pinus resinosa

Height: 70–80 ft, rarely over 98 ft
Needles: 4¼–6½ in long, shiny, dark green, brittle, sharp-pointed, in bundles of 2
Seed cones: 1½–2¼ in long, oval, light brown, woody, hanging at upper branch tips

Red pines live about 200 years. Slow growing at first, once this tree is established, it can shoot up nearly 1 ft per year. • This species is valued for its timber, which is easily preserved because of the high creosote content in the porous wood. It has been popular for building ship masts, poles and cribbing, as well as for other outdoor uses. The yellowish to reddish color of the wood is not desirable for furniture. • The bark and seeds provide winter forage for birds and mammals. **Where found:** dry sand and gravelly, well-drained soils; from New England south to PA, at elevations of 700–1400 ft. **Also known as:** Norway pine.

Northern White-cedar

Thuja occidentalis

Height: 40–70 ft
Needles: 1/8 in long, dull green, scale-like, overlapping, gland-dotted
Seed cones: 1/4–1/2 in long, upright, green becoming reddish brown with age

Fragrant cedar lumber is known for resisting decay, but living trees are frequently hollow from heart rot. Near water, the wood is often used in cedar-strip canoes, shingles and dock posts. • Deer often browse the lower branches of this tree, and pine siskins are fond of the seeds. • Northern white-cedars can live for over 1000 years. It is commonly named arborvitae, which means "tree of life." • Native Americans and early settlers used parts of this tree to prevent scurvy. **Where found:** humid habitats; swamps and high snowfall areas, often in pure stands; from ME south to NY, at elevations to 3000 ft. **Also known as:** arborvitae, white cedar.

Eastern Red-cedar

Juniperus virginiana

Height: 40–60 ft
Needles: 1/16–3/8 in long, dark bluish green, flat-lying, scale-like, in overlapping pairs
Seed cones: 1/4–3/8 in long, round, dark blue, berry-like

One of the most widely distributed and commonly utilized trees since pioneering days, the eastern red-cedar is native to 37 states. • The aromatic wood was prized for furniture, particularly for cedar chests. The oil from the wood and leaves has practical, medicinal and aromatic benefits. • This tree is resistant to drought, heat and cold, and the berries are relished by wildlife, particularly cedar waxwings, which are named for this tree. **Where found:** dry uplands to floodplains, swamps, abandoned fields and fencerows; from ME south. **Also known as:** red juniper.

Tulip Tree

Liriodendron tulipifera

Height: 80–120 ft
Leaves: 3–6 in long, alternate, bright green above, paler beneath, squared and notched at the tip, 2–3-lobed sides, almost square base
Flowers: 1½–2 in across, showy, cup-shaped, 6 petals, greenish yellow with orange base, single at branch tips
Fruit: dry, green to yellowish, long-winged nutlets, 1–1½ in long, overlapping in cone-like clusters, 2½–3 in long

This tall eastern hardwood is gorgeous in spring when it is covered in tulip-like flowers. It was so admired that it was introduced to Europe and the Pacific coast. Early colonialists documented some of the massive trees that once existed but were cut down for their wood. The trunks were so large that a single log could be hollowed out into a canoe. Today we see diameters of only 2 to 3 ft on this tree. **Where found:** moist, well-drained soils in valleys and on slopes; from VT to RI south, at elevations to 1000 ft. **Also known as:** yellow poplar.

Sassafras

Sassafras albidum

Height: 30–60 ft
Leaves: 4–10 in long, 2–4 in wide, alternate, elliptical or broadly 2–3-lobed, bright green, fragrant
Flowers: 3/8 in across, yellow-green, inconspicuous, 6 tepals, in loose clusters
Fruit: 3/8–5/8 in across, bluish-black, berry-like drupes, each in a red cup

Popularly known as a flavoring for root beer, this aromatic tree's roots and bark have been made into teas and used in scent for soap. Early explorers assumed that the spicy taste of the twigs and leafstalks meant they had medicinal properties and shipped quantities to Europe, but no cures for any maladies have ever been derived. • The leaves turn yellow, orange or red in fall. New England marks the extreme northern limit for this tree, which is also the northernmost representative of its tropical family. **Where found:** moist, sandy soils in uplands, valleys, old fields, clearings and forest openings; from southwestern ME throughout New England and south, at elevations to 5000 ft.

Sycamore

Platanus occidentalis

Height: 60–100 ft
Leaves: 4–8 in across, alternate, bright green above, paler beneath, 3–5 shallow lobes (maple-leaf-like), coarsely toothed
Flowers: tiny, yellowish green, in dense, drooping clusters
Fruit: brownish, hairy, club-like nutlets, about ½ in long, clustered into "balls," ¾–1¼ in across

Many people have enjoyed the pleasure of sitting under the shade of a sycamore tree. This tree has a larger trunk diameter than any other native hardwood, up to 11 ft and historically to 15 ft, and can live for 250 years. The large, sometimes crooked branches spread widely, creating a canopy under which one can rest and escape the summer heat. **Where found:** wet soils, streambanks, floodplains, lake edges, swamps and mixed forests; from southwestern ME throughout New England and south, at elevations to 3200 ft.

American Elm

Ulmus americana

Height: to 100 ft
Leaves: 3–6 in long, alternate, oval, rounded and asymmetrical at the base, pointed at the tip, prominently veined
Flowers: ⅛ in across, greenish, in tassel-like clusters
Fruit: 1-seeded samaras, ⅜–½ in long

Large, graceful elm trees once lined our city streets and parks, but hundreds of thousands have been lost to Dutch elm disease since its arrival in the United States in 1930. This species is abundant in the wild, but seldom gets very large before being attacked and killed by the fungal infection. Occasional giants still occur as isolated specimens in the midst of agricultural fields, where the disease cannot readily reach them. • The American elm is important as a host for many species of moths and butterflies. It is the state tree of Massachusetts. **Where found:** valleys, floodplains, stream terraces, sheltered slopes and moist soils; also mixed hardwood forests; from New England south to central FL, at elevations to 2500 ft.

Butternut

Juglans cinerea

Height: 40–70 ft
Leaves: 1–2 ft long, alternate, aromatic, pinnately divided into 11–17 leaflets, each 2–4¼ in long
Flowers: tiny, greenish; male flowers in hanging catkins, 2½–5½ in long; female flowers in erect catkins, 1½–2¾ in long
Fruit: lemon-shaped, green nuts, 1½–2½ in long, in drooping clusters

Within each sticky, hairy fruit of the butternut tree is an oily seed—the butternut. They are edible and must be collected as soon as they are ripe or they pass their best-before date seemingly overnight and turn rancid. Traditional uses for the oil derived from the nuts were diverse. • The husks stain fingers brown but make a yellow or orange dye. **Where found:** moist soils, valleys, slopes, some dry, rocky sites and hardwood forests; from southern ME throughout New England and south, at elevations to 4800 ft.

Shagbark Hickory

Carya ovata

Height: 70–100 ft
Leaves: 6–12 in long, alternate, aromatic, divided into 5 leaflets, each 3–7 in long, finely toothed
Flowers: tiny, greenish; male flowers in hanging catkins, 4–6 in long; female flowers in small, erect clusters at twig tips
Fruit: round, aromatic, greenish to dark reddish brown nuts, 1¼–2½ in across

The edible, tasty nuts of this tree and other subspecies throughout North America led to improved cultivated varieties for commercial hickory nuts. • The name "hickory" comes from the original Native American word *pawcohiccora*, which was not the name for the tree, but for the meal or nut milk that was derived from pounding and boiling the kernels. **Where found:** moist soils, valleys, upland slopes and mixed hardwood forests; from southwestern ME throughout New England and south, at elevations to 3000 ft. **Also known as:** scalybark hickory, shellbark hickory.

American Beech

Fagus grandifolia

Height: 60–80 ft
Leaves: 2½–5 in long, alternate, narrowly oval, parallel veins each end in a coarse tooth
Flowers: male flowers ¾–1 in long, in dense, hanging clusters; female flowers ¼ in long, in small, erect clusters
Fruit: prickly burs ½–¾ in long, greenish to reddish brown, enclosing pairs of 3-angled, shiny, brown nuts

The edible nuts of mature beech trees are said to taste best after the first frost but should be eaten in moderation to avoid an upset stomach. Ground, roasted beechnuts were traditionally used as a coffee substitute. The oil was extracted and used as food and lamp oil. Beechnuts have a high fat content and are an important food for animals, including squirrels and black bears. • A tiny, parasitic wildflower called beechdrops (*Epifagus virginianus*) grows on the roots of beeches and is found on or near the host tree. **Where found:** moist, well-drained slopes and bottomlands; from New England south to northern FL, at elevations to 3000 ft.

White Oak

Quercus alba

Height: 80–100 ft
Leaves: 4–9 in long, 2–4 in wide, alternate, with 5–9 deep, rounded lobes
Flowers: tiny; male flowers numerous, in hanging catkins; female flowers reddish, in a small spike
Fruit: acorns, ⅜–1¼ in long, single or paired, lower ¼ of nut seated in a shallow cup with overlapping, knobby scales

This oak species is a classic eastern tree, with its wide spreading branches, mighty trunk (3–4 ft in diameter) and distinctive acorns, which are a staple in the diets of many species of wildlife. • Oak barrels are prized by wine and whiskey producers—the wood makes tight seams, does not warp and adds desirable flavor and aroma to the liquid within as it ages. The qualities of this wood also made it popular with shipbuilders. • White oak is the state tree of Connecticut. **Where found:** moist, well-drained soils in uplands or lowlands; from southern ME throughout New England and south, at elevations to 5500 ft. **Also known as:** stave oak.

Red Oak

Quercus rubra

Height: 60–90 ft
Leaves: 4–9 in long, alternate, dull yellowish green, with 7–11 deep, nearly triangular lobes
Flowers: tiny; male flowers in hanging catkins 4–5 in long; female flowers in small clusters
Fruit: acorns, ⅝–1⅛ in long, lower ¼ of nut seated in a saucer-shaped cup

This common eastern tree is a member of the red or black oak group, which includes black oak (*Q. velutina*) and pin oak (*Q. palustris*). These species all have deep, pointed leaf lobes, bitter acorns that ripen in 2 years and non-scaly bark. • Although the acorns contain tannins that are toxic to humans, they are an important food for squirrels, raccoons, black bears, white-tailed deer and birds. • The copious flowers of mature oaks attract masses of insects, which are consumed by birds traveling from the tropics to boreal nesting grounds. **Where found:** rich, moist, loamy, sandy or clay soils, often in pure stands, on the lower and middle slopes of forests; from New England south to GA, at elevations to 5500 ft.

Yellow Birch

Betula alleghaniensis

Height: 70–100 ft
Leaves: 3–5 in long, alternate, yellowish green, toothed, bright yellow in fall
Flowers: tiny; male flowers in catkins 2–4 in long; female flowers in erect, cone-like catkins ½–¾ in long
Fruit: small, flat, 2-winged nutlets, in hanging catkins ¾–1¼ in long

North American birches are divided into two groups: yellow birches, which include the yellow birch and cherry birch (*B. lenta*), and white birches, which include the white birch and gray birch (*B. populifolia*). Members of the yellow birch group have leaves with 8 to 12 straight veins per side, slender, cone-like catkins and inner bark that smells and tastes like wintergreen; white birches have leaves with fewer veins and inner bark without a distinct fragrance. • Yellow birch sap can be boiled into syrup or fermented into beer; the leaves and twigs be used to make a fragrant tea. **Where found:** rich, moist, often shady sites; from New England south to extreme northeastern GA, at elevations to 2400 ft.

White Birch

Betula papyrifera

Height: 50–70 ft

Leaves: 2–4 in long, alternate, dull green, toothed, slender-pointed, 5–9 straight veins per side

Flowers: tiny; male flowers in hanging catkins 2–4 in long, in clusters of 1–3; female flowers in erect catkins ¾–1½ in long

Fruit: small, flat, broadly 2-winged nutlets, in narrow, brown, hanging catkins 1½–2 in long

The smooth, pale bark of this birch peels off in papery sheets and was used by Native Americans to make birchbark canoes, baskets and writing paper. Never peel the bark off a living tree because the tree can be scarred or killed. • Betulic acid, the compound that makes birch bark white, is being studied for use in sunscreens and in the treatment of skin cancer. • White birch is the state tree of New Hampshire. **Where found:** dry to moist, open or disturbed sites (prefers full sun and nutrient-rich soils) and forest edges; from New England south to NY, at elevations to 4000 ft. **Also known as:** paper birch, canoe birch.

American Basswood

Tilia americana

Height: 60–100 ft

Leaves: 3–7 in long, alternate, heart-shaped, sharply toothed, asymmetrical at base

Flowers: ½–⅝ in across, 5 creamy yellowish petals, fragrant, in loose, hanging clusters

Fruit: brown, woolly, round, nut-like capsules ⅜ in across, in long-stalked clusters

American basswood, with its fragrant flowers, large leaves and rounded crowns, is often planted in urban parks and gardens. It is the northernmost basswood species. • Linden flower tea, sold in health-food stores, provides a remedy for coughs, colds and bronchitis. • Bees, attracted in droves to the hanging clusters of flowers, produce strongly flavored honey. **Where found:** cool, moist, rich woodlands, often near water and mixed with other hardwoods; from ME south to western NC, at elevations to 3200 ft. **Also known as:** American linden, bee-tree.

Balsam Poplar

Populus balsamifera

Height: 60–80 ft (twice that height possible)
Leaves: 3–5 in long, alternate, dark green above, silvery below, oval, blunt-toothed, tapered to a point
Flowers: tiny, male and female flowers on separate trees; male catkins ¾–1¼ in long; female catkins 2–3½ in long
Fruit: oval capsules, ¼–5⁄16 in across, numerous in hanging catkins 4–5 in long; capsules release fluffy masses of tiny, brown seeds tipped with soft, white hairs

This tree is both the largest poplar species and the largest hardwood in general in North America. • In spring, many Native American groups ate the young catkins and sweet inner bark. Medicinally, the leaves, bark and resinous aromatic buds were important for treating many conditions and ailments—the resins are still used today in salves, cough medicines and painkillers. • The wood is ideal for campfires because it does not crackle and makes clean smoke. **Where found:** moist to wet, low-lying sites, often on shorelines; also foothills to subalpine zones; from New England south to PA, from sea level to mid elevations. **Also known as:** black cottonwood, balm-of-Gilead; *P. trichocarpa.*

Quaking Aspen

Populus tremuloides

Height: 40–70 ft, sometimes taller
Leaves: 1¼–3 in long, alternate, oval with a short point, finely blunt-toothed
Flowers: tiny, in slender, hanging catkins 1–2½ in long, male and female catkins on separate trees
Fruit: light green, cone-shaped capsules, ¼ in long, in hanging catkins; capsules release many tiny, cotton-tipped seeds

The common names "quaking" and "trembling" refer to the way the leaves flutter in the slightest breeze because of the narrow leaf stalks; this trait is a good way to differentiate this tree from the similar balsam poplar. • Aspen trunks were once used for tipi poles and canoe paddles; today, aspen wood is harvested primarily for pulp and for making chopsticks. • Suckers from the shallow, spreading roots of this deciduous tree can colonize many hectares of land. Single trunks are short-lived, but a colony of clones can survive for thousands of years. **Where found:** dry to moist sites; from New England south to VA, from near sea level in the north to elevations of 6500–10,000 ft in the south. **Also known as:** trembling aspen, aspen poplar.

Black Willow

Salix nigra

Height: 60–100 ft
Leaves: 3–6 in long, alternate, uniformly green above and below, narrow, tapering to a pointed tip, finely toothed
Flowers: tiny, male and female flowers in catkins on separate trees
Fruit: light brown, hairless capsules, 3⁄16 in long, in loose, hanging catkins, 1–3 in long

Black willows grow in riparian areas and are valuable in binding soil banks and preventing erosion and flooding. • This large willow can reach 140 ft in height in other parts of its range and attains commercial timber size quickly. The wood has been used for furniture, doors, cabinetwork and pulp. In earlier days, it was a source of charcoal for gunpowder. • The small flowers are popular with honey bees. **Where found:** wet soils, streambanks, lakes and floodplains; from ME south. **Also known as:** swamp willow.

Sugar Maple

Acer saccharum

Height: 70–100 ft
Leaves: 3½–5½ in long and wide, opposite, 5 palmate lobes, irregularly coarse-toothed
Flowers: 3⁄16 in across, yellowish green, on slender, hairy stalks in tassel-like clusters
Fruit: winged samaras, 1–1¼ in long, hanging in pairs

Sugar maples are famous worldwide for their sap, the main source of pure maple syrup and tasty maple sugar. Each spring, festivals celebrate the traditions of boiling sap and making maple syrup. About 40 qt of sap yields 1 qt of maple syrup. Sugar maple, which is sometimes referred to as a "hard maple," is also prized for its wood. It is used in high-quality furniture, and the famous Longaberger baskets that are manufactured in Ohio. • Maples have winged seeds that "helicopter" downward. The foliage turns an exceptionally showy orange-red in fall. • Sugar maple is the state tree of Vermont. **Where found:** deep, rich, moist soils, often with American beech; from ME south to NC, at elevations to 2500 ft.

Red Maple

Acer rubrum

Height: 60–90 ft
Leaves: 2½–4 in long and wide, opposite, palmately 3–5 lobed, irregularly double-toothed
Flowers: ⅛ in across, reddish, in tassel-like clusters
Fruit: reddish or yellow, winged samaras, ½–1 in long, hanging in pairs

The red twigs, buds, flowers and fall leaves of Rhode Island's state tree add color to North America's eastern forests. The bright red flower clusters appear in early spring. • Red maple leaves have palmate lobes separated by shallow notches. The samara wings spread at a 50° to 60° angle. • The even, straight-grained wood is used in cabinets, furniture and flooring, and the bark can be boiled into a red ink or dark brown dye. The sap yields syrup that is semisweet. **Where found:** cool, moist sites near swamps, streams and springs; sometimes in drier upland sites; from ME south to FL, at elevations to 6000 ft.

White Ash

Fraxinus americana

Height: to 80 ft
Leaves: 8–12 in long, opposite, dark green, paler beneath, smooth margins, compound, pinnately divided into 5–9 (usually 7) sharp-pointed leaflets, 2½–5 in long
Flowers: ¼ in across, purplish to yellow, in compact clusters along twigs
Fruit: slender, winged samaras, 1–2 in long, hanging in clusters

This tree is North America's main source of commercial ash. The strong, flexible wood is used in sporting goods (especially baseball bats), tool handles, boats and church pews. Historically, plough, airplane and automobile frames were made from ash. • Native Americans made a yellow dye from the bark. • Ash leaves can be crushed and applied to skin to soothe mosquito and bee stings. **Where found:** among other hardwoods on upland sites with rocky to deep, well-drained soils; from ME to northern FL, to elevations of 2000 ft in the south.

SHRUBS & VINES

The difference between a tree and a shrub is sometimes rather sketchy, but in general, shrubs are small, woody plants less than 20 feet tall , though many may grow to over 30 ft if conditions permit. They are typically bushy, with multiple small trunks and branches that emerge from near the ground, and many species produce soft berries. Some shrubs occur in open, sunny areas, whereas others are important dominant components of the forest understory. Shrubs provide habitat and shelter for a variety of animals, and their berries, leaves and often bark are crucial sources of food. The tasty berries of some shrubs have long been a staple of Native and traditional foods, and they are still enjoyed by people throughout our region.

Birches
p. 158

Vines are climbing or trailing woody-stemmed plants. The growth form of a vine is based on long stems, which enables the plant to quickly colonize large areas or to take advantage of small patches of fertile soil—the vine can root in the soil, but grow so that its leaves have access to areas with more light. Vines use different climbing methods—some twine their stems around a support, whereas others use tendrils. Most vines are flowering plants and can be woody or herbaceous.

Witch-hazel
p. 158

Spicebush
p. 159

Baccharis
p. 159

Heaths
pp. 159–160

Roses
pp. 161–163

Dogwoods
pp. 163–164

Winterberry
p. 164

Sumac & Poison Ivy
pp. 164–165

Buttonbush
p. 165

Honeysuckles
pp. 165–166

Bayberry
p. 166

Hog-peanut
p. 166

American Hornbeam

Carpinus caroliniana

Height: 10–35 ft
Leaves: 2–4½ in long, alternate, arranged in 2 rows, oval, tapering to a sharp point, hairless, double toothed
Flowers: tiny, greenish; male flowers in dense, cylindrical, hanging catkins 1–1½ in long; female flowers hairy, in loose catkins ⅜–¾ in long
Fruit: ribbed nutlets ¼–⅜ in long, in the axils of green, leaf-like bracts

This short-lived shrub has exceptionally dense, strong wood. Despite its toughness, however, the wood rots quickly when left in contact with soil. • American hornbeam is a member of the birch family. **Where found:** moist, rich soils, streambanks, ravines and the understory of hardwood forests; from central ME south. **Also known as:** musclewood, blue-beech, ironwood.

Eastern Hop-hornbeam

Ostrya virginiana

Height: 20–50 ft
Leaves: 2–5 in long, alternate, pointed, sharply double toothed
Flowers: tiny; male flowers greenish, in cylindrical, hanging catkins ½–2 in long; female flowers reddish green, in small, loose catkins ½–¾ in long
Fruit: hop-like, in hanging clusters of flat, yellowish, papery sacs ¼–¾ in long

Often planted as an ornamental, eastern hop-hornbeam is slow growing. • The dense, resilient wood is used to make tool handles, fence posts and other durable wood items. It is so hard that it is difficult to split with an ax. • The fruits resemble hops, an ingredient in beer, hence this tree's common name. **Where found:** moist understory in hardwood forests; throughout New England. **Also known as:** ironwood.

Witch-hazel

Hamamelis virginiana

Height: 30 ft
Leaves: 2½–6 in long, alternate, oval, scalloped
Flowers: small, fragrant, bright yellow, 4 ribbon-like petals, clustered in 3s along twigs
Fruit: woody, light brown capsules, ⅜ in across

Well known for its astringent properties and ability to stop bleeding, witch-hazel preparations are widely available commercially for topical use. The leaves and bark of this shrub are used in medicinal extracts, skin cosmetics, shaving lotions, mouthwashes, eye lotion, ointments and soaps. **Where found:** moist, shaded areas and transitional forests; throughout New England south to central FL. **Also known as:** winterbloom.

Spicebush

Lindera benzoin

Height: 6–17 ft
Leaves: 2–5½ in long, alternate, ovate to elliptical, thin, smooth-edged
Flowers: ¼–⅜ in across, honey yellow, fragrant, 6 tepals, in dense clusters, ¾ in wide
Fruit: red, shiny, football-shaped drupes, ¼–½ in long

All parts of spicebush, especially the bark and berries, have an agreeable spicy fragrance and flavor. The leaves and twigs are commonly used for tea. • Bark extracts have been shown to inhibit *Candida albicans*, the yeast-like fungus that causes thrush and yeast infections. • In early spring, spicebushe's tiny, pale yellow flowers bloom before the first green leaves bud. **Where found:** swamps and wet woods; from ME south. **Also known as:** forsythia of the wilds, wild-allspice, spicewood.

Eastern Baccharis

Baccharis halimifolia

Height: 6–12 ft
Leaves: 1–2½ in long, alternate, oval, gray-green, thick, coarsely toothed
Flowers: tiny, white to green, crowded in bell-shaped heads less than ¼ in long
Fruit: silvery white, plume-like achenes, ½ in long, in clusters

Eastern baccharis is the only tall shrub in the aster family. • This attractive ornamental is tolerant of saltwater spray, making it one of the few eastern shrubs suitable for planting near the ocean. **Where found:** moist soils, salt marshes, streambanks, roadsides, open woods and waste places; from southernmost ME south. **Also known as:** aster tree, white cloud tree, snow bush, groundsel-bush, pencil-tree.

Rosebay Rhododendron

Rhododendron maximum

Height: to 20 ft
Leaves: 4–10 in long, evergreen, alternate, leathery, oblong, dark green
Flowers: 1–1½ in wide, white or pale pink with yellow-green spotting, bell-shaped, 5 petals, in large clusters 5–8 in across
Fruit: elongated, dark reddish brown capsules, ½ in long

This species is one of the largest evergreen rhododendrons that is hardy in our climate. • The wood has been used in tool making, and this shrub's dense growth habit provides winter shelter for wildlife. However, if bees access these flowers, the resultant honey is poisonous. **Where found:** moist soils, streambanks and the understory of forests; from ME south.

Pinxter Flower

Rhododendron periclymenoides

Height: 2–7 ft
Leaves: 2–4 in long, alternate, appearing whorled at branch tips, oval to elliptical, leathery
Flowers: 1½–2 in wide, pink or white, 5 petals, tubular, protruding stamens, in clusters of 5–16
Fruit: slender, erect, hairy capsules

The dark leaves of this shrub cluster near the ends of the twigs, creating a leathery backdrop to the clusters of delicately fragrant flowers. Often the flowers bloom before the leaves appear. • "Pinxter" is the Dutch word for "Pentecost," the 50th day after Easter, referring to the blossoming time for this shrub. **Where found:** upland woods, thickets, swamps and bogs; from MA south. **Also known as:** pink azalea; *Azalea nudiflora, R. nudiflorum.*

Mountain Laurel

Kalmia latifolia

Height: 20 ft
Leaves: 2½–4 in long, alternate, evergreen, elliptical, glossy
Flowers: ¾–1 in wide, saucer-shaped, white to rose pink with purple markings, 5 fused petals, in showy clusters
Fruit: round, dark brown capsules, ¼ in across

The large flower clusters make the state flower of Connecticut one of our most beautiful native shrubs. • Mountain laurel contains poisonous andromedotoxin compounds that have been known to kill livestock. Even honey made from the nectar is said to be poisonous. **Where found:** dry to moist, acidic soils in the understory of mixed forests, upland slopes, valleys and shrub thickets; from southeastern ME south. **Also known as:** spoonwood, ivybush, sheep laurel, lambkill.

Highbush Blueberry

Vaccinium corymbosum

Height: 5–15 ft
Leaves: 2–4 in long, alternate, elliptical, turn red in fall
Flowers: ¼ in across, greenish white to pinkish, urn-shaped, waxy, in clusters
Fruit: dull blue to black berries, ⅜ in across

Plentiful blueberries were an important fruit for Native American peoples, and blueberry picking remains a favorite tradition today. • There are many *Vaccinium* species native to New England, with many more that have been introduced and cultivated, including huckleberries and cranberries. **Where found:** variety of habitats; reaches peak abundance in bogs, sometimes dry, sandy areas and open, upland woods; also transitional forests; throughout New England.

American Mountain-ash

Sorbus americana

Height: 12–35 ft
Leaves: 6–8 in long, alternate, compound with 9–17 lance-shaped, finely sharp-toothed leaflets, 1½–4 in long
Flowers: ¼ in wide, white, 5 round petals, bell-shaped, in flat-topped clusters
Fruit: orange-red, berry-like pomes, 3/16–¼ in across, in branched, flat-topped clusters

This native shrub is often found interspersed with the similar European mountain-ash (*S. aucuparia*) that has spread throughout the region. Both produce a bounty of red berries in fall that remain on the tree through winter, providing food for wildlife. **Where found:** open woodlands, roadsides, moist soils, valleys and coniferous and transition forests; from Maine south to northern GA. **Also known as:** rowan tree, dogberry.

Pin Cherry

Prunus pensylvanica

Height: to 30 ft
Leaves: 1½–6 in long, alternate, oval to lance-shaped
Flowers: ⅜–½ in wide, white, 5 round petals, in flat-topped clusters
Fruit: bright red cherries, ¼ in across

Unpopular raw because of their sourness and tiny pits, pin cherries are nonetheless a bountiful fruit that is delicious in pies, jelly and wine. Native Americans dried them and pounded them into animal fat and meat to make pemmican, which was once an important staple. • This shrub is one of the first trees to regenerate after fire. **Where found:** moist, forested areas, clearings, burned areas and transitional forests; throughout New England. **Also known as:** fire cherry.

American Plum

Prunus americana

Height: to 30 ft
Leaves: 2½–4 in long, alternate, oval, finely sawtoothed
Flowers: ¾–1 in across, white, saucer-shaped, 5 petals, fragrant, in clusters of 2–4
Fruit: yellow to red-purple plums (drupes), ¾–1 in long, with a waxy bloom

Domestic varieties of plums have long been cultivated to improve the fruit of this native shrub, whose wild fruit is not bad, but simply smaller, sour, thicker skinned and with a large seed. • American plum is grown for erosion control because it has spreading roots. **Where found:** moist soils, valleys and low upland slopes; from NH south to FL.

Chokecherry

Prunus virginiana

Height: to 30 ft
Leaves: 1–4 in long, alternate, thick, waxy, dark green above, finely toothed
Flowers: ¼–⅜ in across, white, 5 petals, in racemes 3–6 in long
Fruit: bright red to black, sour cherries (drupes), ¼–⅜ in across

High in antioxidant anthocyanins and used in the past to treat colds and flus, chokecherries need sweetening in preserves and baking. • The name "chokecherry" refers to poisoning that can occur to humans and ruminants from ingesting the seeds, stems or leaves, which contain hydrocyanic acid (cyanide). **Where found:** pastures and deciduous woodlands; throughout New England. **Also known as:** bitter-berry, bird cherry, chokeberry (misnomer), wild cherry, jamcherry, cabinet cherry, chuckleyplum, sloe tree, caupulin.

Downy Serviceberry

Amelanchier arborea

Height: up to 40 ft
Leaves: 2–4 in long, alternate, oval, finely sharp-toothed
Flowers: ⅝–1 in across, white, 5 long, narrow petals, in elongated, drooping clusters
Fruit: dark reddish purple, dry, berry-like pomes, ¼–⅜ in wide

Serviceberry's beautiful white flowers are among the first of spring. • The name "serviceberry" is derived from "sarvissberry," which comes from the Old English "sarviss." The alternate name "shadbush" refers to the shad fish migration, which occurs about the same time this shrub blooms. **Where found:** dry, often sandy woods, rocky sites and transitional forests; throughout New England. **Also known as:** smooth serviceberry, smooth juneberry, shadbush.

Black Raspberry

Rubus occidentalis

Height: under 6 ft
Leaves: 2–5 in long and wide, palmately compound, with 3–5 irregularly toothed leaflets
Flowers: 1 in wide, white, 5 petals, in clusters of 3–7
Fruit: black, seedy raspberries, ½ in across

This shrub provides cover for wildlife in winter, and both humans and animals enjoy the fruit. Fresh or completely dried raspberry leaves make excellent tea, but wilted leaves can be toxic. • The numerous species of blackberries and raspberries in the genus *Rubus* can be difficult to separate. This distinctive species has strongly whitened, or glaucous, stems. **Where found:** thickets, clearings and open woodlands; throughout New England.

Swamp Rose

Rosa palustris

Height: 2–7 ft
Leaves: alternate, pinnately compound, with 7 finely toothed, elliptical leaflets, each 1–2 in long
Flowers: up to 2 in wide, pink, 5 petals, solitary or in small clusters
Fruit: smooth, red hips, ½ in long

As its name implies, swamp rose commonly grows in swampy, wet areas and will even survive in standing water. It is distinguished from other roses by its large, pink flowers, compound leaves with 7 leaflets and downcurved thorns. • Rose hips are rich in vitamins A, B, C, E and K. **Where found:** swamps and bottomlands; throughout New England.

Flowering Dogwood

Cornus florida

Height: to 30 ft
Leaves: 2½–6 in long, opposite, elliptical to oval, slightly wavy-edged
Flowers: tiny, yellowish, in a dense 20–30-flowered cluster at the center of 4 white or pinkish, petal-like bracts, resembling a single, showy, blossom, 2–4 in wide
Fruit: shiny, red, berry-like drupes, ⅜–½ in long

With its beautiful spring flowers, showy, bird-attracting fruits and red fall leaves, eastern flowering dogwood is one of our finest native ornamentals, but its delicate flower buds are not frost hardy. • The aromatic bark yields a red dye. **Where found:** moist and dry soils, valleys, uplands, old fields, roadsides and the understory of hardwood forests; from southwestern ME south to FL.

Red-osier Dogwood

Cornus sericea

Height: 1½–10 ft
Leaves: ¾–4 in long, opposite, oval to lance-shaped, pointed at the tip, prominently veined
Flowers: less than ¼ in wide, white to greenish, in flat-topped clusters
Fruit: white, berry-like drupes, about ¼ in across

This attractive, hardy, deciduous shrub has distinctive purple to red branches with white flowers in spring, red leaves in fall and white, berry-like fruits in winter. • A similar species, alternate-leaved dogwood (*C. alternifolia*) has green bark and is sometimes called "green-osier dogwood." • An "osier" is a flexible branch that may be used to weave baskets and such. **Where found:** moist sites and transitional forests; from Newfoundland south to northern VA. **Also known as:** *C. stolonifera.*

Black Tupelo

Nyssa sylvatica

Height: 35–65 ft
Leaves: 2–5 in long, alternate, shiny, dark green, elliptical to oval or obovate
Flowers: tiny, greenish white, male and female flowers on separate trees, in clusters at the ends of long stalks
Fruit: blue-black, plum-like drupes, ⅜–½ in long

Black tupelo is an attractive tall shrub or shade tree that is often planted as an ornamental. • Bees are attracted to the tiny flowers, making black tupelo a well-known honey plant. • The juicy fruits are too sour for human tastes, but they are an important food for many animals. **Where found:** moist soils, valleys, uplands and hardwood and pine forests; from southwestern ME south, at elevations to 4000 ft. **Also known as:** black gum, sourgum, pepperidge.

Winterberry

Ilex verticillatus

Height: 3–10 ft
Leaves: 1½–3½ in long, alternate, elliptical, shiny, leathery
Flowers: ¼–½ in across, yellowish to greenish white, 4–8 petals, solitary or in small clusters
Fruit: glossy, red, berry-like drupes, less than ¼ in across

A member of the holly family, winterberry's thick, green foliage and bright red "berries" make it a popular ornamental, particularly at Christmas. The most commonly used decorative species is American holly (*I. opaca*), which also occurs in New England. • The berries are toxic and can cause nausea, diarrhea and vomiting. **Where found:** wet areas, swamps, damp woods, pond edges and transitional forests; throughout New England. **Also known as:** Canada holly, coralberry.

Staghorn Sumac

Rhus typhina

Height: to 30 ft
Leaves: 12–24 in long, alternate, compound with 11–31 lance-shaped leaflets; central stalks reddish, hairy
Flowers: ⅛–3/16 in across, yellowish green, in erect, cone-shaped clusters, 6–8 in long
Fruit: red, hairy drupes, 3/16 in across, in erect, cone-shaped clusters

Showy, red fruit clusters and colorful fall leaves make this shrub a favorite ornamental. In winter, the wide, woolly branches resemble velvet-covered deer antlers, inspiring the name "staghorn." • Delicious pink "lemonade" can be made by soaking the crushed fruit in cold water (to remove the hairs), then adding sugar. **Where found:** open, often disturbed sites, typically on dry, rocky or sandy soil; roadsides, abandoned fields and transitional forests; throughout New England.

Poison Ivy

Toxicodendron radicans

Height: to 4 ft, trailing or erect
Leaves: 7–10 in long, alternate, compound with 3 shiny, oval, irregularly toothed leaflets, each 2 in long
Flowers: ⅛ in across, greenish white, 5 petals, in loose clusters
Fruit: round, greenish white berries, ¼ in across, in hanging clusters

This species is the one plant that anyone venturing outdoors should learn to recognize. Identification difficulties are compounded by its variable growth habit; it can appear as trailing groundcover, a small, erect shrub or a vine climbing high into trees or on other objects. A brush with poison ivy can cause a severe allergic reaction, obvious in an itchy rash and swelling. To hyper-responders, contact can even be life threatening. **Where found:** various dry to moist upland sites; throughout New England. **Also known as:** *Rhus radicans.*

Buttonbush

Cephalanthus occidentalis

Height: up to 20 ft
Leaves: 2–6 in long, opposite or rarely in whorls of 3, elliptical, glossy, dark green, smooth edges
Flowers: small, creamy white, fragrant, funnel-shaped with 4 petal lobes, protruding style, in dense, spherical heads, 1–2 in across
Fruit: reddish green to red-brown nutlets, in dense clusters, ¾–1 in across

This species often forms a distinctive wetland plant community known as a buttonbush swamp. These shrubs can grow in fairly deep water, sometimes choking woodland pools. • Traditionally, the bark was used for stomach ailments and toothaches, as an eyewash for inflamed or irritated eyes and as a quinine substitute to treat malaria. **Where found:** wooded wetlands, marsh borders, edges of ponds and lakes, and transitional forests; from New England south to FL.

Southern Arrowwood

Viburnum dentatum

Height: 5–9 ft
Leaves: 2–4½ in long, opposite, oval, pointed at tip, prominently veined, coarsely toothed
Flowers: ¼ in across, creamy white, in flat-topped clusters, 2–3½ in wide
Fruit: blue-black, berry-like drupes, ¼–⅜ in across

This shrub's common name has its roots in a Native American use—the straight, young shoots were used for arrow shafts. • Closely related northern arrowwood (*V. recognitum*) has hairless twigs, whereas southern arrowwood has downy twigs. Some authorities treat these species as one. **Where found:** moist and sandy soils; throughout New England, except northernmost areas.

Nannyberry

Viburnum lentago

Height: 13–22 ft
Leaves: 2½–4 in long, opposite, elliptical, finely sawtoothed, smell unpleasant when bruised
Flowers: ¼ in across, white, 5-lobed corolla, in round-topped clusters 3–5 in wide
Fruit: red to bluish black, berry-like drupes, ½ in across

This shrub's summer leaves are shiny and green above, and yellow-green with tiny, black dots beneath. • Nannyberry's true beauty is revealed in fall, when the leaves turn shades of purple, red or orange and the fruits ripen to deep red, blue or almost black. • Although the fragrance of the fruits has been compared to dirty socks, their flavor is sweet and tasty. **Where found:** shady and moist sites, mixed woodlands, open pastures, streambanks and along lakes and roadsides; from ME south to WV.

Bayberry

Morella pensylvanica

Height: 3–15 ft
Leaves: ¾–4 in long, alternate, oval to oblong, leathery, toothed, aromatic when crushed
Flowers: tiny, yellowish green, in catkins ¾ in long
Fruit: round, blue to gray berries, ¼–⅜ in across, with a waxy bloom

The leaves and twigs of this aromatic shrub are collected for their fragrance, and the leathery leaves can be used in cooking and give off a spicy aroma. • This beneficial shrub provides forage for wildlife and also adds nitrogen-fixing bacteria to the soil. **Where found:** dry sites, sandy soils, protected dunes, open and rocky woodlands and abandoned fields; throughout New England. **Also known as:** candleberry; *Myrica pensylvanica.*

Hog-peanut

Amphicarpaea bracteata

Height: twining vine to 5 ft long
Leaves: long-stalked, compound, divided into 3 broadly oval leaflets, each 1–3 in long
Flowers: ½–¾ in long, white to pink or lavender, pea-like, in nodding racemes
Fruit: flat pods, 1½–2 in long, pointed at both ends

Hog-peanuts are edible and a good source of protein and carbohydrates, but they must be fully cooked; otherwise, compounds in the beans prevent them from being properly digested. • After pollination, the flowers bury themselves in the soil and form beans underground. **Where found:** dry or damp woodlands and streambanks; throughout New England. **Also known as:** American licorice, wild peanut.

HERBS, GRASSES, FERNS & SEAWEEDS

Herbs include all non-woody, flowering plants that are not grass-like (grasses, sedges and rushes are all graminoids). They are often perennials that grow from a persistent rootstock, but many are short-lived annuals. A great variety of plants are herbs, including all our spring wildflowers, several flowering wetland plants, herbs grown for food or medicine and numerous weeds. Many herbs are used for adding flavor to foods and in herbal remedies, aromatherapy and dyes. Culinary herbs are typically made from the leaves of non-woody plants, but medicinal herbs are made from the flowers, fruit, seeds, bark or roots of both non-woody and woody plants. Herbs are also vital to the ecology of the plant communities in which they occur as food sources for pollinating insects and other animals, host plants for moths and butterflies, nest material for birds and cover for many animal species.

The herbs illustrated here are only the most frequent and likely to be seen. Of the many herbaceous plants in New England, just a sampling from the various plant families appears in this guide. We have included common, widespread, ecologically important species, as well as representatives found in the various habitats of forests, coastlines, open fields, low valleys and high elevations. These species should provide a good starting point for those wishing to delve further into the spectacular and diverse flora of our region.

Ferns are flowerless plants with feathery or leafy fronds and reproduce by means of spores. These plants first appeared in the fossil record 360 million years ago, though many of the current species did not evolve until the late Cretaceous period, about 145 million years ago. Some fern species can be gathered as food (fiddleheads) or medicine, or used as ornamental plants and for remediating contaminated soils, whereas others are considered weeds.

Seaweeds are algae and can be classified into 3 major groups: green, red and brown. They absorb all the required fluids, nutrients and gases directly from the water and, unlike terrestrial plants, do not require an inner system for conducting fluids and nutrients. However, seaweeds do contain chlorophyll to absorb the sunlight needed for photosynthesis. They also contain other light-absorbing pigments, which give some their red or brown coloration. Instead of roots, seaweeds have "holdfasts" to anchor them to the sea floor, and many have hollow, gas-filled floats that help keep the photosynthetic structures of these organisms buoyant and close to the water's surface so they can absorb sunlight. Seaweeds provide food and shelter for marine animals, and dense, underwater seaweed "forests" are an important part of many marine ecosystems.

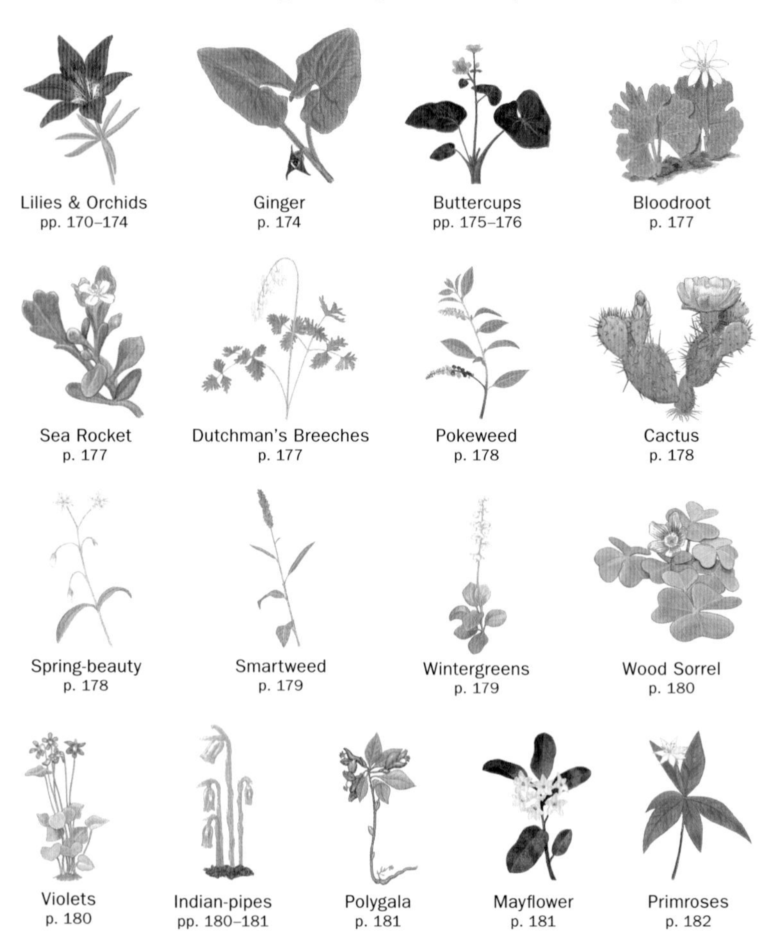
Lilies & Orchids
pp. 170–174
Ginger
p. 174
Buttercups
pp. 175–176
Bloodroot
p. 177
Sea Rocket
p. 177
Dutchman's Breeches
p. 177
Pokeweed
p. 178
Cactus
p. 178
Spring-beauty
p. 178
Smartweed
p. 179
Wintergreens
p. 179
Wood Sorrel
p. 180
Violets
p. 180
Indian-pipes
pp. 180–181
Polygala
p. 181
Mayflower
p. 181
Primroses
p. 182

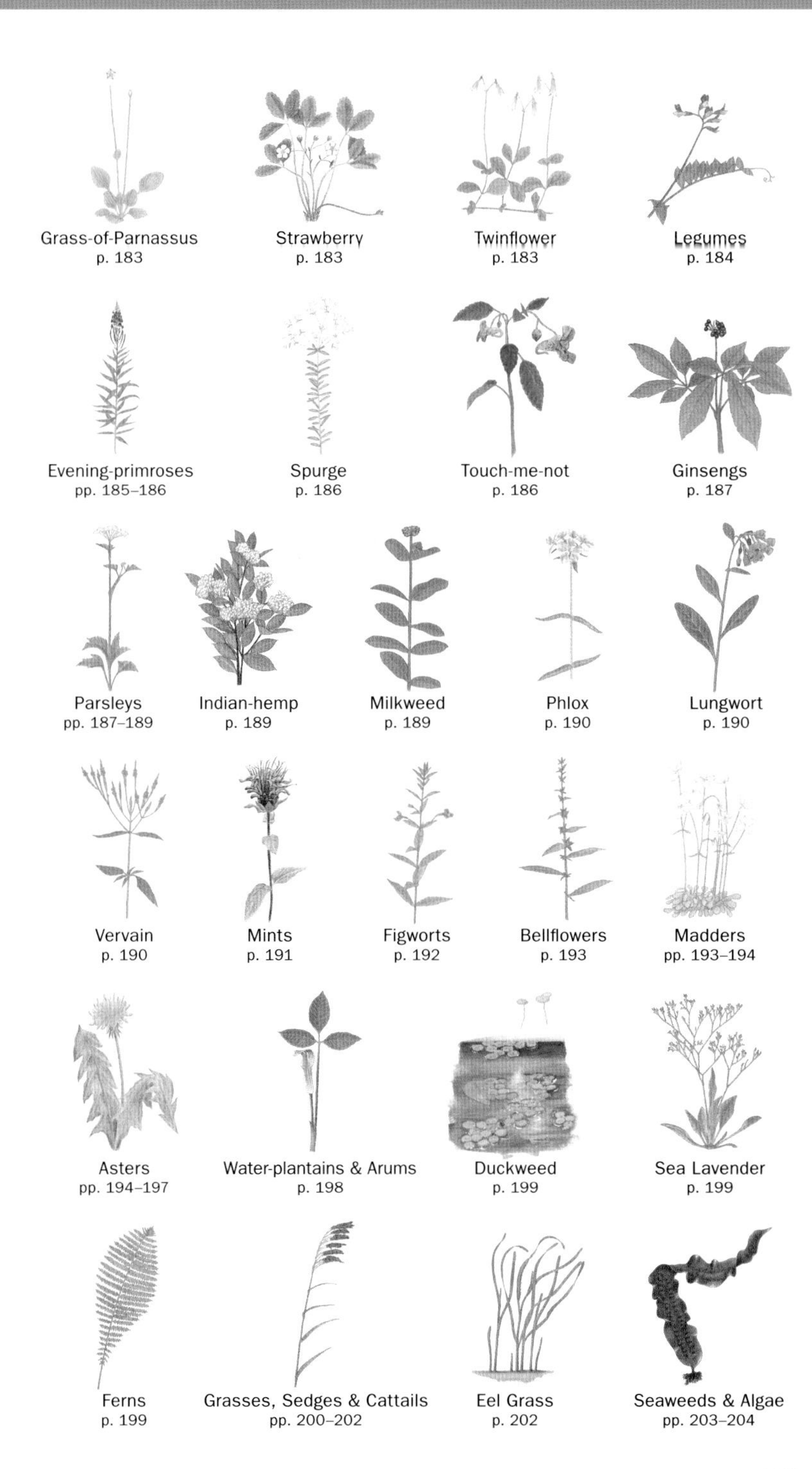
Grass-of-Parnassus
p. 183
Strawberry
p. 183
Twinflower
p. 183
Legumes
p. 184
Evening-primroses
pp. 185–186
Spurge
p. 186
Touch-me-not
p. 186
Ginsengs
p. 187
Parsleys
pp. 187–189
Indian-hemp
p. 189
Milkweed
p. 189
Phlox
p. 190
Lungwort
p. 190
Vervain
p. 190
Mints
p. 191
Figworts
p. 192
Bellflowers
p. 193
Madders
pp. 193–194
Asters
pp. 194–197
Water-plantains & Arums
p. 198
Duckweed
p. 199
Sea Lavender
p. 199
Ferns
p. 199
Grasses, Sedges & Cattails
pp. 200–202
Eel Grass
p. 202
Seaweeds & Algae
pp. 203–204

Wood Lily

Lilium philadelphicum

Height: 1–3 in
Leaves: 2–4 in long, usually in whorls of 3–8, lance-shaped
Flowers: 2 in across, 6 tepals, reddish orange, yellow with dark spots at base, 1–5 flowers per stem
Fruit: oblong capsules, 1–2 in long

A showy woodland flower, the wood lily has a simple beauty with a symmetric 6 tepals, 6 stamens and whorls of leaves usually in threes. • As with most lilies, this species has bulbous roots, and if you can tell the good (edible) lilies from the bad (poisonous) ones, you could use the bulbs as a starchy food source, much like the early Native Americans did. However, misidentifying a lily can be a lethal mistake. **Where found:** dry woods and thickets; throughout New England.

Painted Trillium

Trillium undulatum

Height: 8–20 in
Leaves: 2½–5 in long, oval, waxy, in a whorl of 3
Flowers: 2–2½ in across, 3 white petals, each with a dark pink, V-shaped stripe near the base, wavy margins, solitary
Fruit: shiny, red, ovoid berries, ½–¾ in across

Everything about this plant seems to be in threes—3 leaves, 3 petals, 3 sepals—which is what the name "trillium" refers to. • The ripe fruits split open to reveal numerous sticky seeds that have oily elaiosomes attached to them, which are irresistible snacks for ants. The ants carry the seeds to their nests and bite off the treat, leaving the seed to grow far from the parent plant. **Where found:** acidic soils and cool, coniferous forests; throughout New England.

Large-flowered Trillium

Trillium grandiflorum

Height: 12–18 in
Leaves: 5–8 in long, 3–6 in wide, in a whorl of 3, oval, pointed at tip, prominently veined
Flowers: 2–4 in across, 3 petals, white turning pink with age, 3 pointed, green sepals between the petals, 6 yellow stamens, solitary
Fruit: 6-angled, berry-like capsules, ½–⅝ in long

This species is one of the showiest and most common trilliums in North America. • At first bloom, the petals are the whitest of whites, eventually blushing to pink or violet as they age. **Where found:** cool, moist, rich deciduous or mixed forests; throughout New England, though extirpated in parts of its historic range. **Also known as:** white wake-robin, snowy trillium, grand trillium, great-flowered trillium, large-flowered wake-robin, beth root, birthroot, wood lily.

Yellow Trout-lily

Erythronium americanum

Height: 4–10 in
Leaves: 2–8 in long, 2 near the base of the stem, opposite, elliptical, green-mottled purplish brown
Flowers: 1–2 in across, 6 backward-curved tepals, yellow, often red-spotted inside, solitary, nodding on long stalks
Fruit: flat, rounded capsules, ½ in long

This lily was likely named for its leaf markings, which somewhat resemble the patterns on a brook trout. • The edible underground bulbs were collected as a food staple by many Native American groups. All lilies have a degree of toxicity and some are deadly poisonous, so it took astute observation and skilled preparation to use lilies for food and medicine. **Where found:** shaded and moist meadows and transitional forests; throughout New England south to GA. **Also known as:** dogtooth violet.

False Solomon's-seal

Maianthemum racemosum* ssp. *racemosum

Height: 12–36 in
Leaves: 3–6 in long, alternate, in 2 rows, elliptical, finely hairy beneath, prominent parallel veins
Flowers: ⅛ in across, white, numerous in a dense terminal cluster
Fruit: round, red berries (may be green with red splotches), ¼ in across

In traditional medicine and alchemy, Solomon's-seal was thought to have mystical as well as healing properties, and it is still used today by herbalists. False Solomon's-seal was used for its similar appearance, but it is a different plant from the former, which is a *Polygonatum* species. **Where found:** moist, typically deciduous woods and clearings; throughout New England. **Also known as:** Solomon's plume; *Smilacina racemosa*.

Canada Mayflower

Maianthemum canadense

Height: less than 10 in
Leaves: 1–3 in long, alternate, broadly heart-shaped to oval, pointed at tip, somewhat hairy
Flowers: ⅛ in across, white, 4-parted, in clusters at stem tips
Fruit: hard, brown-spoltched, green berries, 3/16 in across, becoming red and soft with age

Spreading by underground rhizomes, this flower often forms dense carpets of green leaves adorned with delicate flowers in spring, hence the name. • Many parts of this herb were used traditionally for food and medicine. **Where found:** upland woods, clearings and transitional forests; throughout New England. **Also known as:** wild lily-of-the-valley, false lily-of-the-valley, heartleaf, tobacco berry, bead ruby.

Bluebead Lily

Clintonia borealis

Height: 6–15 in
Leaves: 5–8 in long, basal, 2–5 (usually 3), oblong to elliptical, glossy, dark green
Flowers: ¾–1 in long, greenish yellow, bell-shaped, nodding, in clusters of 3–8
Fruit: ellipsoid, bright blue berries, ½ in long

The shiny, almost metallic-looking, blue berries inspired the name for this lily. They are attractive but poisonous. • The genus name honours DeWitt Clinton (1769–1828), a New York governor who was a respected naturalist but also responsible for the construction of the Erie Canal. **Where found:** shady, moist woodlands, acidic soils and transitional forests; throughout New England. **Also known as:** balsam bell, bear plum, calf corn, Canada mayflower, cow tongue, wood lily, yellow clintonia.

Indian Cucumber Root

Medeola virginiana

Height: 1–2½ in
Leaves: 2½–5 in long, in 1–2 whorls of 3–11 leaves, narrowly elliptical, tapered at both ends, veined
Flowers: ½ in long, greenish yellow, 6 backward-curved tepals, nodding on long stalks, in clusters of 3–9
Fruit: round, dark bluish purple berries, ⅜ in across

The crisp, juicy rhizome of this plant tastes and smells quite like a cucumber. It is white and brittle, with much the same texture as a cucumber, as well. It can even be pickled! • The berry-like fruits are favored by birds. • Flowers only appear on plants with 2 tiers of leaves and bloom from May to June. **Where found:** moist woodlands and hardwood and mixed coniferous-hardwood forests; throughout New England south to FL.

Sessile Bellwort

Uvularia sessilifolia

Height: 6–12 in
Leaves: 1¾–3 in long, alternate, sessile, narrowly elliptical
Flowers: 1 in long, pale yellow, bell-shaped, 6 tepals, solitary, nodding
Fruit: sharply 3-angled capsules similar to a beechnut, ⅝–¾ in long

This common woodland flower gets its name from the shape of its flowers, which resemble the uvula in the throat. Because of this, early homeopaths surmised that the plant might be used to cure sore throats, which was incorrect. • The flowers have a rich, spicy fragrance, but this does not translate into flavor. **Where found:** deciduous woods, thickets and transitional forests; throughout New England. **Also known as:** wild oats, cornflower, straw lily, sessileleaf bellwort.

Grass-pink

Calopogon tuberosus

Height: 12–18 in
Leaves: 6–20 in long, basal, usually single, lance-shaped, strongly ribbed
Flowers: 1–1½ in across, pale pink to bright magenta, 3 petals, uppermost petal narrow with a triangular lip and a patch of orange-yellow bristles, 2 lateral petals and 3 sepals widely spreading
Fruit: erect, cylindrical to ellipsoid capsules, ¾–1½ in long

The genus name *Calopogon* means "beautiful beard" in Greek, which on this orchid refers to the hair-like projections on the lip of the flower. The flower's intricate architecture is designed to aid in pollination—when a bee lands on the flower, pollen is brushed all over its back, or pollen from a previously visited orchid is brushed off. **Where found:** wet meadows, fens and open seepage slopes; throughout New England. **Also known as:** bearded pink, meadow gift.

Calypso

Calypso bulbosa

Height: 3–8 in
Leaves: ¾–1½ in long, solitary, basal, ovate, dark green
Flowers: 1–2 in long, solitary, rose purple, 3 erect sepals and 2 erect, twisted petals, 1 large slipper-like lower petal, yellow to whitish, streaked and spotted with purple and with a cluster of golden hairs
Fruit: erect, ellipsoid capsules, ¾–1¼ in long

This wildflower is special in our region, being the only member of its genus that braves our northern climes. • The solitary basal leaf of this perennial withers after the flower booms and is replaced with an overwintering leaf. **Where found:** cool, damp, mossy woods, typically in coniferous forests; throughout New England. **Also known as:** fairy slipper.

Stemless Lady's-slipper

Cypripedium acaule

Height: 6–15 in
Leaves: 4–8 in long, 5–8 cm wide, basal, 2, elliptical, sparsely hairy
Flowers: 1¼–2½ in long, yellowish brown to maroon sepals and petals and a large white, pink or magenta pouch, drooping, solitary at stem tips
Fruit: erect capsules, 1¾ in long

The distinctive lower petal of the flower looks like a tiny slipper, giving this plant its demure name. It is not a slipper for the Cinderellas of the forest, however, as it is one of our largest native orchids. Surely exciting for anybody with a shoe fetish, this flower often appears by the hundreds in small areas. **Where found:** humus-rich or sandy soils in dry forests and pine woodlands; occasionally moist forests; throughout New England. **Also known as:** pink lady's-slipper, pink moccasin-flower.

Large Purple Fringed Orchid

Platanthera grandiflora

Height: 2–4 in
Leaves: to 8 in long, 2–5, alternate, lance-shaped, keeled, reduced to bracts above
Flowers: 1 in long, fragrant, showy, lavender to rose purple, 3 erect, oval sepals and 2 small, upward curved lateral petals, large lip petal has 3 deeply fringed lobes, flowers in a dense, cylindrical raceme
Fruit: ellipsoid capsules, ½–¾ in long

This lovely orchid is delicately colored and scented, but it is a hardy perennial despite its seeming fragility. • The sticky nectar from the fragrant flowers attracts moths, which pollinate the flowers during their evening dining forays. **Where found:** cool, moist woods, wet meadows, swamps and transitional forests; throughout New England. **Also known as:** *Habenaria fimbriata.*

Showy Orchis

Galearis spectablilis

Height: 5–12 in
Leaves: 4–8 in long, basal, nearly opposite, elliptical, glossy, dark green
Flowers: 1 in long, pink to lavender, 2 petals and 3 sepals form a hood over a white, spade-shaped lip, in racemes
Fruit: ellipsoid capsules, ¾–1 in long

Despite its exotic-looking blossoms, the showy orchis is a native wildflower of our eastern forests. • This orchid is insect pollinated, but while the insect may get a nectar treat, the pollen is contained in a packet called a "pollinia" that cannot be used as food by insects. It sticks to the pollinator and is dropped into the flower of the next orchid. **Where found:** rich, damp woods and swamps; throughout New England. **Also known as:** *Orchis spectabilis.*

Wild Ginger

Asarum canadense

Height: 6–12 in
Leaves: 3–6 in wide, opposite, heart-shaped, downy
Flowers: 1¼–1½ in across, tan to purple, urn-shaped with 3 long, pointed sepals, solitary
Fruit: inconspicuous capsules

Wild ginger flowers lie on the ground, hidden under the large leaves, and are pollinated by crawling as well as flying insects. • This plant looks and smells like commercial ginger and can be used in much the same way. The roots can be used to flavor foods and drinks and to treat certain ailments. The leaves have antifungal and antibacterial properties. • Wild ginger and commercial ginger (*Zingiber officinale*) are not even closely related. **Where found:** rich woodlands, usually deciduous, and transitional forests; throughout New England south to SC.

Wild Columbine

Aquilegia canadensis

Height: 12–24 in
Leaves: 4–6 in wide, compound, divied 1–3 times into 3s
Flowers: 1–2 in long, nodding, 5 yellow petals with red spurs, 5 red sepals, solitary on stems above the leaves
Fruit: dry, 5-parted pods

Wild columbine has hanging, bell-like flowers with distinctive, showy, backward-pointing spurs. The tubular spurs store the nectar that attracts long-tongued pollinators such as moths and butterflies, as well as hummingbirds. Some nectar-robbing insects will bite into the flower spurs and steal a meal. • This is the only native columbine of eastern North America. **Where found:** rocky, wooded or open slopes; throughout New England.

Marsh-marigold

Caltha palustris

Height: 24 in
Leaves: 1–5 in long, round to kidney-shaped, heart-shaped at base, serrated, waxy
Flowers: 1–1½ in across, bright yellow, 5–9 petal-like sepals, solitary
Fruit: clusters of 6–12 curved, beaked pods (follicles), ⅝ in long

This sunny yellow flower brightens up its swampy habitat. Although the genus name *Caltha* is Latin for "marigold," this plant is a member of the buttercup family. • Marsh-marigold was traditionally used for a variety of medicinal and culinary purposes, but do not eat this plant unless you know precisely how to prepare it. It contains poisonous glycosides and protoenemonin and helleborin poisons. Contact with the skin may cause blistering. **Where found:** marshes and other wet areas; also boreal forest; throughout New England.

Roundlobe Hepatica

Anemone americana

Height: 4–6 in
Leaves: 2–3 in across, basal, dark green, leathery, 3-lobed with rounded tips
Flowers: ½–1 in across, pale pink to lavender or white, 5–12 petal-like sepals, numerous yellow stamens, subtended by 3 green bracts
Fruit: several, hairy, seed-like achenes

The three-lobed leaves of this plant were thought to resemble the shape of the liver, which is how this plant got its name. • Bees and flies are the main pollinators, but ants disperse the seeds later in the season. **Where found:** rich, upland woods, acidic soils and mixed forests; throughout New England. **Also known as:** *Hepatica americana.*

Bristly Buttercup

Ranunculus hispidus

Height: 12 in
Leaves: 2–4 in long, basal and alternate on the stem, on long, hairy stalks, deeply divided into 3 toothed or lobed leaflets
Flowers: ¾–1 in across, 5 shiny, yellow petals, 5 yellow-green sepals, many yellow stamens, solitary on hairy stalks
Fruit: smooth, flattened achenes, ⅛ in long

The genus name *Ranunculus* comes from the Latin, *rana*, meaning "frog," because buttercups tend to grow in moist places; *hispidus* means "covered in stiff coarse hairs" and refers to the hairs that cover the entire plant. • The seeds are eaten by birds and mammals such as grouse and chipmunks, but the foliage is toxic to mammals. **Where found:** medium-moist to moist woodlands, slopes and valleys, as well as swamps and wetlands; throughout New England. **Also known as:** hispid buttercup.

Goldthread

Coptis trifolia

Height: 3–6 in
Leaves: 1–2 in long, basal, evergreen, shiny, divided into 3 wedge-shaped, toothed leaflets
Flowers: ½ in across, white with a yellow center, 5–7 petals, solitary
Fruit: 3–9 dry, long-stalked, beaked pods, splitting open along one side

One wonders why, with its dark evergreen leaves and solitary white flowers, this plant is called goldthread. The yellow, thread-like underground stem is the hidden treasure of this species; it has many medicinal properties and is used to treat mouth sores (hence the name "cankerroot") and to make an eyewash to sooth eye irritations. **Where found:** cool woodlands, swamps, bogs and transitional forests; throughout New England. **Also known as:** cankerroot; *C. groenlandica*.

Red Baneberry

Actaea rubra

Height: 12–24 in
Leaves: 2½–4 in long, alternate, 2–3 times divided into 3s, coarsely toothed
Flowers: ¼ in across, white, 5–10 petals, numerous stamens, in rounded clusters
Fruit: clusters of glossy, red (occasionally white) berries on slender stalks

Baneberries are toxic but poisoning is rare because of the bitterness of the berries. The high toxicity of the plant is attributed to either the glycoside ranunculin or to an as-yet-unidentified essential oil. • Herbalists have taken advantage of medicinal properties in the roots of this plant, prescribing it as an antispasmodic, anti-inflammatory, vasodilator and sedative. **Where found:** woods and thickets, streambanks, swamps and deciduous, mixed coniferous and transitional forests; throughout New England.

Bloodroot

Sanguinaria canadensis

Height: 10–16 in
Leaves: 4–8 in long, single, round, pale green, 3–9-lobed
Flowers: 1–2 in across, 8–16 white petals, numerous yellow stamens, solitary
Fruit: 2-parted capsule, pointed at both ends

Bloodroot bleeds a brilliant crimson sap when the rhizome is cut. It is well known for its antimicrobial, anti-inflammatory and antioxidant properties and was traditionally used to treat any blood-related disease or malady. Bloodroot was also, more logically, used as a red dye, and, more romantically, as a love charm or aphrodisiac. **Where found:** streambanks, rich woodlands, thickets and transitional forests; throughout New England.

Sea Rocket

Cakile edentula

Height: 6–20 in
Leaves: 1–2 in long, ¼–½ in wide, fleshy, oblong, lobed, edges wavy or toothed
Flowers: ¼ in wide, pale lavender to white, 4 petals, in small clusters
Fruit: elongated seedpods (silicles), about 1 in long

The rocket-shaped seed capsules for which the plant is named form after the pale lavender flowers finish blooming. The stems and leaves are fleshy and thick to store water and to withstand the desiccating effect of sand and sun. • Sea rocket is a pioneer species that colonizes sandy beaches. It helps to bind and stabilize the sand and adds nutrients to the impoverished soil. **Where found:** above the high-tide line on sandy beaches; from New England south to FL.

Dutchman's Breeches

Dicentra cucullaria

Height: 4–12 in
Leaves: 3–6 in, trifoliate with finely divided leaflets
Flowers: ¾ in across, white, pantaloon-shaped, hanging on an arching stalk
Fruit: oblong capsules, opening into 2 parts when mature

This plant's common name refers to the flowers, which resemble the baggy breeches once worn by "Dutchmen." • *Dicentra* species contain several alkaloids that negatively affect the nervous system if ingested. If cattle graze upon these plants, one of the most common symptoms of poisoning is a staggering gait, which gives this plant the alternate name "staggerweed." **Where found:** fresh to moist hardwood forests, rich woodlands and transitional forests; throughout New England. **Also known as:** staggerweed, white hearts.

Pokeweed

Phytolacca americana

Height: 6–10 ft
Leaves: 3½–12 in long, alternate, lance-shaped, smooth
Flowers: ¼ in across, greenish white, 5 petal-like sepals, numerous stamens, in upright or drooping racemes
Fruit: dark purple, nearly round berries, less than ½ in across, on pink stalks

Despite the berries, seeds, roots and mature stems and leaves of this plant being very poisonous, it was somehow discovered that the young shoots and leaves are edible after they have been boiled multiple times. A less risky use of this plant was as a dye made from the red juice of the berries. • **Where found:** damp, rich soil, in clearings, pastures, thickets and disturbed sites and along roadsides; throughout New England. **Also known as:** inkberry, American nightshade, pigeon berry, redweed.

Prickly-pear

Opuntia humifusa

Height: 6–10 in, prostrate
Leaves: absent; spreading stems are segmented into oval pads, 4–6 in wide, with spines to 2 in long
Flowers: 4–8 cm wide, brilliant yellow, bell-shaped, solitary
Fruit: red-purple, fleshy, spiny berries, 1–2 in long

The fleshy pads of this cactus are dotted with clusters of fine spines and single long spines. If you can navigate your way past these defenses, both the pads and the ripe fruits, known as prickly pears, are edible. They can be peeled and cooked like a vegetable, and the red, fleshy fruit is sweet raw. **Where found:** rock outcrops, gravelly soils, sand dunes and cedar glades; throughout New England. **Also known as:** barberry, devil's tongue, old man's hand, Indian fig.

Spring-beauty

Claytonia virginica

Height: 6–12 in
Leaves: 2–8 in long, opposite (usually a single pair), narrow, stalk-less
Flowers: ½–¾ in across, bright pink to white with dark pink veins, 5 petals, 2 sepals, in loose terminal clusters
Fruit: small, ovoid capsules enclosed by the 2 sepals

This perennial makes a spectacular appearance in the first awakenings of botanical life in spring, often forming large patches of fresh, bright pink flowers. • The corms can be collected and eaten like potatoes. • The genus *Claytonia* is named for American botanist John Clayton (1686–1773). **Where found:** moist woods, thickets and clearings; southern New England. **Also known as:** fairy spuds, good morning spring, grass flower, mayflower, wild potato.

Water Smartweed

Persicaria amphibia

Height: to 6 ft on land; to 10 ft when aquatic
Leaves: 2–6 in long, alternate, lance-shaped to elliptical, tapered to the tip; somewhat hairy when terrestrial
Flowers: ¼–½ in across, pink, 5-lobed, in dense, terminal clusters
Fruit: shiny, brown, lens-shaped achenes, ⅛ in long

On the water, this plant has long, floating stems and forms large colonies that extend across the surface. Water smartweed can also be terrestrial, with hairier, lance-shaped leaves; the aquatic form has elliptical leaves that are more rounded at the tip. • The seeds are edible and can be pounded into meal or flour. • This is an introduced species from Europe. **Where found:** low, wet habitats including ponds, swamps and damp meadows; throughout New England. **Also known as:** scarlet smartweed; *Polygonum amphibium*.

Shinleaf

Pyrola elliptica

Height: 5–12 in
Leaves: 1–3 in long, evergreen, basal, oval, rounded at the tip
Flowers: ¼– ½ in wide, waxy, white to pinkish, 5 oval, often green-veined petals, cluster of orange-tipped stamens, pale green style curves down and out like an elephant's trunk, in racemes of 3–16
Fruit: flattened, spherical capsules, less than ½ in wide

The pear-shaped leaves are one of the distinguishing characteristics of this plant, and the genus name *Pyrola* comes from the Latin *pyrus,* which means "pear-shaped." • The leaves and roots were used medicinally to make infusions, gargles and, particularly, poultices and plasters, which is the likely etymology of the common name. **Where found:** bogs, fens, swamps and moist to wet woodlands; throughout New England. **Also known as:** white wintergreen, waxflower.

Spotted Wintergreen

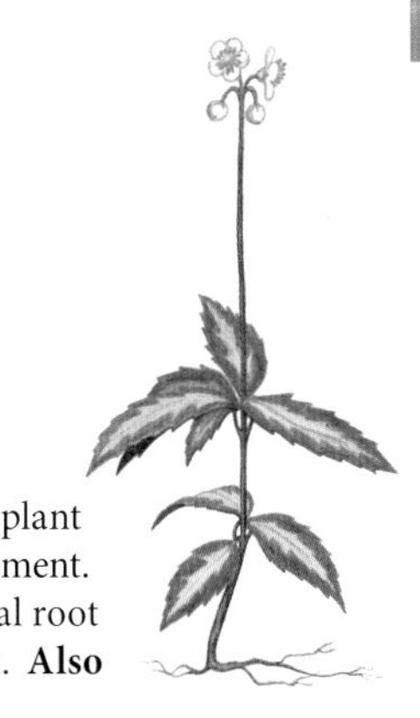

Chimaphila maculata

Height: 3–8 in
Leaves: 1½–2 in long, opposite, lance-shaped, toothed, dark green with a whitish stripe down the middle
Flowers: ½–¾ in across, waxy, white with a green center, 5 petals, nodding, in clusters of 2–5 at the top of the plant
Fruit: erect, brown capsules

The white and green evergreen leaves make this a conspicuous plant in summer and winter. • The leaves can be chewed for refreshment. At one time, this plant was used as an ingredient in commercial root beer. **Where found:** dry woods; from southern NH south. **Also known as:** pipsissewa, striped prince's pine.

Common Wood Sorrel

Oxalis montana

Height: 4–6 in
Leaves: 2–2½ in long, basal, long-stalked, palmately divided into 3 heart-shaped leaflets
Flowers: ½–1 in across, white veined with pink, 5 petals, usually solitary
Fruit: tiny, hairy, seed-like capsules

Although common throughout our woodlands, this plant is difficult to grow in gardens—many have tried to include the pink to white flowers and clover-like leaves in their flowerbeds with limited success. • *Sorrel* is German for "sour" and refers to the tangy taste of the leaves, which are delicious in salads. The leaves are also rich in vitamin C and were once used to treat scurvy. **Where found:** damp coniferous forests; throughout New England. **Also known as:** sour grass, sour clover.

Blue Violet

Viola cucullata

Height: 6–8 in
Leaves: 2–4 in long, basal, heart-shaped, on long stalks
Flowers: ½ in long, violet-blue to white, usually darker at the center, 5 petals, on tall stalks
Fruit: ovoid capsules with dark seeds

Violets are more than just pretty flowers, with lengthy lists of culinary, medicinal and practical uses. The flowers can be eaten raw or candied, and the leaves used as potherbs or thickeners. This plant is extremely rich in vitamins A and C. Obscure additional uses include being a substitute for litmus paper. • The blue violet is the state flower of Rhode Island. **Where found:** moist meadows; throughout New England. **Also known as:** marsh blue violet.

Indian-pipe

Monotropa uniflora

Height: 3–9 in
Leaves: to ⅜ in long, alternate, scale-like
Flowers: ½–1 in long, white to salmon pink, 5 petals, narrowly bell-shaped, nodding
Fruit: ovoid capsules, ⅜ in long, becoming erect when mature

This unusual fleshy, waxy plant is easily mistaken for a fungus because its lack of chlorophyll imbues no green coloration. Rather than using photosynthesis, this parasitic perennial obtains nutrients from nearby plants through connections with mycorrhizal fungi. This adaptation also allows it to grow in darkness. **Where found:** humus-rich soils in dense, moist woodlands and transitional forests; throughout New England. **Also known as:** corpse plant, ghost flower, ice plant.

Pinesap

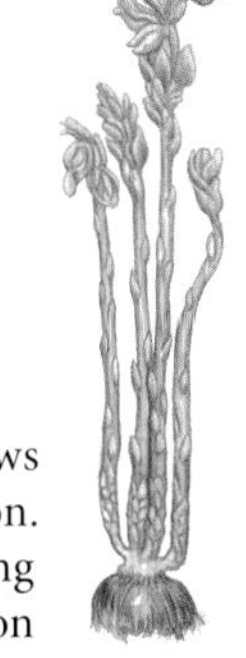

Monotropa hypopitys

Height: 4–16 in
Leaves: ½ in long, reduced to scales
Flowers: about ½ in long, nodding, urn-shaped, 4–5 petals, in a raceme of 2–11 flowers at the tip of the stalk
Fruit: erect, ovoid capsules

Pinesap blooms at different times of the year and the entire plant shows different colors—red, pink, lavender or yellow—depending on the season. In the fall, the plant and flowers are typically red; early spring flowering pinesaps are yellow. • This plant is saprophytic. It does not carrying on photosynthesis but obtains its nourishment from fungi associated with tree roots, usually those of oaks or pines. **Where found:** upland forests and acidic soils; throughout New England.

Fringed Polygala

Polygala paucifolia

Height: 3–7 in
Leaves: alternate and scale-like near the stem base, upper leaves ¾–1½ in long, oval
Flowers: ¾ in long, showy, rose purple, yellow or white, 2 oval wings, fringe-tipped corolla tube, in a terminal cluster of 1–4
Fruit: capsules

This milkwort species has exquisite flowers that look like little airplanes or birds in flight with their wings held aloft. Three petals form a tube and 2 sepals are the wings. • The milkwort family gets its name for the long-forgotten belief that nursing mothers or dairy cows could increase their milk production if they ate these plants. **Where found:** rich, moist woodlands; throughout New England. **Also known as:** gaywings, bird-on-the-wing.

Mayflower

Epigaea repens

Height: creeping
Leaves: ¾–3 in long, leathery, elliptical with rounded or heart-shaped bases
Flowers: ½ in wide, pink-white, fragrant, tubular corolla flares into 5 lobes, in clusters at the ends of small branches
Fruit: round capsules splitting into 5 parts with over 100 seeds

Stewards of pristine environments may be rewarded with the exquisite fragrance of this lovely native plant, which trails a string of flowers along the forest floor. Once plentiful, mayflower is becoming scarcer owing to its sensitivity to environmental disturbances. • It is the floral emblem of Massachusetts. **Where found:** sandy, acidic soils in exposed sites within coniferous and mixedwood forests; throughout New England. **Also known as:** trailing arbutus.

Fringed Loosestrife

Lysimachia ciliata

Height: 1–4 ft
Leaves: 2–5 in long, opposite, oval, pointed at the tip
Flowers: ½–1 in across, bright yellow, deeply 5-lobed, bell-shaped, 1–3 on slender stalks
Fruit: egg-shaped capsules, ¼ in across

The name of this plant comes from the belief that it could calm, or loosen, strife. Legend says that the Sicilian king Lysimachus, successor to Alexander the Great, was once being chased by a mad bull; the king forced a sprig of loosestrife at the animal, and it was instantly calmed. Traditionally, loosestrife was used to soothe yoked animals and prevent them from fighting. **Where found:** moist or wet woodlands; throughout New England.

Starflower

Trientalis borealis

Height: 4–8 in
Leaves: 1¾–4 in long, lance-shaped, in whorls of 5–9 at stem tips
Flowers: ½ in across, white, 5–9 pointed petals, solitary or 2–3 on slender stalks
Fruit: spherical, 5-valved capsules

This plant's pure white flowers against a background of dark leaves resemble stars in the sky. The leaves of this perennial herb wither back and disappear in autumn but reappear fresh and green in spring to provide the backdrop to a galaxy of flowers by May or June. **Where found:** cool, rich woodlands, peaty slopes, bogs and transitional forests; throughout New England. **Also known as:** chickweek, evergreen, maystar.

Sea-milkwort

Glaux maritima

Height: to 12 in
Leaves: ¼–1 in long, opposite, fleshy, oval, blunt-tipped
Flowers: less than ¼ in long, white or pinkish, 5 petal-like sepals, solitary and stalkless at leaf bases
Fruit: tiny, spherical capsules

Called "milkwort" for its use in infusions for nursing mothers, this plant is actually a member of the primrose family. • Native Americans cooked and ate the rhizomes, and Europeans pickled the leaves. • The genus name *Glaux*, from the Greek *glaucos*, means "bluish green," which aptly describes the color of the foliage; *maritima* refers to this plant's coastal habitat. **Where found:** coastal tidelands; also inland salt marshes and wet meadows; throughout New England. **Also known as:** black saltwort.

Fen Grass-of-Parnassus

Parnassia glauca

Height: 6–24 in
Leaves: 1–2 in long, almost as wide, basal, leathery; 1 rounded leaf on the lower part of the stem
Flowers: ¾–1½ in wide, 5 petals, white with greenish veins, solitary on long stalks
Fruit: 4-valved capsules

This plant looks nothing like a grass—its name is a poor translation of the Latin name *Parnassia*, which derives from Parnassus, a Greek island sacred to Apollo and the Muses. The ancient naturalist Dioscorides named the genus for a grass-like plant observed there, though *P. glauca* is native to North America. • The lines on the petals are believed to be helpful guidelines for pollinators to follow. **Where found:** wet habitats; prefers lime-rich soil; throughout New England.

Common Strawberry

Fragaria virginiana

Height: up to 6 in
Leaves: 1–4 in long, divided into 3 coarsely toothed leaflets
Flowers: ¾ in across, white, 5 petals, in open clusters
Fruit: small, red strawberries dotted with achenes

Few things beat running into a patch of fresh wild strawberries. The fruit is delicious, and many animals enjoy it as well. • There are several species of strawberry throughout the U.S., always distinguishable by the spreading runners, white flowers and, of course, sweet, red fruits. • This plant is the ancestor of 90 percent of our cultivated strawberries. **Where found:** dry fields and open forests; throughout New England.

Twinflower

Linnaea borealis

Height: flowering branches 3–6 in high, arising from semi-woody runners
Leaves: ½–¾ in long, opposite, evergreen, oval
Flowers: ¼–⅝ in long, whitish to pink, trumpet-like, fragrant, in pairs on Y-shaped stalks
Fruit: tiny, dry, egg-shaped nutlets

The small, delicate pairs of pink bells are easily overlooked among other plants on the forest floor, but their strong, sweet perfume may draw you to them in the evening. • Hooked bristles on the tiny nutlets catch on fur, feathers or the clothing of passersby, who then carry these inconspicuous hitchhikers to new locations. **Where found:** moist, cool, open or densely shaded forests, shrub thickets, muskeg, bogs, rocky shorelines and transitional forests; throughout New England.

Beach Pea

Lathyrus japonicus

Height: 12–60 in, stems trailing
Leaves: 2–4 in long, waxy, compound with 2–5 pairs of leaflets
Flowers: 1¼ in long, pea-like, reddish purple to blue, in racemes of 2–7
Fruit: pods, 1½–2¾ in long

Long, curly tendrils cling to other plants as the beach pea spreads along the ground, anchoring itself against strong winds and blowing sand. • Although these legumes are edible, they should not be consumed in large amounts. They contain a non-protein amino acid that is a neurotoxin and causes a type of cumulative poisoning called lathyrism. **Where found:** sandy or gravelly beaches and dunes along coastlines and large lakes; throughout New England.

Lupine

***Lupinus* spp.**

Height: to 30 in
Leaves: to 2¾ in long, gray-green, hairy, compound with multiple, pointed leaflets
Flowers: ⅝–¾ in long, showy, pea-like, yellow to purple, in tall, erect clusters
Fruit: hairy pods, ¾–2½ in long

These attractive perennials, with their showy flower clusters and fuzzy seedpods, enrich the soil with nitrogen. • The seedpods look like hairy garden peas, and children may incorrectly assume that they are edible. Many lupines contain poisonous alkaloids, and it is difficult to distinguish between poisonous and non-poisonous species. **Where found:** wet, open areas and disturbed sites; naturalized throughout New England.

Red Clover

Trifolium pratense

Height: 12–24 in
Leaves: alternate, compound, divided into 3 leaflets, ¾–1 in long, each leaflet with a pale "V"
Flowers: tiny, pink to purple, densely clustered in heads 1–1½ in across
Fruit: 1-seeded pods

Native to Europe, this plant is widely used around the world as fodder. It was originally cultivated in North America for this purpose and eventually became naturalized. Although weedy, it increases soil fertility by fixing nitrogen. • Red clover is the state flower of Vermont. **Where found:** open, disturbed sites such as roadsides, fields and lawns; throughout New England.

Purple Loosestrife

Lythrum salicaria

Height: to 5 ft
Leaves: to 3 in long, mostly opposite or whorled, dark green, lance-shaped
Flowers: 3/8–1/2 in long, red-purple, usually 6 narrow, wrinkled petals, in spikes
Fruit: capsules with numerous seeds

Beautiful but noxious, purple loosestrife is an invasive weed on the most-wanted list for eradication in North America. It was introduced from Eurasia and took to its new land with enthusiasm. The biggest threats are its invasiveness in wetlands and its ability to hybridize with plants in the native *Lathyrum* genus. Purple loosestrife chokes waterways, pushing out native plants such as cattails. A single one of these plants can produce millions of seeds. **Where found:** wet areas; throughout New England. **Also known as:** kill weed, rosy strife.

Fireweed

Epilobium angustifolium

Height: 1–10 ft
Length: 3/4–8 in long, alternate, narrowly lance-shaped
Flowers: 1–2 in across, pink to purple, 4 petals, in long clusters at stem tips
Fruit: linear pods, 2–3 in long

Fireweed helps heal landscape scars such as burned forests by blanketing the ground with colonies of plants, producing a sea of deep pink flowers. The erect, linear pods split lengthwise to release hundreds of tiny seeds tipped with fluffy, white hairs. • Young fireweed shoots can be eaten like asparagus and the flowers added to salads. **Where found:** open, often disturbed sites and transitional forests; throughout New England.

Common Evening-primrose

Oenothera biennis

Height: 1 1/2–5 ft
Leaves: 1–6 in long, alternate, lance-shaped, slightly toothed
Flowers: 1–2 in across, bright yellow, tube-shaped
Fruit: erect, cylindrical capsules, 3/4–2 in long

The flowers of this well-named species open near dusk, bloom throughout the night and generally close by midmorning, making moths the prime pollinators. The flowers open amazingly quickly, going from shrivelled wisps to robust blossoms in just 15 to 20 minutes. • Evening-primrose oil, which is produced from the seeds, has potent medicinal properties and is being tested as a treatment for a wide variety of conditions, mostly pain relief. **Where found:** dry, open sites, woods and meadows; throughout New England. **Also known as:** cure-all, fever-plant.

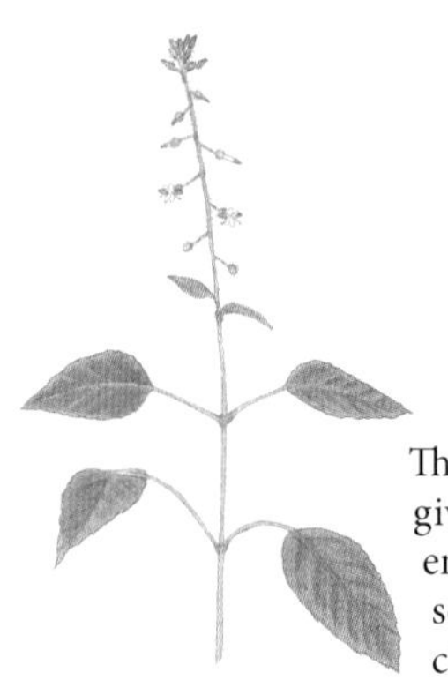

Enchanter's-nightshade

Circaea lutetiana

Height: 1–2 ft
Leaves: 2–4 in long, opposite, oval, shallowly and irregularly toothed
Flowers: small, numerous, white or pinkish, 2 deeply notched petals, well spaced in terminal racemes
Fruit: small, nut-like pods

The name of Circe, the mythological Greek enchantress, was given to this charming, delicate wildflower perhaps for its own enchanting beauty or, according to some sources, because the sorceress made a love potion from this nightshade. Some claim that Circe used poisonous *Circaea* plants in her magic. • To truly appreciate these miniscule flowers, you'll have to use a magnifying lens. **Where found:** moist, rich woodlands; throughout New England.

Flowering Spurge

Euphorbia corollata

Height: 1–3 ft
Leaves: 1–1½ in long, alternate, broadly linear or narrowly oblong
Flowers: ⅛–¼ in across, white with a yellow center, 5-parted, in loose umbels
Fruit: tiny, round, 3-lobed capsules

Each flowerhead consists of a tiny, yellow central flower surrounded by 5 white, modified leaves that look like petals. • A milky liquid oozes from all parts of this plant when it is bruised or cut and can cause skin irritation. It is toxic when ingested. Birds seem immune to these effects, and many species eat the seeds of this plant. **Where found:** dry fields and woodlands; throughout New England.

Spotted Touch-me-not

Impatiens capensis

Height: 3–5 ft
Leaves: 1–4 in long, alternate, oval, serrated margins
Flowers: 1 in long, orange-yellow, sac-like sepal is heavily spotted with reddish brown, flowers hang from thread-like stalks
Fruit: green capsules, ¾ in long, open explosively when touched

Exceptionally succulent, this plant will wilt in your hands like melting ice if picked, hence it begs you to "touch it not." • The seeds are enclosed in fleshy capsules and held by tightly coiled, elastic attachments. Press a ripe pod, and the seeds shoot forth explosively. Catch the seeds in your hand, pop them in your mouth and enjoy the taste of walnuts. **Where found:** moist, shaded woodlands, damp sites and lakesides; throughout New England. **Also known as:** jewelweed.

Dwarf Ginseng

Panax trifolius

Height: 4–8 in
Leaves: 3 in long, whorl of 3, compound, palmately divided into 3–5 coarsely toothed leaflets
Flowers: tiny, whitish or yellow-green, 5 petals, in a round cluster that rises above the leaves
Fruit: yellow, berry-like drupes with 2–3 seeds

Ginseng root has a rich 5000-year history of herbal use. According to traditional Chinese medicine, it regulates the balance between yin and yang, promotes health, vigor and long life, and is considered an aphrodisiac. In the West, ginseng root is known for its ability to boost the immune system, increase mental efficiency, improve physical performance and aid in adapting to stress. **Where found:** moist, rich woodlands; throughout New England.

Wild Sarsaparilla

Aralia nudicaulis

Height: 8–28 in
Leaves: 8–15 in long, single leaf is divided into 3, each division with 3–5 oval to lance-shaped, finely toothed leaflets, 1–4 in long
Flowers: ¼–⅜ in across, greenish white, 5 petals, in clusters of 2–7
Fruit: purplish black berries, ¼ in across

The sweet, aromatic rhizomes of this plant were traditionally used to make tea, root beer and mead. The berries, generally inedible, have also been used in making beer and wine. • The rhizomes were pulverized into poultices to heal wounds, burns and other skin ailments, and to reduce swelling and inflammation. **Where found:** moist, shaded woods and transitional forests; throughout New England.

Woolly Sweet-cicely

Osmorhiza claytonii

Height: 1–3 ft
Leaves: 12 in long, compound, 2 times pinnately divided into fern-like, serrated leaflets
Flowers: tiny, less than ¼ in across, white, 5 petals, in branched clusters
Fruit: capsules with flattened nutlets

With a reputation as a good-luck charm or a love charm, woolly sweet-cicely was widely used medicinally for its mild anise quality, which is soothing to upset stomachs. The leaves, stems and roots were pulverized and used in infusions for stomach discomforts and kidney troubles. Root decoctions were consumed as an energizing drink, and poultices prepared with the root were applied to wounds and boils. **Where found:** moist to dry woodlands; throughout New England. **Also known as:** sweet anise, aniseroot.

Water Parsnip

Sium suave

Height: 20–40 in
Leaves: alternate, pinnately divided into 5–17 slender, sawtoothed leaflets, 2–4 in long
Flowers: tiny, white, in dense umbels 2–7 in wide
Fruit: pairs of seed-like schizocarps, ¼ in long

All members of the carrot/parsnip family have characteristic umbels of tiny, clustered flowers. • The young stems and roots of water parsnip are edible, crisp and bitter like parsnips, and were eaten raw, roasted or fried by Native American peoples. • The flowerheads are poisonous. This plant is also very similar to the extremely poisonous water-hemlocks (*Cicuta* spp.). **Where found:** wet sites, fields and hillsides; throughout New England.

Cow Parsnip

Heracleum sphondylium* ssp. *montanum

Height: up to 8 ft
Leaves: 4–12 in wide, alternate, compound, divided into 3 lobed, coarsely toothed leaflets
Flowers: tiny, white, in compound umbels up to 1 ft wide
Fruit: flattened, egg-shaped capsules (schizocarps), ¼–½ in long

The tiny flowers contrast with the overall largeness of this member of the carrot/parsley family. • Cow parsnip is edible and was a valuable staple to many Native American groups. However, it can cause skin problems in photosensitive people because of irritative furanocoumarins. • Be careful not to confuse this plant with highly poisonous water-hemlocks (*Cicuta* spp.), which are similar in appearance. **Where found:** streambanks, moist slopes and clearings, upper beaches and marshes; throughout New England. **Also known as:** *H. lanatum*, *H. maximum*.

Marsh-pennywort

Hydrocotyle americana

Height: 2–5 in
Leaves: ¼–2¼ in long, oval to round, scalloped edges
Flowers: to ⅛ in across, greenish white, 5 petals, in small clusters in leaf axils
Fruit: tiny, dry capsules, splitting into 2 seeds

This aquatic plant has leaves reminiscent of nasturtiums. The name "pennywort" comes from the European species, whose round leaves are the size of coins. • Historically, marsh-pennywort was used to treat skin ailments, but it is highly poisonous, making the cure worse than the disease. • *Hydrocotyle* species have long, creeping stems that form dense mats in aquatic habitats. **Where found:** damp, shady sites, marshes, ponds and swamps; throughout New England. **Also known as:** navelwort.

Angelica

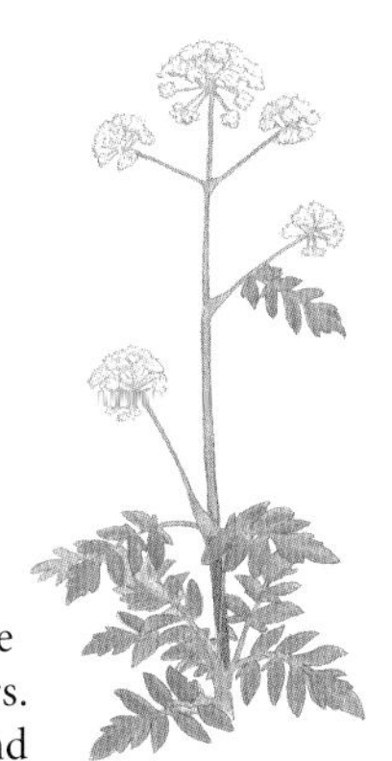

Angelica atropurpurea

Height: to 6 ft
Leaves: compound with 3 major divisions, pinnately divided into sharp-toothed leaflets, 1–4 in long
Flowers: small, greenish white, in large, ball-like clusters
Fruit: flat, winged and ribbed capsules (schizocarps), less than ¼ in long

Angelica in bloom, with its large, spherical clusters of whitish flowers, suggests a display of exploding fireworks. • The leaves smell like parsley and have a strong but pleasant taste. They were traditionally used in soups and stews or to flavor gin and liqueurs. Teas and extracts made from the roots and seeds aid digestion and relieve nausea and cramps. **Where found:** wet, open sites; throughout New England.

Indian-hemp

Apocynum cannabinum

Height: to 4 ft
Leaves: 2–4 in long, opposite, oval, often hairy beneath
Flowers: less than ¼ in long, greenish white, bell-shaped, 5-petaled, in open clusters
Fruit: pairs of slender pods (follicles), 4 in long

This common, weedy native plant is tough and can even push through asphalt. • The stem's long, strong fibers make a durable, fine thread. Traditionally, mature stems were soaked in water to remove the coarse outer fibers, then rolled against the leg into thread. • This plant is poisonous. The milky sap can cause skin blistering; ingestion has resulted in sickness and death. **Where found:** fields, roadsides, woodland edges and open sites; throughout New England. **Also known as:** dogbane.

Common Milkweed

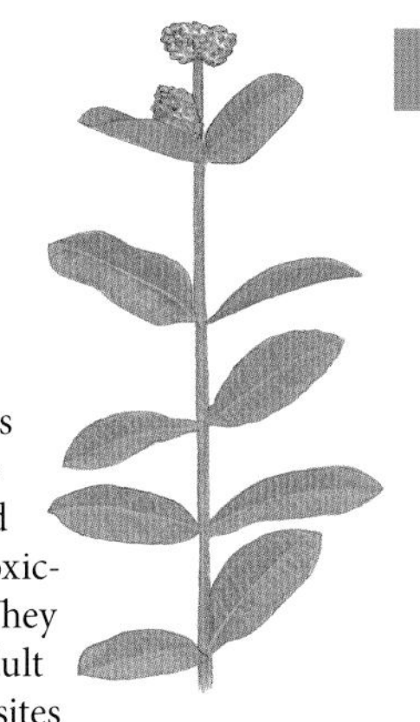

Asclepias syriaca

Height: 3–5 ft
Leaves: 4–10 in long, opposite, oblong, hairy beneath
Flowers: tiny, pinkish lavender, fragrant, numerous, in rounded clusters
Fruit: spiny follicles in erect clusters

By far our most common milkweed, this weedy plant contains glycosides that are toxic to both animals and humans. The insects adapted to feed on these plants become poisonous and tend to be brightly colored and conspicuous, advertising their toxicity. Monarch butterfly larvae feed solely on milkweed leaves. They absorb the glycosides into their bodies, so both larvae and adult butterflies become poisonous to predators. **Where found:** open sites such as fields, meadows and roadsides; throughout New England.

Blue Phlox

Phlox divaricata

Height: to 20 in
Leaves: 1¼–2 in long, mostly opposite, oblong, pointed at tip, veined
Flowers: ¾–1¼ in wide, purple to blue, fragrant, tubular with 5 lobes, in loose clusters
Fruit: 3-valved capsules, ¼ in long

Blue phlox is a characteristic and abundant May-blooming wildflower of rich woodlands. Each sweet-smelling blossom is a pinwheel-like fan of 5 petals fused at their bases into a long corolla tube, which butterflies and moths with long tongues are perfectly adapted to pollinate. **Where found:** rich, moist woodlands and fields; throughout New England.

Sea Lungwort

Mertensia maritima

Height: 4–14 in
Leaves: ½–1 in long, succulent, pale blue-green, oval or nearly round
Flowers: ¼–⅜ in across, blue (pink in bud), bell-shaped, 5 lobed, in small clusters on stems above the leaves
Fruit: 4-chambered capsules (schizocarps)

Sea lungwort is a plant of beaches and coastal areas. It is easily recognized by its blue flowers and, when not in bloom, by its succulent, blue-green leaves. • This member of the borage family is considered edible. • The genus name *Mertensia* honors Franz Karl Mertens (1764–1831), a renowned German botanist who was primarily a collector of algae. **Where found:** beaches; throughout New England. **Also known as:** oysterleaf, sea bluebells.

Blue Vervain

Verbena hastata

Height: 1½–6 ft
Leaves: 2–6 in long, opposite, lance-shaped, coarsely toothed
Flowers: ¼ in wide, violet-blue, 5 petals, densely clustered in blunt-tipped spikes
Fruit: 2-parted capsules

An abundant and conspicuous denizen of damp, open ground, blue vervain produces spikes of showy blossoms that bloom in spirals, working their way up the flower spike. This pretty wetland plant is important for insects, attracting numerous bees and butterflies. • The steamed leaves are palatable, and the flowers make a pretty garnish or addition to salads. **Where found:** marshes, ditches, wet meadows and shorelines; throughout New England.

Wood Sage

Teucrium canadense

Height: to 3 ft
Leaves: 2–6 in
Flowers: ½–¾ in long, scentless, white, pink or lavender, 2-lipped, the lower lip much larger, in a crowded, spike-like cluster
Fruit: tiny, yellowish brown, ellipsoid nutlets

This member of the mint family has an unpleasant taste, and for perhaps this reason alone, it was thought to have medicinal properties (since culinary ones were lacking). • Teucer, the first king of Troy, was reputedly the first to use this plant medicinally. It has been used to heal sores and treat ulcers, and is sometimes sold commercially as "pink skullcap." **Where found:** thickets, woods and shorelines; throughout New England. **Also known as:** Canada germander.

Wild Bergamot

Monarda fistulosa

Height: 2–4 ft
Leaves: 2–4 in long, opposite, lance-shaped, somewhat serrated
Flowers: 1 in long, pale to bright lavender, fragrant, tubular, densely clustered in a head-like inflorescence
Fruit: tiny, shiny, oblong nutlets

North American wild bergamot smells very similar to the tropical tree orange bergamot (*Citrus aurantium*), which gives Earl Grey tea its characteristic flavor and aroma. It is a member of the mint family, and the leaves can be used much the same way as mint, either dried or for the essential oil. They can also be made into a tea to soothe an upset stomach. **Where found:** dry fields, thickets and woodland borders; from western New England south. **Also known as:** horsemint.

Heal-all

Prunella vulgaris

Height: 6–20 in
Leaves: 1–3 in long, opposite, lance-shaped, finely toothed
Flowers: ½–1 in long, purplish to pink, tubular, hood-like upper lip arches over 3-lobed lower lip, in spike-like clusters
Fruit: dark, shiny, ribbed nutlets

Introduced from Eurasia, this abundant and often weedy little mint ranges throughout North America. As its name suggests, this plant has been used to treat just about every type of ailment. Research indicates that the entire plant has antibacterial compounds and inhibits the growth of a number of disease-causing bacteria. **Where found:** open, weedy areas, lawns, fields and roadsides; throughout New England.

Downy False Foxglove

Aureolaria virginica

Height: 1–5 ft
Leaves: 2½–5 in long, opposite, upper leaves lance-shaped, lower leaves with pointed lobes
Flowers: 1 in across, yellow, funnel-shaped, 5 rounded lobes, in terminal clusters
Fruit: smooth, ovoid capsules

Aureolaria species are known as oak leeches because they partly parasitize the roots of native oaks, catching an easy meal by deriving nutrients from the tree. • This wildflower looks very similar to garden foxglove (*Digitalis purpurea*), which is where the common name comes from, but the species are not related. • This plant has some anti-inflammatory qualities and was used traditionally for treating wounds. **Where found:** dry, open woods, under oak trees; from NH south.

Common Monkeyflower

Mimulus ringens

Height: 2–4 ft
Leaves: 2–4 in long, opposite, lance-shaped, clasping the stem
Flowers: ¾–1¼ in long, lavender, 2-lipped corolla, yellow "throat," on long stalks
Fruit: oblong capsules with many yellow seeds

When looked at head on, this flower resembles a monkey's face, hence the plant's common name. • This relative of garden snapdragons brightens moist, open habitats with its pale purple blooms. After the flowers drop, the oblong fruit capsules appear, formed by the sepals fusing into inflated balloons full of seeds. **Where found:** marshes, wetlands and damp, open sites; throughout New England.

Wood-betony

Pedicularis canadensis

Height: 6–18 in
Leaves: 2–6 in long, basal or alternate on the stem, elliptical, fern-like
Flowers: ¾ in long, pale yellow, maroon or bicolored, 2-lipped with a hood-like upper lobe, leaf-like bracts, in a spike
Fruit: dry capsules, ¼ in long

This odd-looking plant depends on mycorrhizal fungi for nutrient intake and should not be transplanted or disturbed because it will not survive. • The genus name is derived from the Latin word *pediculus*, meaning "louse." It was once thought that if cattle consumed wood-betony, they would become louse-ridden. **Where found:** moist to dry, forested habitats; throughout New England. **Also known as:** lousewort.

Harebell

Campanula rotundifolia

Height: 6–20 in
Leaves: ½–3¼ in long, basal leaves oval to heart-shaped and toothed, stem leaves alternate and narrowly lance-shaped
Flowers: ½–1¼ in long, purple-blue, 5-lobed, bell-shaped, nodding
Fruit: nodding, oblong to cone-shaped capsules

The genus name *Campanula* means "little bell" and describes the nodding, bell-like flowers. However, some eastern species have flared petals. • The common garden bellflower (*C. rapunculoides*) frequently escapes from gardens and shows up in natural areas; it differs by having heart-shaped leaves. • Victorians attributed the sentiments of humility or grief to harebell, with its downcast face. **Where found:** rocky banks and slopes, meadows and shorelines; throughout New England. **Also known as:** bluebell.

Cardinal-flower

Lobelia cardinalis

Height: 2–4 ft (occasionally reaches 7 ft)
Leaves: 2–6 in long, alternate, lance-shaped, toothed
Flowers: ¾–1½ in long, intense red or scarlet, 2-lipped, in showy spikes
Fruit: spherical capsules with brown seeds

Cardinal-flower gets its name from the striking color of its flowers, which matches that of the robes of cardinals in the Roman Catholic Church. The brilliant red blossoms with their long corolla tubes are well adapted to attract hummingbirds, this plant's primary pollinators. • Some *Lobelia* species, including cardinal-flower, have therapeutic properties, but large doses can cause nausea, vomiting, drowsiness, respiratory failure and potentially death. **Where found:** wet woods, meadows and damp areas; throughout New England.

Bluets

Houstonia caerulea

Height: to 6 in
Leaves: ¼–½ in long, mostly basal, stem leaves opposite, spatulate
Flowers: ½ in wide, tubular, light blue to white, yellow center, 4 petals, solitary on long stalks
Fruit: flattened capsules, ⅛ in long

Bluets grow in masses, carpeting the ground in spring. The small flowers' bright yellow center acts like a bull's-eye for insects, guiding tiny bees to the pollen inside the tubular flowers. • Bluets cannot withstand much competition from other plants and typically grow in barren soil. **Where found:** dry, barren soil in clearings, deciduous woodlands and transitional forests; throughout New England.

Partridgeberry

Mitchella repens

Height: 4–12 in, trailing along the ground
Leaves: 1/4–3/4 in long, opposite, oval to round, leathery
Flowers: 1/2–3/4 in long, white, fragrant, trumpet-shaped, usually 4 petals, fuzzy inside
Fruit: scarlet berries, 3/8 in wide

The reddish berries of this plant are edible, though not very tasty. Some Native American peoples ate them fresh or cooked into a jam. • Wildlife such as ruffed grouse and wild turkeys eat the buds, leaves, flowers and fruit of this plant. • The trailing stems and berries make good Christmas decorations, though taking plants from the wild is discouraged. **Where found:** dry or moist woodlands, rich, mixed forests with acidic soils (especially under conifers) and transitional forests; throughout New England.

Cleavers

Galium aparine

Height: 1–3 ft
Leaves: 1–3 in long, opposite, narrowly oblanceolate, in whorls of 8
Flowers: tiny, white, 4 lobed, in 3-flowered clusters
Fruit: dry nutlets with bristles

Cleavers are so named because their bristled fruits cleave (adhere) to animals and clothing, aiding in seed dipersal. This plant's nickname is "Velcro-weed." • Species in the genus *Galium* are also called "bedstraw" because early Americans used dried stems to stuff mattresses. • Cleavers is related to coffee (*Coffea* spp.), and the tiny nutlets can be dried, roasted and ground as a coffee substitute. **Where found:** open woods, fields and roadsides; throughout New England. **Also known as:** bedstraw, tangleweed.

Giant Ragweed

Ambrosia trifida

Height: 3–12 ft
Leaves: 2–4 in long, opposite on lower stem, alternate on upper stem, deeply pinnately divided into 3–5 lobes
Flowers: ray flowers absent; disk flowers 1/4–1/2 in long, greenish; flowerheads in terminal spikes to 15 cm tall
Fruit: reddish brown, beaked achenes, 1/4 in long

Huge stands of this abundant plant sometimes cover old fields, and its airborne pollen causes much hayfever suffering. • Ragweed seeds 4 to 5 times larger than today's wild species have been found in archaeological digs in North America, suggesting that this plant was once selectively bred, perhaps for its seed oil. **Where found:** moist soils, disturbed sites in old fields and along roadsides; throughout New England.

Common Yarrow

Achillea millefolium

Height: 4–30 in
Leaves: 2–6 in long, basal and alternate on the stem, fern-like
Flowers: ray flowers white (rarely pinkish), usually 5, 3-toothed; disk flowers whitish, minute, flowerheads ¼–⅜ in wide, in dense, flat-topped clusters
Fruit: flattened achenes, less than ½ in long, with a single seed

This hardy, aromatic perennial has served for thousands of years as a fumigant, insecticide and medicine. • The Greek hero Achilles, for whom the genus was named, reportedly used it to heal his soldiers' wounds after battle. • Yarrow is an attractive ornamental, but its extensive underground stems (rhizomes) are invasive. **Where found:** dry to moist, open sites; throughout New England.

Oxeye Sunflower

Heliopsis helianthoides

Height: 2–5 ft
Leaves: 2–6 in long, opposite, lance-shaped, serrated margins
Flowers: ray flowers golden yellow, 8–16; disk conical, yellow; flowerheads to 3 in wide, solitary to several on long stalks
Fruit: 4-angled, slightly hairy achenes

This plant is a member of the sunflower/aster family, as are daisies, asters and the sunflowers (*Helianthus* spp.) that we are familiar with for producing giant heads of "spits" from the disk flowers (the ray flowers do not produce seeds). • Both the ray and disk flowers of oxeye sunflower produce fruits, but it is mainly American goldfinches that feast upon the tiny seeds. **Where found:** semi-shaded woodland borders; throughout New England. **Also known as:** false sunflower.

Golden Ragwort

Packera aurea

Height: 12–30 in
Leaves: to 5 in long, basal leaves heart-shaped, purplish beneath, with scalloped edges, stem leaves alternate and lobed
Flowers: ray flowers yellow, 10–12, ¼–½ in long; disk yellow, ¼–½ in wide; flowerheads several on long stalks in open clusters
Fruit: brownish, cylindrical achenes with tufted white pappus

In early spring, colonies of golden ragwort brighten shady roadsides and low-lying meadows. The basal leaves are dark purple below, possibly allowing the plant to absorb additional heat to aid growth during cool spring weather. • Historically, ragwort tea was used medicinally, but this plant contains toxic alkaloids and should not be consumed. **Where found:** moist woods and fields; throughout New England.

Canada Goldenrod

Solidago canadensis

Height: 2–5 ft
Leaves: 3–6 in long, narrowly lance-shaped, stalkless, rough-hairy, sawtoothed
Flowers: ray flowers yellow, 10–17, ⅛ in long; disk flowers yellow, 6–12; flowerheads numerous in plume-like clusters
Fruit: hairy achenes with tufted, white pappus

Canada goldenrod is a classic pioneer forb of old fields. Growth-inhibiting enzymes released from its roots discourage other plants from flourishing. • Many people think that goldenrod flowers cause hayfever, but the real culprit is probably ragweed, which shares the same habitat. • The goldenrod gall fly (*Eurosta solidaginis*) lays its egg in the stem, which causes the plant to form a hardened, perfectly round mass of tissue that looks like it swallowed a golf ball. **Where found:** moist to dry fields and open sites; throughout New England.

New England Aster

Symphyotrichum novae-angliae

Height: 2–5 ft
Leaves: 1–4 in long, lance-shaped, clasping the stem
Flowers: ray flowers violet, rose or magenta, 45–100, ¾ in long; disk yellow-orange, ½–¾ in wide; flowerheads showy, in leafy clusters
Fruit: hairy achenes with tufted, bristly pappus

Of the many asters in our region, this one is the showiest. Though considered an aggressive weed, New England aster is admired for its attractive flowers, and it is often deliberately planted in flowerbeds. The flowers are typically rich purplish magenta but can vary to lilac and almost white, and the blooms persist after the first autumn frosts. **Where found:** moist to dry meadows, wet thickets, swamps and open sites; throughout New England.

Common Boneset

Eupatorium perfoliatum

Height: 2–4 ft
Leaves: 3–8 in long, opposite, fused at base, lance-shaped, sparsely hairy, serrated margins
Flowers: ray flowers absent; disk flowers white, 9–23; flowerheads ¼ in high, in flat-topped clusters
Fruit: resinous achenes with tufted, white pappus

Early herbalists believed the perforated leaves of this wetland plant indicated that the herb was useful in setting bones, so the leaves were wrapped with bandages around splints. There is little scientific proof that the leaves help bones heal, but researchers in Germany have found compelling evidence that this plant boosts the immune system. **Where found:** wet meadows and low, moist sites; throughout New England.

Canada Thistle

Cirsium arvense

Height: 2–5 ft
Leaves: 2–6 in long, alternate, usually stalkless, deeply lobed, spiny-toothed, wavy edges
Flowers: ray flowers absent, disk flowers numerous, tubular, purple or pink; flowerheads ½–1 in across
Fruit: seed-like achenes

Introduced from Europe in the 17th century, Canada thistle is considered a noxious weed, choking out other plants and reducing crop yields. Its deep underground runners contain a substance that inhibits the growth of nearby plants. Each year, one plant can send out up to 20 ft of runners, and female plants can release up to 40,000 seeds. **Where found:** disturbed sites; throughout New England.

Common Dandelion

Taraxacum officinale

Height: 2–20 in
Leaves: 2–16 in long, in a basal rosette, oblanceolate, lobed
Flowers: ray flowers numerous, yellow; disk flowers absent; flowerheads 1–2 in wide, solitary on hollow stalks
Fruit: tiny achenes with white, fluffy pappus

Emerald green lawns sprinkled with yellow dandelion blossoms create a rather showy palette but rankle fastidious lawn-keepers. • Introduced from Eurasia, dandelions were cultivated for food and medicine. Young dandelion leaves and flowerheads make nutritious salad greens. The roots can be ground into a caffeine-free coffee substitute. **Where found:** disturbed sites; throughout New England.

Black-eyed Susan

Rudbeckia hirta

Height: 1–3 ft
Leaves: 2–6 in long, alternate, elliptical, bristly-hairy
Flowers: ray flowers yellow, 8–21, 1–1½ in long; disk dark brown, conical, ½–¾ in across; flowerheads 2–3 in across, 1–several on long stalks
Fruit: tiny, blackish, angular achenes

This sun-shiny member of the sunflower/aster family is a native wildflower that is also a popular ornamental. • This species has been used therapeutically for boosting the immune system and treating inflammation. In colonial times, it was used to treat saddle sores on horses. • Nectar-loving insects dine from the flowers until they go to seed, when seed-loving birds take their turn. **Where found:** open woods, meadows, grasslands, roadsides, disturbed sites, sand hills and bogs; throughout New England.

Broad-leaved Arrowhead

Sagittaria latifolia

Height: to 40 in, aquatic
Leaves: 6–16 in long, basal, arrowhead-shaped, long-stalked
Flowers: ¾ in long, white, 3 petals, in whorls of 3 on erect stalks
Fruit: beaked achenes in clustered heads

The leaves of this marsh plant vary in shape but always have long basal lobes. • The entire rootstock is edible, but the corms are preferred. When cooked, they taste like potatoes or chestnuts but are unpleasant raw. Native Americans often camped near arrowhead sites for weeks, harvesting the crop or seeking out muskrat caches of corms. **Where found:** shallow water or mud in sunny marshes, ditches and other wetlands; throughout New England. **Also known as:** duck potato.

Skunk Cabbage

Symplocarpus foetidus

Height: 1–2 ft
Leaves: 15–22 in long, basal, heart-shaped, cabbage-like
Flowers: tiny, yellowish, star-like, clustered on a ball-like spadix inside a brownish purple, hooded spathe 4–6 in high
Fruit: brown-black berries in rounded clusters

This odd-looking plant is our first wildflower to bloom each year. As early as late February, the spathes push from the boggy ground, aided by heat produced through cellular respiration that melts nearby snow and ice. The giant, cabbage-like leaves emerge after the flowers have bloomed. • This wetland plant emits a mild odor when left alone but reeks when damaged. The smell attracts pollinating insects but repels animals that may eat or otherwise damage the plant. **Where found:** spring-fed, boggy wetlands; throughout New England.

Jack-in-the-pulpit

Arisaema triphyllum

Height: 1–3 ft
Leaves: 3–6 in long, basal, 1–2, compound with 3 oval, pointed leaflets
Flowers: tiny, in clusters on a greenish, club-shaped spadix, 3 in long, encircled by a green to purplish, flanged spathe
Fruit: smooth, shiny, red berries

Jack-in-the-pulpit's odd flowers are composed of a spadix ("Jack") covered with tiny male and female flowers and surrounded by a hood-like spathe (the "pulpit"). • The entire plant and the bright red berries are poisonous if eaten fresh. Native peoples cooked the fleshy taproots as a vegetable or dried and pounded them into flour. **Where found:** moist hardwood forests, damp woodlands and swamps; throughout New England. **Also known as:** Indian turnip.

Lesser Duckweed

Lemna minor

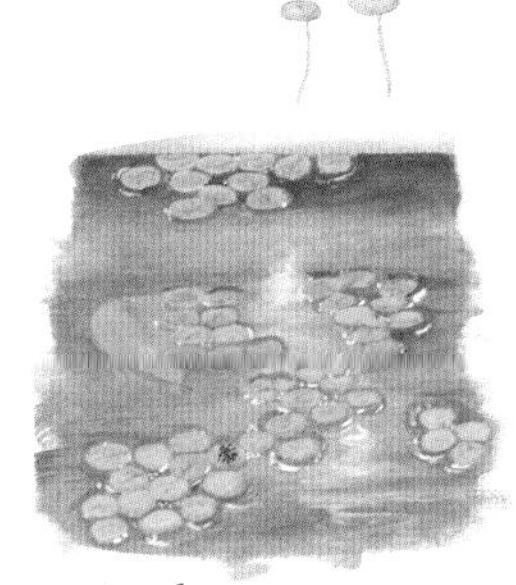

Height: tiny, in colonies
Leaves: ⅛–¼ in across, oval
Flowers: minute, usually 3, without sepals or petals
Fruit: tiny, thin walled, bladder like utricles

Lesser duckweed is the most common of a number of tiny, floating, aquatic plants that are often mistakenly called algae. Sometimes regarded as a nuisance, duckweed removes unwanted phosphorus and nitrogen from the water, acting as a natural filter and improving water quality. • The tiny flowers are seldom seen because flowering is rare. Most reproduction is vegetative, with existing leaves dividing into new ones. **Where found:** surface of ponds, lakes and rivers; throughout New England.

Sea Lavender

Limonium carolinianum

Height: 8–20 in
Leaves: to 12 in long, spoon-shaped, leathery, in a basal rosette
Flowers: ⅛–⅜ in across, light purple or lavender pink, tubular, 5 petals, along one side of the stem
Fruit: small capsules with a single seed

This seaside perennial is not related to the herb lavender; the common name is merely a reference to the flower color. Dense colonies of this plant grow in some salt marshes, salt meadows and dunes. • The rootstock was once made into a mouthwash because of the astringent tannins, which have been and are still used today for a variety of home remedies. **Where found:** coastal salt marshes; all along the coast. **Also known as:** harsh rosemary.

Ostrich Fern

Matteuccia struthiopteris

Height: 1½–5 ft
Leaves: 2 types of fronds; sterile fronds lance-shaped, to 12 in wide, tapered at both ends, with 20–60 leaflet pairs, fronds form a crown-like cluster; fertile fronds 8–24 in tall, narrow, erect, olive green becoming dark brown, arising from the center of the clump

These lovely ferns give a lush, primitive feeling to any forest and are popular ornamentals in gardens. • The emerald green fiddleheads are a traditional dish in New England, particularly in Maine. They are collected in spring when they are about 6 in tall and still tightly coiled. Do not overharvest from a single plant—leave more than half, or at least 3 tops, or the plant may die. **Where found:** rich, moist or wet soils, stream and riverbanks, open forests and swamps; throughout New England.

Beach Grass

Ammophila breviligulata

Height: up to 3 ft
Leaves: ¼–½ in wide, up to 15 in long, deeply veined above, smooth below
Flowers: tiny, inconspicuous, in spike-like panicles to 10 in long
Fruit: minute seeds

Beach grass is a very important pioneer plant that stabilizes sand dunes. The stems continue to grow higher as blowing sand builds up around them. The buried stems eventually become roots that reach and spread far and wide under the sand. • The tough, thin, green blades roll up to conserve moisture on hot days and unroll to catch moisture. **Where found:** beaches and sand dunes close to the sea; throughout New England.

Common Reed

Phragmites australis

Height: 3–10 ft
Leaves: 8–15 in long, 1–1½ in wide, flat, stiff
Flowers: tiny, purple-brown, in plume-like panicles 4–16 in long
Fruit: seed-like grains

This giant non-native grass is conspicuous, forming massive stands that tower over other plants. • The stem contains a sugary substance with many uses. Dried, ground stalks can be turned into a sugary flour that will bubble and brown like a marshmallow when heated, and sugar crystals from dried stems or the sweet, gummy substance that bleeds from cut stems can be eaten like candy. • Probably the most common use of reeds, both historically and still today, is for weaving mats and baskets and for thatching roofs. **Where found:** marshes, ditches, wetlands and shorelines; throughout New England.

Rush

Juncus spp.

Height: to 5 ft
Leaves: 1–2 mm wide, basal, flattened or round
Flowers: small, greenish to brown, usually 3 petals and 3 sepals, in open clusters or dense, terminal heads
Fruit: brown capsules with many tiny seeds

Rushes are a type of grass that stabilizes dunes and provides shelter for a variety of wildlife. Few other plants can tolerate tidal environments that transition between terrestrial and underwater. Rushes occur around the world, mostly in temperate zones. **Where found:** salt marshes, coastal and freshwater beaches, estuaries, wetlands, lakes, riparian zones and rural or disturbed sites; throughout New England.

Cord Grass

Spartina patens

Height: 6–32 in
Leaves: 4–20 in long, ⅛–¼ in wide, light green, rolled inward
Flowers: inconspicuous, in heads 2–9 in long, with 1–4 spikes, each ½–3 in long
Fruit: wheat-like seeds

Dense mats of cord grass appear tousled and messy, and each year, new grass adds density to the previous year's growth, producing increasingly thick and dense mats. Cord grass grows from rhizomes as well as seeds and can grow in salt water because root membranes screen out much of the salt. • In earlier times, this "wild hay" was used as fodder for livestock or as bedding in barns. **Where found:** salt marshes along the coast; throughout coastal New England. **Also known as:** saltmarsh hay, salt-meadow cord grass.

Beach Sedge

Carex silicea

Height: 1–3 ft
Leaves: 4–10 in long, ⅛–½ in wide, basal
Flowers: inconspicuous, clustered in silvery green spikes 1½–3 in long, arching or nodding

Sedges are grass-like herbs, and the genus name *Carex* is a Latin word that translates as "grasses with sharp leaves." However, unlike grasses, the stems of *Carex* species are solid and often triangular in cross-section. • *Carex* species are found around the world, and their edible grains have served as famine foods. The whitish leaf base is often tender and edible as well. **Where found:** beaches; throughout New England.

Spike Grass

Distichlis spicata

Height: 4–20 in
Leaves: 1–4 in long, narrow, flat, stiff
Flowers: inconspicuous, clustered in greenish to purple spikelets to 3 in long

This coastal grass is typical of salt marshes but also occurs in forests, desert-scrub and montane zones. Its heavy root system develops into a thick sod layer over time. • This plant can excrete salt from its tissues, and stems are often covered in salt crystals. It is valuable as a grazing crop for livestock for its ability to use salt water, important in times of drought. **Where found:** salt marshes; throughout New England. **Also known as:** seashore salt grass.

Cottongrass Bulrush

Scirpus cyperinus

Height: 2–6 ft
Leaves: to 12 in long, 1/8–3/8 in wide, grass-like, rough
Flowers: inconspicuous, in greenish spikelets in large, arching, terminal clusters that become fuzzy as they mature
Fruit: tiny, sharply beaked, yellowish achenes

Like other grass-like plants, bulrushes are great for weaving, and many species are edible. The seeds are food for ducks and other marsh birds. The long stems offer cover to wildlife and are eaten by raccoons, muskrats and geese. • Bulrushes anchor sandy soil and build up land in low-lying, flooded areas. **Where found:** open, wet places and shorelines; throughout New England. **Also known as:** wool grass.

Broad-leaved Cattail

Typha latifolia

Height: 3–10 ft
Leaves: up to 10 ft long, 1/2–1 in wide, flat, grass-like
Flowers: tiny, numerous, in dense spikes 6–8 in long; female flowers dark brown, on lower portion of spike; male flowers cone-shaped, on upper portion of spike, disintegrating and leaving stem tip bare
Fruit: tiny, ellipsoid achenes clustered in a fuzzy, brown spike (cattail)

Cattails rim wetlands and line lakeshores and ditches across North America, providing critical habitat for marsh birds. • The long rhizomes were traditionally eaten fresh in spring. Later in the season, they were peeled and roasted or dried and ground into flour. • Narrow-leaved cattail (*T. angustifolia*) has narrower leaves and a gap between the male and female flowers on the spike. **Where found:** wetlands, marshes, ponds, ditches and damp ground; throughout New England.

Eel Grass

Zostera marina

Height: 3–10 ft, aquatic
Leaves: up to 4 ft long, 1/8–1/2 in wide, alternate, veined
Flowers: inconspicuous, in a spike 1–2 1/2 in long of unstalked male and female flowers alternating in 2 rows
Fruit: translucent, ribbed, flask-shaped nutlets, 3/8 in long

Neither algae nor a grass, but a flowering plant, this species is a type of sea grass. Eel grass is truly marine, spending almost its entire life underwater. Rarely, it is exposed at low tide, when its long, narrow, bright green strands can be seen in shallow, rocky waters. • Sea grass flowers are tiny and inconspicuous because there is no need to attract insects for pollination. • **Where found:** low intertidal and subtidal zones; all along the coast.

Rockweed – Brown Algae

Fucus distichus

Height: to 20 in

There are 3 types of algae—brown, red and green. This small, tufted, brown alga lacks the air bladders that are fun to pop on other rockweeds known as bladder wrack (*F. vesiculosus*), though the tips of the fronds do swell when mature. The rockweed family includes many of the most widely distributed seaweeds in the world and gets its name from the habit these plants have of adhering to rocks and other solid foundations. **Where found:** in tidal pools on rocky shores; middle and lower intertidal zones all along the coast.

Sugar Kelp – Brown Algae

Laminaria saccharina

Length: up to 10 ft

Kelp is a brown alga and has root-like anchors that affix to rocks while the wide (6 in), leathery blades float with the currents. • Forests of kelp create habitat for marine animals such as sea urchins, sea stars, periwinkles, crabs and small fish, and are among the most biodiverse forests, including terrestrial ones. • A sweet-tasting powder forms on the blades when they dry out. Sugar kelp has a nutty flavour and makes a tasty snack when dried. **Where found:** low littoral rock pools; low tide and subtidal zones to below 64 ft; all along the coast. **Also known as:** sugar wrack.

Encrusting Corralline Algae – Red Algae

Corallina officinalis

Length: 2½–5 in

Red algae are the largest group of seaweeds. A red pigment typically masks the chlorophyll that would otherwise render these algae green in color. • This red alga looks like coral because of its branching, calcified fronds and its whitish pink to lilac coloration. Most tidal rock pools will have corralline algae, and it provides habitat for many small sea creatures. • Encrusting corralline algae has been used in the research of bone replacement therapies. **Where found:** often forms a distinct zone just below the rim of rock pools, in middle and lower shore zones; all along the coast. **Also known as:** coral weed.

Dulse – Red Algae

Palmaria palmata

Length: fronds 2–12 in

This rubbery alga can be eaten raw like a vegetable and is commercially harvested to be dried and sold in local grocery stores. Dried dulse can be added to soup and to seafood and Asian dishes. • Nori or laver (*Porphyra* spp.), another type of red algae in our waters, is cultivated in East Asia and is routinely used in Japanese cooking. • Dulse grows best in deeper waters because the red pigment photosynthesizes better in dim underwater light. **Where found:** on rocks and mussels; epiphytic on several algae; intertidal (particularly near low water) and shallow subtidal zones; all along the coast. **Also known as:** *Ptilota elegans, Rhodymenia palmata.*

Irish Moss – Red Algae

Chondrus crispus

Length: 6 in

Clumps of this seaweed on the beach or floating in shallow water look like moss and give the species its analogous common name. • The walls of this and similar red algae are made up of cellulose, agars and carrageenans—long-chain polysaccharides—that have widespread commercial uses. Agars are used as thickeners in soups and dairy products and as mediums for growing cultures in laboratories. Carrageenan is used as a thickener in cooking and baking and as an ingredient in cough syrups. **Where found:** on rocks and in pools; lower intertidal and shallow subtidal zones; all along the coast. **Also known as:** carrageenan moss.

Sea Lettuce – Green Algae

Ulva lactuca

Length: tissue thin sheets, 7–12 in

Among the few green algae species found in the intertidal zone, perhaps the most visible and abundant is the bright green sea lettuce, either attached to rocks or free-floating. This seaweed has a very simple structure and is only 1 or 2 cells thick. • Sea lettuce is of high caloric value and is eaten by crabs and mollusks. Although it looks like salad lettuce, it is not tasty. • Sea lettuce is tolerant of fresh water or minor pollution for short periods. **Where found:** shallow bays, lagoons, harbors and marshes, on rocks and other algae; intertidal and high-tide zones; all along the coast.

REFERENCES

AmphibiaWeb. amphibiaweb.org.

BirdFellow. www.birdfellow.com.

The Cornell Lab of Ornithology. www.birds.cornell.edu.

Carwardine, Mark. 2000. *Whales, Dolphins and Porpoises.* Dorling Kindersley Handbooks. Dorling Kindersley Publishing, New York.

DeGraaf, Richard M., and Mariko Yamasaki. 2001. *New England Wildlife.* University Press of New England, Lebanon, NH.

Eder, Tamara. 2012. *Whales and Other Marine Mammals of the East Coast.* Lone Pine Publishing International, Auburn, WA.

FAO Fisheries and Aquaculture Department. www.fao.org/fishery/en.

FishBase. www.fishbase.org.

Horn, Dennis, and Tavia Cathart. 2005. *Wildflowers of Tennessee, the Ohio Valley and the Southern Appalachians.* Lone Pine Publishing, Edmonton, AB.

Leatherwood, Stephen, and Randall R. Reeves. 1983. *The Sierra Club Handbook of Whales and Dolphins.* Sierra Club Books, San Francisco.

National Audubon Society. 1998. *Field Guide to North American Seashore Creatures.* Chanticleer Press, Toronto, ON.

National Audubon Society. 1998. *Field Guide to North American Fishes, Whales & Dolphins.* Chanticleer Press, Toronto, ON.

The Nature Conservancy. www.nature.org.

New England Botanical Club. www.rhodora.org.

New England Herpetological Society. www.neherp.com.

NOAA Fisheries Service. www.nmfs.noaa.gov.

Petersen, Wayne, and Roger Burrows. 2004. *Birds of New England.* Lone Pine Publishing International, Auburn, WA.

Sheldon, Ian, Tamara Hartson, and Mark Elbroch. 2000. *Animal Tracks of New England.* Lone Pine Publishing, Edmonton, AB.

St. John, Alan. 2002. *Reptiles of the Northwest: California to Alaska, Rockies to the Coast.* Lone Pine Publishing, Edmonton, AB.

Sutton, Ann, and Myron Sutton. 1985. *Eastern Forests.* Audubon Society Nature Guides. Alfred A. Knopf, NY.

University of Michigan Museum of Zoology, Animal Diversity Web. animaldiversity.ummz.umich.edu/site/index.html.

USDA Natural Resources Conservation Service, PLANTS Database. plants.usda.gov.

World Register of Marine Species (WoRMS). marinespecies.org.

GLOSSARY

A

achene: a seed-like fruit (e.g., sunflower seed)

alcid: a seabird of the family Alcidae, which includes murres, auklets and puffins, characterized by wings well suited to diving and swimming and that beat rapidly in flight

alga (*pl.* algae): simple photosynthetic aquatic plants lacking true stems, roots, leaves and flowers, and ranging in size from single-celled forms to giant kelp

alternate: an arrangement of leaves along a stem in which the leaves are unpaired

anadromous: fish that migrate from salt water to fresh water to spawn (e.g., salmon)

annual: a plant that lives for only one year or growing season

aquatic: water frequenting

arboreal: tree frequenting

Arctic: the region north of the Arctic Circle (66°33' N latitude)

aril: an extra or specialized seed covering, often fleshy, hairy or brightly colored (e.g. the red, translucent flesh that surrounds a pomegranate seed)

arthropod: an invertebrate with a heard, segmented exoskeleton and paired, jointed legs (e.g., insects, spiders, crustaceans)

awn: a stiff, bristle-like projection, especially from the seed of a grass or grain

axil: the point at which a leaf attaches to a stem

B

baleen: strands of keratin that hang in sheets from the upper jaws of some whales and are used to filter food from water

barbels: fleshy, whisker-like appendages found on some fish

barren: a mainly treeless area with low-growing plants tolerant of exposure and low-nutrient soils; also known as a **heath** for the dominant plant family found there

basal leaf: a leaf arising from the base of a plant

benthic: living at or near the bottom of a sea or lake

benthos: the community of organisms (plants and animals) that lives at or near the bottom of a lake or sea

berry: a fleshy fruit, usually with numerous seeds

bog: a wetland with poor drainage and a thick layer of peat that only receives nutrients from rainfall; mosses, particularly sphagnum moss, are common vegetation in bogs; *see also* **fen**, **string bog**

bow riding: a behavior seen in dolphins in which the animals swim in the bow waves of boats

bract: a leaf-like structure arising from the base of a flower or inflorescence

breach: a whale display in which the animal rises vertically into the air, clearing the water's surface with almost all of its body before splashing back in

brood parasite: a bird that parasitizes other birds' nests by laying its eggs and then abandoning them for the parasitized birds to raise (e.g., brown-headed cowbird)

bulb: a fleshy underground organ with overlapping, swollen scales (e.g., onion)

C

calyx: a collective term for the sepals of a flower

cambium: inner layers of tissue that transport nutrients up and down a plant stalk or trunk

canopy: the fairly continuous cover provided by the branches and leaves of adjacent trees

capsule: a dry fruit that splits open to release seeds

carapace: a protective bony shell (e.g., of a turtle) or exoskeleton (e.g., of a beetle)

carnivorous: feeding primarily on meat

carrion: decomposing animal matter or a carcass

catadromous: fish that migrate from fresh water to the sea to spawn (e.g., eels)

catkin: a spike or hanging cluster of small flowers

cetacean: a marine mammal of the order Cetacea, which includes whales, dolphins and porpoises

compound leaf: a leaf separated into 2 or more divisions called leaflets

cone: the fruit produced by a coniferous plant, composed of overlapping scales around a central axis

coniferous: cone bearing; seed (female) and pollen (male) cones are borne on the same tree in different locations

corm: a swollen underground stem base that resembles a bulb and is used by some plants as an organ of propagation

corvid: a member of the family Corvidae, which includes crows, jays, magpies and ravens

crepuscular: active primarily at dusk and dawn

cryptic coloration: a coloration pattern designed to conceal an animal

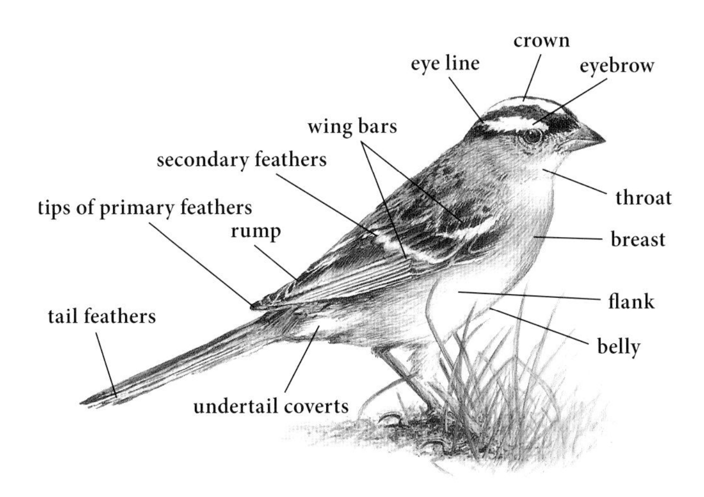

D

deciduous: a tree whose leaves turn color and are shed annually; can also refer to petals that fall after a plant flowers

defoliate: to drop leaves

disk flowers: the small florets in the center, or disk, of a composite flower (e.g., aster, daisy or sunflower)

diurnal: active primarily during the day

dorsal: the top or back

drupe: a fleshy fruit with a stony pit (e.g., peach, cherry)

E

echolocation: navigation by rebounding sound waves off objects to target or avoid them

ecoregion: a geographical region distinguished by its geology, climate, biodiversity, elevation and soil composition

ectotherm: an animal that regulates its body temperature behaviorally from external sources of heat, i.e., from the sun

eft: the terrestrial juvenile stage of a newt

endotherm: an animal that regulates its body temperature internally

epiphyte: a plant that grows on another plant but is not a parasite (e.g., many mosses and lichens)

estivate: a state of inactivity and a slowing of the metabolism to permit survival during extended periods of high temperatures and inadequate water supply

estuary: a partly enclosed coastal body of water where fresh water from one or more rivers mingles with salt water from an ocean or sea

eutrophic: a nutrient-rich body of water with an abundance of algae and a low level of dissolved oxygen

evergreen: having green leaves through winter; not deciduous

exoskeleton: a hard outer encasement that provides protection and points of attachment for muscles (e.g., on insects and crustaceans)

F

fen: a wetland with poor drainage and a thick layer of peat into which water seeps from nearby soils, making the fen's soil more nutrient rich than that of a bog; primary vegetation includes mosses and some grass species; *see also* **bog**

flight membrane: a membrane between the fore and hind limbs of bats and some squirrels that allows these animals to glide through the air; *see also* **patagium**

fluke: *n.* either of the lobes of a whale's tail; *v.* a whale behavior in which the animal raises its tail above the water before diving

follicle: the structure in the skin from which hair or feathers grow; a dry fruit that splits open along a single line on one side when ripe; a cocoon

food web: the elaborate, interconnected feeding relationships of living organisms in an ecosystem

forb: a broad-leaved plant that lacks a permanent woody stem and loses its above-ground growth each year; may be annual, biennial or perennial

fry: the young of fish

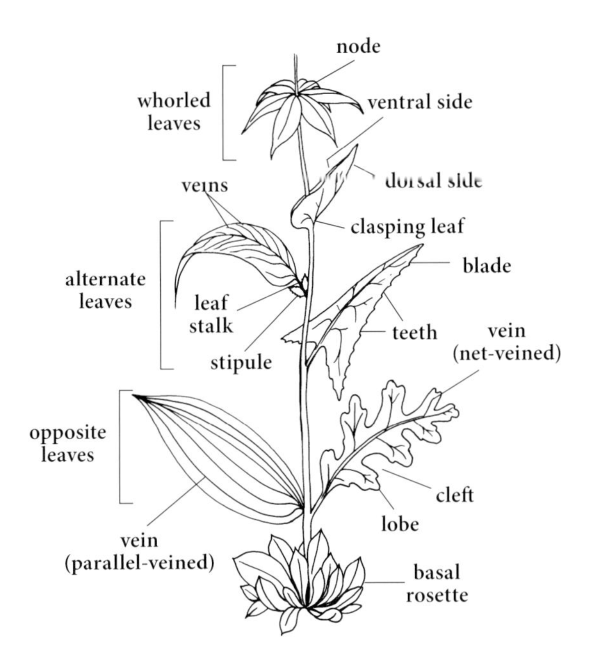

G

gillrakers: long, thin, fleshy projections that protect delicate gill tissue from particles in the water

glandular: similar to or containing glands

glaucous: covered with a waxy, whitish coating or "bloom"

graminoid: a herbaceous plant with narrow leaves growing from the base; includes grasses and grass-like plants such as sedges and rushes

H

habitat: the physical area in which an organism lives

hawking: feeding behavior in which a bird leaves a perch, snatches its prey in midair and returns to the perch

haw: the small, berry-like fruit of a hawthorn

herbaceous: feeding primarily on vegetation

hibernaculum (*pl.* hibernacula): a shelter in which an animal, usually a mammal, reptile or insect, chooses to hibernate

hibernation: a state of decreased metabolism and body temperature and slowed heart and respiratory rates to permit survival during long periods of cold temperatures and diminished food supply

hip: the berry-like fruit of some plants in the rose family (Rosaceae)

hybrid: the offspring from a cross between parents belonging to different varieties or subspecies, and sometimes between different subspecies or genera

I

incubate: to keep eggs at a relatively constant temperature until they hatch

inflorescence: a cluster of flowers on a stalk

insectivore: feeding primarily on insects

invertebrate: any animal lacking a backbone (e.g., worms, slugs, crayfish, shrimp)

involucral bract: one of several bracts that form a whorl below a flower or flower cluster

K

key: a winged fruit, usually of an ash or maple tree; also called a **samara**

kype: the hook-like protrusions that develop on the mandibles of a spawning trout or salmon

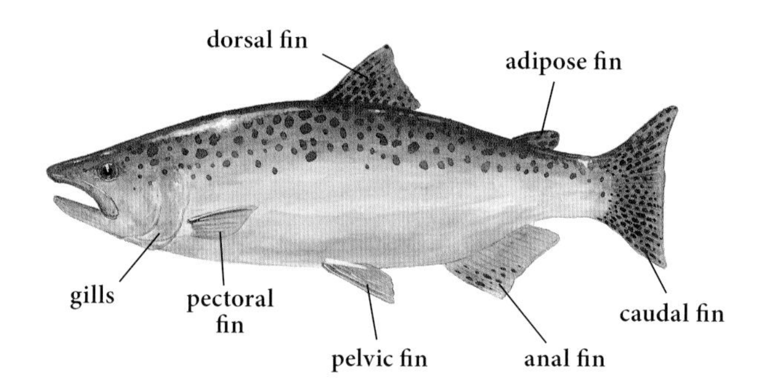

L

larva (*pl.* larvae): the immature form of an animal that differs from the adult

leaflet: a division of a compound leaf

lenticel: a slightly raised portion of bark where the cells are packed more loosely, allowing for gas exchange with the atmosphere

leveret: a young hare

littoral: along the shore of a river, lake or sea

lobate: having each toe individually webbed

lobe: a projecting part of a leaf or flower, usually rounded

lobtail: a display in which a whale forcefully slaps its tail flukes on the water's surface

M

metabolic rate: the rate of chemical processes in an organism

metamorphosis: the developmental transformation of an animal from a larval stage to a sexually mature adult stage

midden: the pile of cone scales found on the territories of tree squirrels, usually under a favorite tree

molt: when an animal sheds old feathers, fur or skin in order to replace them with new growth

montane: the ecological zone located below the subalpine; montane regions generally have cooler temperatures than adjacent lowland regions

myccorhizal fungi/myccorhizae: fungi that have a mutually beneficial relationship with the roots of some seed plants

N

neotropical: the biogeographical region that includes Mexico, Central and South America and the West Indies

neritic: that part of the ocean extending from the low-tide mark to the continental shelf, i.e., to a depth of about 200 m

nocturnal: active primarily at night

node: a slightly enlarged section of a stem where leaves or branches originate

notochord: a primitive backbone

nutlet: a small, hard, single-seeded fruit that remains closed

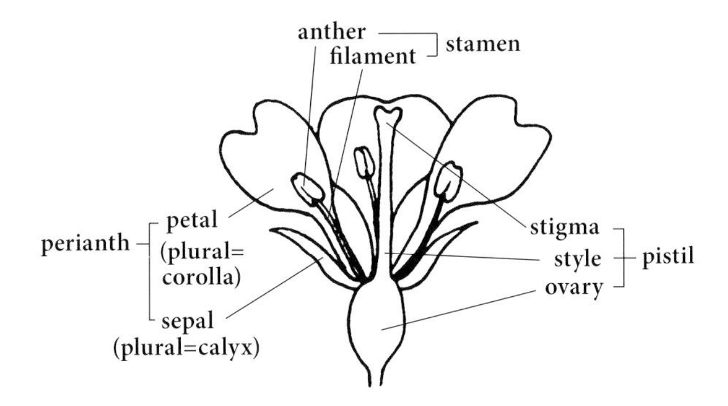

O

oblanceolate: having a rounded tip that is wider than the base (usually in reference to leaves)

omnivorous: feeding on both plants and animals

operculum: a lid or covering, especially the plate that closes the shell of a gastropod (e.g., snail) when the animal is retracted

opposite: an arrangement of leaves along a stem in which the leaves are paired and directly opposite one another

ovoid: egg-shaped

P

palmate: having leaflets, lobes or veins arranged around a single point, like the fingers on a hand (e.g., a maple leaf)

panicle: a branched flower cluster in which the lower blossoms develop first

pappus: the tuft of hairs on a seed (e.g., dandelion or thistle) that aids in wind dispersal

parasitic: a relationship between 2 species in which one benefits at the expense of the other

patagium: the skin that forms a flight membrane (e.g., in bats and flying squirrels)

pelage: the fur or hair of a mammal

pelagic: open-ocean habitat far from land

perennial: a plant that lives for several years

petal: a member of the inside ring of modified flower leaves, usually brightly colored or white

petiole: a leaf stalk

photosynthesis: the conversion of carbon dioxide and water into sugars via the energy of the sun

pinniped: a carnivorous, aquatic mammal with a streamlined body specialized for swimming and limbs modified into flippers (e.g., seals, sea lions, walruses)

pinnate: having branches, lobes, leaflets or veins arranged on both sides of a central stalk or vein (e.g., fern fronds); feather-like

pioneer species: a plant species that is capable of colonizing an otherwise unvegetated area; one of the first species (plant or animal) to take hold in a disturbed area

piscivorous: feeding on fish

pishing: a noise made to attract birds

pistil: the female organ of a flower, usually consisting of an ovary, style and stigma

plastic species: a species that can adapt to a wide range of conditions

plastron: the lower part of a turtle or tortoise shell

poikilothermic: having a body temperature the same as that of the external environment and varying with it

pollen: the tiny grains produced in the anthers of a plant and that contain the male reproductive cells

polyandry: a mating strategy in which one female mates with several males

pome: a fruit with a core (e.g., apple)

precocial: animals that are active at birth or hatching

prehensile: able to grasp

proboscis: the elongated tubular and flexible mouthpart of many insects

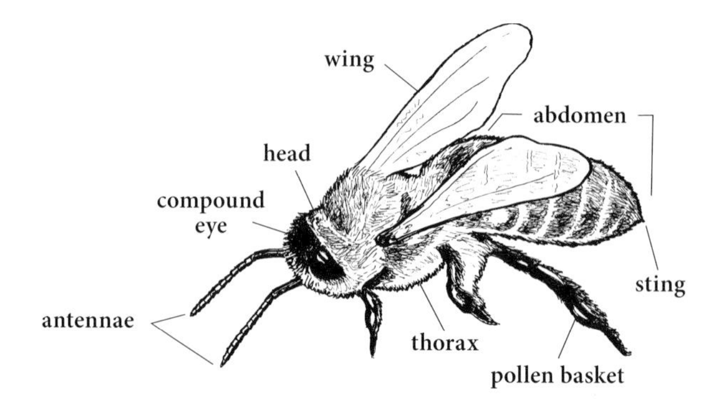

R

raceme: a simple, unbranched inflorescence with flowers on short stalks along an elongated central stalk

ray flowers: in a composite flower (e.g., aster, daisy or sunflower), the strap-like outer florets that resemble petals

redd: a spawning nest for fish

rhizome: a horizontal underground stem

rictal bristles: hair-like feathers found around the mouths of some birds

riparian: on the bank of a river or other watercourse

rookery: a colony of nests

rorqual: a type of baleen whale with pleated, expandable skin on its throat

ruminant: a even-toed mammal with a segmented stomach (e.g., cow, moose, deer)

runner: a slender stolon or prostrate stem that roots at the nodes or the tip

rut: the mating season for members of the deer and sheep families, when stags or rams compete for does or ewes, often engaging in dramatic clashes of antlers or horns

S

samara: a dry, winged fruit, usually of a maple or ash, with typically only a single seed; also called a **key**

salmonid: a member of the Salmonidae family of fishes, which includes trout, char, salmon and whitefish

saprophyte: a plant or other organism that lives on dead or decaying material

schizocarp: a dry fruit that splits into 2 or more parts at maturity, each part with a single seed

scute: a bony or horny plate (e.g., on a turtle's shell or the underside of a snake)

sepal: the outer, usually green, leaf-like structures that protect the flower bud and are located at the base of an open flower

sessile: without a stem or stalk

silicle: a fruit of the mustard family (Brassicaceae) that is two-celled and usually short, wide and often flat

silique: a long, thin fruit with many seeds; characteristic of some members of the mustard family (Brassicaceae)

sorus (*pl.* sori): a collection of spore-producing structures on the underside of a fern frond

spadix: a fleshy spike made up of many small flowers

spathe: the leaf-like sheath that surrounds a spadix

spur: a pointed projection

spyhop: a whale behavior in which the animal, while in an almost vertical position, raises its head out of the water just far enough to look around

stamen: the pollen-bearing organ of a flower

stigma: in a flower, a receptive tip that receives pollen for fertilization

stolon: a long branch or stem that runs along the ground and often propagates more plants

string bog: a bog with raised ridges of vegetation perpendicular to the flow of water and islands of woody plants alternating with sedge mats; also known as a **strong mire**

Subarctic: the region in the Northern Hemisphere that is immediately south of the true Arctic, generally between 50° and 70° N latitude, and covering much of Canada, Alaska, Scandinavia and Siberia

subtend: to be directly below; also to enclose or surround

suckering: a method of tree and shrub reproduction in which shoots arise from an underground runner or spreading roots

syrinx: a bird's vocal organ

T

taproot: the main, large root of a plant from which smaller roots arise (e.g., a carrot)

tendril: a slender, clasping or twining outgrowth from a stem or leaf

tepal: a term used for sepals and petals when there is no clear distinction between the two

terrestrial: land frequenting

territory: a defended area within an animal's home range

test: the external skeleton ("shell") of a sea urchin

torpor: a state of physical inactivity

tragus: a prominent structure of the outer ear of a bat

trifoliate: divided into 3 leaflets

tubular flower: a type of flower with all or some of the petals fused at the base

tundra: a high-latitude ecological zone at the northernmost limit of plant growth, where plants are reduced to shrubby or mat-like forms

tympanum: eardrum; the hearing organ of a frog

U

umbel: a round or flat-topped flower cluster in which several flower stalks originate from the same point, like the ribs of an inverted umbrella

ungulate: a hoofed animal

utricle: a dry, thin-walled, single-seeded fruit

V

ventral: of or on the abdomen (belly)

vermiculations: wavy-patterned markings

vertebrate: an animal with a backbone

vibrissae (*sing.* vibrissa): specialized hairs ("whiskers") around the mouths of certain mammals that serve as tactile organs; bristle-like feathers around the beaks of some birds that aid in catching insects

W

whorl: a circle of leaves or flowers around a stem

woolly: bearing long or matted hairs

wrack line: the line of seaweed, grasses and other debris left on the upper beach by a high tide

INDEX

Names and page numbers in **boldface** type refer to primary species.

ABOUT THE AUTHORS

Erin McCloskey spent her formative years observing nature from atop her horse. Erin received her BSc with distinction in environmental and conservation sciences, majoring in conservation biology and management. An active campaigner for the protection of endangered species and spaces, Erin has collaborated with various NGOs and is involved in numerous endangered species conservation projects around the world. Since 2000, she has freelanced as a writer and editor for several magazine and book publishers focused on nature, travel, scientific research and even alternative healthcare. Erin is the author of *The Bradt Travel Guide to Argentina*, *Ireland Flying High*, *Canada Flying High* and *Hawaii from the Air*, and co-author/editor for the *Green Volunteers* guidebook series. Erin is also the author of the *Washington and Oregon Nature Guide*, *Southern California Nature Guide*, *Northern California Nature Guide*, *British Columbia Nature Guide*, *Bear Attacks* and *Wolves of Canada* for Lone Pine Publishing.

Gregory Kennedy has been an active naturalist since he was very young. He is the author of many books on natural history, and has also produced film and television shows on environmental issues and indigenous concerns in Southeast Asia, New Guinea, South and Central America, the High Arctic and elsewhere. He has also been involved in numerous research projects around the world, ranging from studies in the upper canopy of tropical and temperate rainforests to deepwater marine investigations.